We see romantic love as one of the most exquisite of all human opportunities, one of the great adventures of life. . . .

In the daily course of living and in the struggle to make a relationship work, there is so much confusion, bewilderment, and uncertainty that the vision of love's possibilities is all too easily lost. The dream does not have to be abandoned, but we need more than love to make love last.

We need clear thinking, we need an understanding of what love is and what love requires.

—from the Introduction to

What Love Asks Of Us
Solutions to the Challenge of Making Love Work

What Love Asks of Us

Solutions to the Challenge of Making Love Work

Nathaniel Branden and Devers Branden

REVISED AND EXPANDED EDITION

(Originally published as
*The Romantic Love
Question & Answer Book*)

BANTAM BOOKS

TORONTO · NEW YORK · LONDON · SYDNEY · AUCKLAND

WHAT LOVE ASKS OF US

A Bantam Book

PRINTING HISTORY

J. P. Tarcher edition published February 1982
Bantam edition / February 1983
Bantam revised edition / February 1987
2nd printing . . . . .August 1988

ISBN 0-553-27837-1

Published simultaneously in the United States and Canada

Bantam Books are published by Bantam Books, a division of Bantam
Doubleday Dell Publishing Group, Inc. Its trademark, consisting of the
words ''Bantam Books'' and the portrayal of a rooster, is Registered in
U.S. Patent and Trademark Office and in other countries. Marca
Registrada. Bantam Books, 666 Fifth Avenue, New York, New York
10103.

PRINTED IN THE UNITED STATES OF AMERICA

O   11   10   9   8   7   6   5   4   3   2

For our daughters, Vicki and Lorin,
and our grandchildren, Brandon and Ashley

Contents

vii

FIVE / *Living Up to Romantic Love*   59

EIGHT / Jealousy and Infidelity   159

NINE / Balancing Work and Love   190

ELEVEN / Marriage, Children, Relatives   229

TWELVE / Letting Go   258

Introduction

Romantic love, rationally understood, is not an unattainable dream, an adolescent fantasy, or a literary invention. It is an ideal within our power to reach. But reaching it requires a great deal of us, in terms of consciousness, dedication, courage, and personal maturity.

Such is the theme of this book. At a more theoretical level, it is also the theme of my previous book, *The Psychology of Romantic Love*; but here my co-author and I propose to carry it forward and amplify it in very concrete and specific ways.

The Psychology of Romantic Love addresses itself to the task of making love intelligible, of explaining what love is, why it is born, why it sometimes grows, and why it sometimes dies. It is not a "how-to" book, except indirectly and by implication. In contrast, *What Love Asks of Us* addresses itself far more to practical issues: for example, the challenges of balancing a couple's conflicting needs and wants, negotiating differences, and the problems, struggles, and confusions that men and women encounter in their efforts to sustain a love relationship.

This book—a collaboration with my wife and colleague, Devers Branden—took shape from the many questions we have been asked about the nature, pitfalls, and challenges of romantic love. Our questions come from participants in the personal growth workshops we conduct throughout the United States, from our clients undergoing psychotherapy or marriage and couple counseling at the Biocentric Institute in Los Angeles, and from the many people we meet socially in our travels. All have been eager to talk about why love is so difficult. Do we think that marriage still has a chance? Do we know any people who really know *how* to be in a committed relationship? Why don't men understand more about nurturing? Why don't woman understand more about how difficult it is to be a man? Can one really avoid conflict between love and career?

We began making notes on the questions we heard, paying special attention to those that recurred with noticeable frequency. This book is our answer to those questions.

Originally published as *The Romantic Love Question & Answer Book*, this revised and expanded edition contains three essays on love that did not appear in the earlier volume. The first deals with the nature of romantic love. The second deals with the role of communication in love. And the third discusses some of the ways in which men and women sabotage love—and their reasons for doing so. The other changes in this new edition improve the quality of some of our answers.

Not all problems can be solved by reading a book. There are difficulties for which the only solution may be psychotherapy or marriage counseling—or divorce. But we have seen a great deal of absolutely unnecessary ignorance and confusion about man/woman relationships, and this book can illuminate some of the dark corners, providing a rational clarification of what romantic love is, what it asks of us, and how we are to meet its challenges.

We see romantic love as one of the most exquisite of all human opportunities, one of the great adventures of life and a unique pathway to personal growth and self-actualization. We hope this book will inspire readers to confidence in making romantic love a possibility for themselves.

In the daily course of living and in the struggle to make a relationship work, there is so much confusion, bewilderment, and uncertainty that the vision of love's possibilities is all too easily lost. Joy fades into despair, excitement collapses into cynicism. We would like to give back to men and women the hope they had when they started. The dream does not have to be abandoned—but we need more than love to make love last.

We need clear thinking; we need an understanding of

what love is and what love requires; we need courage and determination, flexibility and patience; *we need a higher level of consciousness* than anyone ever told us to attain.

There are important questions for which we need answers, and in many cases, workable solutions to real and painful difficulties.

Before we begin, I want to say a word about the nature of Devers's and my collaboration.

I have already indicated that we each practice Biocentric therapy and that for some years we have conducted workshops, called Intensives, in self-esteem enhancement, man/woman relationships, and personal transformation. Aside from our own experience, our therapy practice and these workshops have been the laboratory for testing the ideas presented in this book. Usually we sketched answers to each question independently, comparing notes and assembling the final version of our response afterward. What made the procedure enriching was the number of times one of us would think of points not included by the other. Generally we speak as a single voice, but occasionally one of us speaks on his or her own behalf, and when this occurs we so indicate.

Readers of *The Psychology of Romantic Love*, who learned something of the background of Devers's and my relationship, and of the stressful and difficult circumstances under which it developed, will perhaps appreciate my profound joy and sense of fulfillment at her being my partner in this venture.

Nathaniel Branden

I. Three Essays on Love
by Nathaniel Branden

SIX / *Communicating Our Emotions* 90

SEVEN / *Intimacy and Sex*   128

One
What Is Romantic Love?

The passionate attachment between man and woman that is known as romantic love can generate the most profound ecstasy. It can also generate, when frustrated, the most unutterable suffering. Yet for all its intensity, the nature of that attachment is little understood. To some, who associate "romantic" with "irrational," romantic love is a temporary neurosis, an emotional storm, inevitably short-lived, which leaves disillusionment and disenchantment in its wake. To others, romantic love is an ideal that, if never reached, leaves one feeling that he or she has somehow missed the secret of life.

Looking at the tragedy and confusion so many experience in romantic relationships, many persons have concluded that the idea of romantic love is somehow fundamentally wrong, a false hope. Romantic love is often attacked today by psychologists, sociologists, and anthropologists, who frequently scorn it as an immature, illusory ideal. To such intellectuals, the idea that an intense emotional attachment could form the basis of a lasting, fulfilling relationship is simply a neurotic product of modern Western culture.

Young people growing up in twentieth-century North America take for granted certain assumptions about their future with the opposite sex, assumptions that are by no means shared by all other cultures: that the two people who will share their lives will choose each other, freely and voluntarily, and that no one, neither family nor friends, church nor state, can or should make that choice for them; that they will choose on the basis of love, rather than on the basis of social, family, or financial considerations; that it very much matters which human beings they choose and, in this connection, that the differences between one human being and another are immensely important; that they can hope and expect to derive happiness from the relationship with the person of their choice and that the pursuit of such happiness is entirely normal, indeed is a human birthright; that the person with whom they choose to share their life, and the person with whom they hope and expect to find sexual fulfillment, are one and the same. Throughout most of human history, all of these views would have been regarded as extraordinary, even incredible.

Only during the past several decades have some of the educated classes in non-Western cultures rebelled against the tradition of marriage arranged by families and looked to the West with its concept of romantic love as a preferred ideal. While in Western Europe the idea of romantic love (in some sense) has had a long history, its acceptance as the proper basis of marriage has never been as widespread as it has been in American culture. As Burgess and Locke write in their historical survey *The Family: From Institution to Companionship*, "It is in the United States that perhaps the only, at any rate the most complete, demonstration of romantic love as the prologue and theme of marriage has been staged."

Why the United States? The answer, at least in part, is philosophical. What was distinctive about the American outlook, and what represented a radical break with its European past, is its unprecedented commitment to political freedom, its individualism, its doctrine of individual rights—and, more specifically, its belief in a person's right to happiness *here on earth*. Both the individualism and the secularism of this country were essential for the ideal of romantic love to take deep cultural root.

And even now, in the midst of the rampant cynicism and despair of the final decades of the twentieth century, and notwithstanding the attacks on romantic love by American intellectuals, people continue to fall in love. The dream dies, only to be reborn. Moved by a passion they do not understand toward a goal they seldom reach, men and women are haunted by the vision of a distant possibility that refuses to be extinguished.

What, at its best, is the nature of that vision? And what does its realization depend on? That is the subject I wish to address.

Let us begin with a definition. There are, after all, different kinds of love that can unite one human being with another. There is love between parents and children. There is love between siblings. There is love between friends. There is a love made of caring and affection but devoid of sexual feeling. And there is the kind of love we call "romantic."

"Romantic love" is *a passionate spiritual-emotional-sexual attachment between two people that reflects a high regard for the value of each other's person*. When I write of romantic love, this is what I mean.

I do not describe a relationship as romantic if the couple does not experience their attachment as passionate or intense, at least to some significant extent (allowing, of course, for the normal ebb and flow of feeling that is intrinsic to life). I do not describe a relationship as romantic love if there is not some experience of spiritual affinity, by which I mean some deep mutuality of values and outlook, some sense of being "soul mates"; if there is not a deep emotional involvement; if there is not a strong sexual attraction (allowing, once more, for normal fluctuations of feeling). And if there is not mutual admiration (if, for example, there is mutual contempt instead, which can certainly coexist with sex attraction), again I do not describe the relationship as romantic love.

Let it be acknowledged that almost any statement we make about love, sex, or man/woman relationships entails something of a personal confession. We tend to speak from what we have lived. I have shared some of the life experiences that lie behind my thoughts on love in *The Psychology of Romantic Love*, and Devers and I will share more in the chapters that follow. But personal contexts aside, my writing about love draws on two primary sources. First, it represents an attempt to reason about and understand man/woman relationships on the basis of facts and data more or less available to everyone, the material of history and of culture. Second, as a psychotherapist and marriage counselor, I have had the opportunity to work with thousands of people over the past thirty years and to see something of their struggle to achieve sexual and romantic fulfillment. I have been keenly interested in the question of what people seek from love—as well as the question of why some people succeed in their quest while others fail.

Love is our emotional response to that which we value highly. I am speaking now of love in general, love as such, of which romantic love is a special case. Love is the experience of joy in the existence of the loved object, joy in proximity, and joy in interaction or involvement. To love is to delight in the being whom one loves, to experience pleasure in that being's presence, to find gratification or fulfillment in contact with that being. We experience the loved being as a source of fulfillment for profoundly important needs. (Someone we love enters the room; our eyes and heart light up. We look at this person; we experience a rising sense of joy within us. We reach out and touch; we feel happy, fulfilled. Note that this might describe our relationship to a spouse, a lover, a parent, a child, a friend—or a pet.)

But love is more than an emotion; it is a judgment or evaluation, and an action tendency. Indeed, all emotions entail evaluations and action tendencies.

Emotions by their nature are value responses. *They are automatic psychological responses, involving both mental and physiological features, to our subconscious appraisal of what we perceive as the beneficial or harmful relationship of some aspect of reality to ourselves.*

If we consider any emotional response, from love to fear to rage, we can see that implicit in every response is a *dual* value judgment. Every emotion reflects the judgment of "for me" or "against me"—and also "to what extent." Thus, emotions differ according to their content and according to their intensity.

Love is the highest, the most intense expression of the assessment "for me," "good for me," "beneficial to my life." In the person of someone we love we see in extraordinarily high measure many of those traits and characteristics that we feel are most appropriate to life—life as we understand and experience it—and therefore most desirable for our own well-being and happiness.

Every emotion contains an inherent action tendency. The emotion of fear is a person's response to that which threatens his or her values; it entails the action tendency to avoid or flee from the feared object. The emotion of love entails the action tendency to achieve some form of contact with the loved being, some form of interaction. (Sometimes a lover will complain, "You say you love me, but I could *never tell it from your actions*. You never want to spend time with me, you don't want to talk with me, so how would you *act differently* if you *didn't* love me?")

Finally, and in a sense more fundamentally, we may describe love as representing an *orientation*, an attitude or psychological state with regard to the loved being, deeper and more enduring than any momentary alteration of feeling. As an orientation, *love represents a disposition to experience the loved being as the embodiment of profoundly important (conscious or subconscious) personal values—and, as a consequence, a real or potential source of joy.*

What is unique about romantic love is that it incorporates or draws on more aspects of the self than any other kind of love—our sense of life, our sexuality, our body, our deepest fantasies or longings regarding man or woman, our self-concept, the cardinal values that energize our existence.

Our spiritual-emotional-sexual response to our partner is a consequence of seeing him or her as the embodiment of our highest values, and as being crucially important to our personal happiness. "Highest," in this context, does not necessarily mean noblest or most exalted; it means most important, in terms of our personal needs and desires and in terms of what we wish to find and experience in life. As an integral part of that response—and this differentiates romantic love from the love for a friend, a parent, or a child—we see the loved object as being crucially important to our *sexual* happiness. The needs of our spirit and body melt into each other; we experience a unique sense of wholeness.

In light of the widespread misunderstandings on this subject, I want to say a few words about what romantic love is not.

Many of the commonest criticisms of romantic love are based on observing irrational or immature processes occurring between people who profess to be "in love," and then generalizing to a repudiation of romantic love per se. In such cases, the arguments are not fact-directed against romantic love at all—not if we understand its roots in genuine appreciation and admiration for the person of another.

There are, for example, men and women who experience a strong sexual attraction for each other, conclude that they are "in love," and proceed to marry on the basis of their sexual attraction, ignoring the fact that they have few values or interests in common, have little or no admiration for each other, are bound to each other predominantly by dependency needs, have incompatible personalities and temperaments, and, in fact, have little or no authentic interest in each other as persons. Of course such relationships are doomed to failure. But they do not represent romantic love.

To love a human being is to know and love his or her person. This presupposes the ability to see, and with reasonable clarity. It is commonly argued that romantic lovers manifest a strong tendency to idealize or glamorize their partners. Of course this sometimes occurs. But it is not in the nature of love that it must occur. To argue that love is *necessarily* blind is to maintain that no real and deep affinities of a kind that inspire love can really exist between persons. This argument runs counter to the experience of men and women who do see the partner's shortcomings as well as strengths and who do love passionately.

Infatuation differs from love precisely in that while love embraces the person as a whole, infatuation is the result of focusing on one or two traits or aspects and reacting as if that were the total. I see a beautiful face, for example, and assume it is the image of a beautiful soul. I see how kindly this person treats me and assume we share significant affinities. I discover we share important values in one area and expand this area to include the whole sphere of life.

It is sometimes argued (by Freud, for example) that the experience of romantic love is generated solely by sexual frustrations and, therefore, must perish shortly after consummation. True, frustration can create obsessive want and can foster a tendency to endow a desired object with temporary value. Yet anyone who argues that love cannot survive sexual fulfillment is making an extraordinary *personal* statement and is also revealing extraordinary blindness or indifference to the experience of others.

Since romantic love, in literature, is dramatized through lovers battling obstacles to their love, some writers have concluded that these obstacles are essential to the experience. "Romantic love," writes Arnold Lazarus in *Marital Myths*, "thrives on barriers, frustrations, separations and delays. Remove these obstacles, replace them with the everyday-ness of married life, and ecstatic passion fades." What is one to say, then, to couples who have been married for twenty years and who have preserved their vision of each other as well as their devotion—to say nothing of their sexuality? Such couples exist. Is psychology to have no place for them? "Romantics," says Lazarus, "ignore the fact that people grow weary of each other unless they have cultivated common interests and values." *Do* they ignore this fact? And is such blindness essential to the romantic experience? I do not think so. This is the kind of straw-man version of romantic love that is typical of its critics.

It is sometimes argued that since so many couples do in fact suffer feelings of disenchantment shortly after marriage, the experience of romantic love must be a delusion. Yet many people experience disenchantment during their careers somewhere along the line, but it is not commonly suggested that the pursuit of a meaningful and fulfilling career is a mistake. Many people experience some degree of disenchantment in their children, but it is not commonly supposed that the desire to have children and to be happy about them is inherently immature and neurotic. Instead, it is generally recognized that the requirements for achieving happiness in one's career or success in child-rearing may be higher and more difficult than is ordinarily supposed.

Romantic love is not omnipotent—and those who believe it is are too immature to be ready for it. Given the multitude of psychological problems that many people bring to a romantic relationship—given their doubts, their fears, their insecurities, their weak and uncertain self-esteem, given the fact that most have never learned that a love relationship, like every other value in life, requires consciousness, courage, knowledge, and wisdom to be sustained—it is not astonishing that most relationships end disappointingly. But to indict romantic love on these grounds is to imply that if *love is not enough*, if love of and by itself cannot indefinitely sustain happiness and fulfillment, then it is somehow in the wrong, a delusion, even a neurosis. But the error lies not in the *ideal* of romantic love, but in the irrational and impossible demands made of it.

Let us now consider: What are the psychological needs that romantic love satisfies? There are, I believe, a network of complementary needs involved.

1) There is our need for *human companionship*: for someone with whom to share values, feelings, interests, and goals; for someone with whom to share the joys and burdens of existence.

2) There is our need *to love*: to exercise our emotional capacity in the unique way that love makes possible. We need to find persons to admire, to feel stimulated and excited by, persons toward whom we can direct our energies.

3) There is our need *to be loved*: to be valued, cared for, and nurtured by another human being.

4) There is our need to experience *psychological visibility*: to see ourselves in and through the response of another person, one with whom we have important affinities. This is, in effect, our need for a psychological mirror. (The concept of psychological visibility, developed in considerable detail in *The Psychology of Romantic Love*, is basic and central to my understanding of man/woman relationships.)

5) There is the need for *sexual fulfillment*: for a counterpart as a source of sexual satisfaction.

6) There is our need for *an emotional support system*: for at least one person genuinely devoted to our well-being, an emotional ally who, in the face of life's challenges, is reliably *there*.

7) There is our need for *self-awareness and self-discovery*: for expanded contact with the self, which happens continually and more or less naturally through the process of intimacy and confrontation with another human being.

Self-awareness and self-discovery attend the joys and conflicts, harmonies and dissonances of a relationship.

8) There is our need *to experience ourselves fully as a man
or woman*: to explore the potentials of our maleness or
femaleness in ways that only romantic love optimally makes
possible. Just as we need a sense of identity as human
beings, as so we need a sense of identity related to
gender—of a kind most successfully realized through interaction with the opposite sex.

9) There is our need *to share our excitement in being alive
and to enjoy and be nourished by the excitement of another*.

I call these *needs*, not because we die without them, but
because we live with ourselves and in the world so much
better with them. They have survival value.

This list does not seem to me to be the slightest bit
speculative. I believe common experience, observation,
and reason support it.

But if I were to be speculative, I might posit a tenth
need, the need *to encounter, unite with, and live out vicari-
ously our opposite gender possibilities*: the need, in males, to
find an embodiment in the world of the internal feminine;
the need, in females, to find an embodiment in the world
of the internal masculine.

There are couples who remain deeply in love for many,
many years. Even allowing for setbacks, frictions, times of
estrangement and the like, they preserve over time the
essential meaning of romantic love. And there are couples
for whom "romance," whatever the term signifies to them,
vanishes almost from the moment of marriage.

Psychologists seem to know a good deal more about the
failures than the successes, just as they know more about
pathology than health. The danger of such one-sided knowledge, of course, is that it may blind us to life's positive
possibilities. The temptation is to believe that "sickness"
is normal and "health" abnormal. Far more attention
needs to be paid to those men and women for whom
romantic love does *not* end in disenchantment.

My own studies suggest that there are at least some
behaviors we can clearly isolate as being far more characteristic of successful couples than the average.

Couples who remain happily in love over long periods
of time more consistently exhibit these behaviors:

1) *They tend to express love verbally.* This simply means saying "I love you," or some equivalent (in contrast to that attitude best summarized by, "What do you mean, do I love you? I married you, didn't I?").

"Saying the words," one married women remarked, "is a way of touching. Words can nurture feelings, keep love strong and in the forefront of the relationship." Her husband commented, "Saying 'I love you' is a form of self-expression. It's putting a bit of myself out there. So my feelings are in reality, not just inside of me."

2) *They tend to be physically affectionate.* This includes hand-holding, hugging, kissing, cuddling, and comforting—with a cup of tea, a pillow, or a woolly blanket.

"Aren't we all touch animals?" one husband remarked. "An infant first experiences love through touch. I don't think we ever lose that need." His wife added, "For me, cuddling is as important as talking or making love."

3) *They tend to express their love sexually.* People who are happily in love are inclined to experience sexual intimacy as an important vehicle of contact and expression. Sex remains vital for them long after the excitement of novelty has passed.

This does not mean that they regard sex as the most significant aspect of their relationship. They are far more likely to regard their connection at the level of soul (for want of a better word) as the core of their relationship. And there are great variations in frequency of love-making among couples who are happily in love. And yet the expression, "With my body I thee worship," is one they understand and relate to.

Sex is integrated with, rather than alienated from, their feelings of love and caring. The importance they attach to sex is to be found in the emotions with which they invest the act.

4) *They express their appreciation and admiration.* Happy couples talk about what they like, enjoy, and admire in each other. As a result, they feel visible, appreciated, valued.

"My husband has always been my best audience," a woman said to me. "Whether I'm telling him about what I did at work that day, or a remark he liked that I made to someone at a party, or the way I dress, or a meal I've prepared—he seems to notice everything. And he lets me see his pride and delight. I feel as if I'm standing in the most marvelous spotlight—his special way of being aware. That kind of awareness—and then talking about it—is what love means to me. I only hope I give as good as I get, because I'll tell you something: being loved may be the second best thing in the world, but loving someone, really being able to appreciate and admire someone, as I do my husband, is the best. And I do let him know that.

5) *They participate in mutual self-disclosure.* This is a willingness to share more of themselves and more of their inner lives with each other than with any other person. They share thoughts, feelings, hopes, dreams, aspirations; hurt, anger, longing, memories of painful or embarrassing experiences. Such couples are far more comfortable with self-disclosure than the average and, as a corollary, more interested in each other's inner life.

Often, of course, one partner is more verbal than the other. One partner may be somewhat awkward at times about verbalizing intimate thoughts and feelings. And yet, on a relative scale, he or she *reaches out* to the partner as to no other person, and *trusts* the partner above all others, and *listens* to the partner above all others.

6) *They offer each other an emotional support system.* They are there for each other in times of illness, difficulty, hardship, and crisis. They are best friends to each other. They are generally helpful, nurturing, devoted to each other's interests and well-being.

In happy marriages, men as well as women tend to understand the importance of nurturing—in contrast to more conventional relationships in which nurturing, at best, is seen as an exclusively female activity.

Nurturing is acting to support the life and growth of another person. To nurture another human being is to accept him or her unreservedly, to respect his or her sovereignty, to support his or her growth toward self-actualization, and to *care* about his or her thoughts, feelings, and wants.

If we can see only our own needs and not the needs of our partner, we relate as a child to a parent, not as an equal to an equal. In mature romantic love, independent equals do not drain or exploit each other; they nurture each other. *Mutual* nurturing is one of the characteristics we tend to find in happy relationships.

"I think," a man said to me, "that one of the most important things we look for in love is one person who will be truly devoted to our interests and well-being. And that's what the other person naturally expects in return. Without that, what is love? What is marriage?"

7) *They express love materially.* They express love with gifts (big or small, but given on more than just routine occasions) or tasks performed to lighten the burden of the partner's life, such as sharing work or doing more than agreed-upon chores.

The desire to give pleasure to the partner is powerfully in evidence here. As regards gifts, price and income level are not relevant; what is relevant is an underlying intention. The reward is to see an expression of joy or satisfaction on the partner's face.

8) *They accept demands or put up with shortcomings* that would be far less acceptable in any other person. Demands and shortcomings are part of every happy relationship. So are the benevolence and grace with which we respond to them.

Another way of thinking about this point is to say that couples who know how to live together happily do not torment themselves or each other over "imperfections." Each knows he or she is not perfect and does not demand perfection of the other. They are clear that, for them, the partner's virtues outweigh the shortcomings—and they choose to enjoy the positives rather than drown the relationship in a preoccupation with the negatives.

This does not mean they do not ask for—and sometimes get—changes in behavior they find undesirable. But they do not catastrophize difficulties they know they can live with.

9) *They create time to be alone together.* This time is exclusively devoted to themselves. Enjoying and nurturing their relationship ranks very high among their priorities: they understand that love requires attention and leisure.

Such couples tend to regard their relationship as more interesting, more exciting, more fulfilling than any other aspect of social existence. Often they are reluctant to engage in social, political, community, or other activities that would cause them to be separated, unless they are convinced there are very good reasons for doing so; they are clearly not looking for excuses to escape from each other, as is evidently the case with many more "socially active" couples.

"We've been called selfish for wanting to spend so much time alone together," one woman said to me, laughing; she was obviously untouched by the accusation. Her husband added, "But we've never heard that from anyone who's happily married." His wife continued, "I once pointed that out to someone who was trying to give me a hard time. Do you know what she answered? 'Happiness is so middle-class.' A loser's consolation prize if ever I heard one."

It can require considerable independence on the part of a couple to treat their relationship as a major priority. But we find that kind of independence among couples who know how to sustain love across many years.

Once, following a lecture in which I was discussing the importance of time and intimacy for a relationship, a young man and woman came over to me, very enthusiastic about the talk, and proceeded to tell me how happily in love they were—which was how they looked. Then the man said to me, "But there's one thing that troubles me. *How do you find the time for that intimacy?*" I asked him what his profession was and he told me was a lawyer. I said, "There's one thing that troubles me. Given how much in love you are with your wife, and looking at you both it seems clear that you are, *how do you find the time to attend to your law practice?*" He looked disoriented and nonplussed. "The question is incomprehensible, isn't it?" I said to him. "I mean, you *have* to attend to your law practice, don't you?—*that's important.*" Slowly a light began to dawn on his face. I went on, "Well, when and if you decide that love really matters to you as much as your work, when success in your relationship with this woman becomes as much an imperative as success in your career, you won't ask: *How does one find time?* You'll know how one does it."

In my observation, the biggest time-threat comes not from our work, but from our social relationships or what we tell ourselves are our social obligations. Often it is against these that our love needs to be protected. The time that we and our partner spend in the company of relatives, friends, or colleagues can be a source of pleasure, but it is not a substitute for time spent alone together. Nothing is. Evenings spent with people who do not matter to us, or do not matter nearly as much as the ones we love, cannot be reclaimed at a later date, cannot be taken back and relived. *Successful couples seem to know it is now or never.*

Now the characteristics I have outlined are not equally present in every happy marriage or love affair. Even within a relationship each partner does not exhibit them equally at all times. But I strongly doubt that anyone could point to a happy relationship if he or she did not show most of these traits.

I have already suggested that if romantic love is to succeed, it asks far more of us than is ordinarily understood.

The first thing it asks is a reasonably good level of a self-esteem.

If we enjoy healthy self-esteem—that is, if we feel competent, lovable, deserving of happiness—we are very likely to choose a mate who will reflect and support our self-concept. If we feel inadequate, unlovable, undeserving of happiness, again we are likely to become involved with a person who will confirm our deepest vision of ourselves.

If we enjoy good self-esteem, we are likely to treat our partner well and to expect that he or she will treat us well, which tends to become a self-fulfilling prophecy. We will not see ourselves as martyrs or victims. We will not feel that suffering is our natural destiny, and we will not put up with it in passive resignation—let alone go looking for it.

If we lack good self-esteem, we are unlikely to treat our partner well, despite our good intentions, because of our fears and excessive dependency. And if our partner treats us badly, some part of us will feel, "But of course." And if and when our relationship ends and we go looking for a new partner, despair can make us not more thoughtful but more blind—so our self-esteem goes on deteriorating and so does our love life.

If we are to choose a mate wisely, we need to feel that we are deserving of love, admiration, and respect, and that only someone we can truly love, admire, and respect is appropriate for us. If we are to treat our relationship with the care and nurturing it deserves, we need to feel that we are deserving of happiness—that happiness is not a miracle or a mirage but our natural and appropriate birthright.

Our sense of self, the way we perceive and assess ourselves, crucially affects virtually *every* aspect of our existence. That has been the central theme of all my work. As regards love, the first love affair we must consummate successfully is with ourselves. Only then are we ready for other relationships.

And how well can we practice "mutual self-disclosure" if we are strangers to ourselves, alienated from our inner life, cut off from feelings and emotions and longings? Self-alienation is the enemy of intimacy, therefore of romantic love (or any other kind of love). Or if we are estranged from our sexuality, or if we are in an adversary relationship to our bodies, we lack the mind-body integration that romantic love celebrates.

If we have not attained a reasonably mature level of independence and self-responsibility, chances are we will overburden our relationship with demands that can't be met, such as to create (rather than express) our self-esteem and our happiness, or to support the illusion that we are not ultimately responsible for our own existence.

Romantic love requires courage—the courage to stay vulnerable, to stay open to our feelings for our partner, even when we are temporarily in conflict, even when we are frustrated, hurt, angry, the courage to remain connected with our love, rather than shut down emotionally, even when it is terribly difficult to do so. When a couple lacks this courage and seeks "safety" from pain in the refuge of withdrawal, as so commonly happens, it is not romantic love that has failed them, but they who have failed romantic love.

My vision of romantic love is presented in some detail in *The Psychology of Romantic Love*, but perhaps I should say a few concluding words on how the view of love I am presenting differs from traditional views.

I do not, for example share the assumption of some champions of "romantic love" that reason and passion are antithetical. I do not believe that "true love conquers all." Nor that there is only one "soul mate" for each person on earth. Nor that love necessarily entails marriage or that marriage necessarily entails children. I do not believe it has necessarily "failed" if it does not last "forever." I do not insist that romantic love, under all circumstances and conditions, necessarily and always entails sexual exclusivity. I do not see romantic love as the prerogative of youth. I do not identify it exclusively with the excitement of what is merely its first phase: the phase of novelty. To say it once more, I see its success over time as a triumph of psychological maturity.

I see its essence as the encounter of two selves who see in each other a mirror; an opportunity for the celebration of self and of life; a doorway to our ultimate psychological (spiritual) home; and a challenge to the best within us.

Two
Love and Communication

When George came home after a day at the office, he could not decipher the meaning of the expression on his wife's face. Laura's glance seemed peculiarly unrevealing.

"You look awful," were the first words she said to him. "So tired. If you don't take a rest, you'll get sick. I think we should go away this weekend, forget everything; we can walk along the beach and you can just rest."

George looked at her with astonishment and laughed. "I feel fine," he said. "Stop worrying."

Without answering, she walked toward the kitchen. "I'll finish getting dinner ready," she said, her voice uninflected.

But a few minutes later, when George came into the kitchen, he found her at the sink, her head bowed, tears rolling down her cheeks.

"What's the matter, darling?" he asked in astonishment.

"Nothing," she snapped, her voice tight and angry.

She was feeling devastated. She had just told her husband how much she loved him, how much she missed him, how much she longed to spend time alone with him, relaxing, making love, reconnecting physically and emotionally—and he had shown complete indifference. That is what she *thought* had happened.

She was unaware of the actual reality of their interaction. She imagined that she had transmitted her thoughts and feelings and that her husband had heard them—and that he had turned his back. Now she was trapped in the pain of what she perceived as unrequited love. What she was actually trapped in, of course, was a fantasy.

There is nothing unusual about this story. It is how people communicate, or fail to communicate, every day. They do not say what they think and feel, openly and honestly. They say something entirely different that feels "safer"—then are left to wonder why they feel so ineffectual in their relationships.

If Laura had conveyed her actual thoughts and feelings, she still would not have been guaranteed a positive response. But she would have given George far greater emotional incentive to say yes. "I love you and I miss you" is a more inspiring invitation than "You look awful," if the goal is a romantic weekend together. But it does require greater emotional honesty.

Communication is the lifeblood of any relationship, and the love relationship in particular requires communication if it is to flourish. Yet many women and men have great difficulty expressing wants and desires in a simple, straightforward, and benevolent way. Why?

When Laura and George came for counseling, I had them sit opposite each other and I proceeded to explain a process I find extraordinarily useful: the sentence-completion technique. "George," I said, "initially your job is only to listen. Laura will do the talking. Laura, I'm going to give you a sentence stem, an incomplete sentence, and I'd like you to keep repeating the stem, ending the sentence a different way each time. Don't worry if each ending is literally true, or if it makes sense, or if one ending conflicts with another. If you get stuck—invent. Okay? Talking to George now, begin with the stem *One of the things I want from you and don't know how to ask for is*————.'"

Repeating my stem each time, as I requested, Laura provided the following endings:

attention.

more time.

for you to care about what I'm thinking and feeling.

nurturing.

more intimate conversation.

"Fine," I said. "Now switch to the stem 'One of the ways I make it difficult for you to give me what I want is_____.'"

I don't say what I want.

I pretend I don't want anything.

I don't allow myself to know what I want.

I act as if no one has anything of value to offer me.

I expect you to know what I want without my telling you.

I signaled her to pause. "Now switch to 'The scary thing about telling you what I want is_____.'"

you may not care.

I might not get it.

I'll have to admit I have needs.

I'll open myself to being hurt.

I'll be too vulnerable.

Then I suggested the stem "If I were to be more straightforward about what I want_____."

I might get it.

I'd give you a chance.

I could relax more.

you would know me.

maybe you would care.

I would be kinder.

I could love you more.

I think these responses speak for themselves. Many of us, when we were young, did not experience having our wants and desires taken very seriously, which is very often one of the frustrations of being a child. We receive many messages which amount to: "Your wants don't count." Many of us grew up believing our wants would never matter to anyone except ourselves. In some cases, we struggled to make our wants not matter even to ourselves, so the pain of others' indifference would not be so acute. If I never express my wants (or if I can teach myself never to know what they are), I never have to find out whether you will care. I never risk being hurt—I think.

There are no guarantees that someone who loves us will always satisfy our wants. But we will certainly achieve more satisfaction than if we keep our desires secret. To express our wants may not guarantee fulfillment, but to suppress them does guarantee frustration.

I gave George the stem "As I sit here listening to you_____" and his responses are interesting.

I realize I make the same mistakes you do.

I feel I could be more important to you.

I understand why we miss each other.

I want us to be more truthful.

I want to feel trusted by you.

I want us to take a chance with each other.

When dealing with couples who complain of communication difficulties, which is of course the most common complaint, I will ask, in effect, "Do you create a context in which your partner can feel free to share feelings, thoughts, fantasies, hurts, and complaints without the fear that you will condemn, attack, lecture, or simply withdraw? And does your partner create such a context for you?" If a couple cannot answer yes to these questions—and alas, most couples cannot—we need not wonder at the difficulties in their relationship.

"I have finally learned to express negative feelings honestly," said Ann, "but Gary only listens without any real interest in finding a solution. There must be a better strategy than just talking louder, Dr. Branden. What is it?"

When someone behaves in a way that bothers, frustrates, or angers us, begin by describing the behavior to the person and describing our feelings about that behavior, without moralizing, psychologizing, or character assassination. Let our partner know what actions we would like taken. I explained this to Ann, who learned to say to Gary:

"It's taken me a long time to speak honestly with you about things that bother me, and it isn't always easy even now. When I talk to you, you listen without responding, and nothing seems to change your behavior. I feel frustrated, helpless, and angry. It would mean a lot to me if, after you've heard what I have to say, you would share with me your own thoughts and feelings about it."

Here are other statements Ann learned that could evoke more responsive behavior from Gary:

I'm sure you have some negative feelings too that you may not feel comfortable in expressing. Let's try for a solution together rather than be silent and suffer.

Your thoughts and feelings about what I'm saying are important to me. Please tell me how you're reacting.

If you feel I'm misunderstanding you or overlooking something, please tell me.

I love you and I want to protect our relationship. I don't want to accumulate unspoken resentments. I hate it when I have bad feelings toward you. What do you think should be done?

It soon became apparent that Gary's silences came not from lack of love but rather from unspoken hurts and resentments of his own, which he had never known how to express. Sometimes silence comes from feelings of inadequacy to cope with what the partner is saying.

But whatever the reasons of our partner's unresponsiveness, the best strategy is to keep inviting the partner to participate in the solution. Keep interspersing our own statements with such questions as:

What do you think about what I'm saying?

How do you feel about what I'm saying?

What do you think we should do about this?

What's happening inside you right now?

By asking such questions, we do not simply go on talking while letting our partner remain, in effect, outside the relationship. Our inquiries make non-participation by our partners close to impossible.

*   *   *

Although there are many ways to facilitate improvements in communication, one of my favorites is to teach individuals and couples how to use sentence completion on their own, without the guidance of a psychotherapist. A book of mine, *If You Could Hear What I Cannot Say*, is addressed to just this task.

For example, Jane senses that there is something bothering Frank that he has difficulty expressing. They sit opposite each other. She, initially, will do the listening; he will do the talking. Frank begins with a stem such as "One of the things that's bothering me is_____." This might be followed by "One of the things I feel hurt about is_____"; "One of the things I feel angry about is_____"; "I feel upset when you _____"; "If I felt free to talk to you openly_____." Then, to allow Frank to integrate whatever has been said, he might end with "I am becoming aware_____"; "I am beginning to suspect_____"; "Right now it seems obvious that_____."

And then Jane might do a series such as "As I sit here listening to you_____"; One of the things I hear you saying is_____"; One of the things I understand you want from me is_____"; I am becoming aware_____"; and so on.

Sometimes couples have difficulty expressing positives, love, appreciation, and the like. Sentence completion might be done face to face, or via written notes, using such stems as "One of the things I enjoy about you is_____"; "One of the things I appreciate about you is_____; "One of the things I admire about you is_____"; One of the things I love about you is_____"; "One of the things I love about our relationship is_____." I have seen couples use sentence completions of this kind on anniversary and holiday cards . . . and I have also heard reports of couples who understand this method launching into it spontaneously at the dinner table or while out for a drive!

While sentence completion can be a powerful tool for the exploration of serious problems, it can also be a delightful aid when communication is inhibited or blocked even in happy relationships.

If, for instance, we enjoy the way our partner moves, if we delight in a particular expression in our partner's eyes, if we appreciate our partner's thoughts, choices, decisions, and actions, we can learn to communicate our admiration. And doing so is the process by which we make our partner feel visible, appreciated, and loved.

Thus: "One of the things I am aware of about you is_____ "; "One of the things I imagine about you is_____"; "One of the things I know about you that you may not know I know is_____." The possibilities are endless.

If our goal is to improve the quality of communication in our relationship, the most important step is to give up any expectation that our partner be a mind-reader; we need to take responsibility for transmitting that which we want our partner to know. This applies to happy information fully as much as to unhappy information.

As I pointed out in the first chapter, one of the characteristics of couples who remain deeply in love for a long time, as opposed to couples for whom love seems to vanish rather quickly, is that they frequently say "I love you" (or the equivalent) and often express what they admire and enjoy about each other. They understand the nurturing power of communication.

But what of couples who seem truly stuck? Sometimes a woman or a man is reluctant even to experiment with sentence completion, insisting "I have nothing to say." When this occurs, assuming that both people are genuinely willing to work on their relationship, I recommend a twelve-hour intimacy marathon.

In essence, the couple agrees to spend a day together, twelve hours, entirely alone. No books, no television, no telephone calls, no distractions of any kind. If they have children, they call a sitter. They are committed to remaining in the same room with each other, except for meal breaks and bathroom visits. (A hotel or motel with room service is ideal.) They further agree that no matter what the other might say, neither will leave the room refusing to talk. They can sit for several hours in total and absolute silence if they like, but they must remain together. And there must be no physical violence.

I have found that if two people love each other but do not know how to communicate effectively, a twelve-hour session (or several, at monthly intervals) produces radical changes in the relationship. Typically they discover skills in communication they did not dream were possible to them.

A couple conducting this experiment for the first time will usually feel stiff and self-conscious during the first hour or two. They may joke or become irritated. But almost always they begin to communicate. Perhaps one partner talks about something that has angered him or her. Perhaps a quarrel develops. In another hour or two, the situation may reverse itself with a growing closeness and a new intimacy. Very often they make love. Afterward they are generally cheerful. But it may be only three o'clock in the afternoon.

One of them, out of nervousness, frequently proposes that the experiment has worked so why don't they go off to the movies or visit friends or *do something*. But if they stay with their original commitment, as I urge them to do, they soon move down to a much deeper level of contact and intimacy than the earlier one. Often couples share feelings they have never discussed, dreams and longings they have never revealed. They are free during this twelve-hour marathon to talk about anything, *providing it is personal.* No talk of business, the children's schoolwork, redecorating the living room. They must talk about themselves or each other or the relationship.

Having placed themselves in a situation where all other sources of stimulation (or distraction) are absent, they have only themselves, and they begin to learn the meaning of intimacy.

In this context, of course, the use of the sentence-completion process can be powerfully helpful.

Effective "ice-breaking" stems include "One of the things I'd like you to know about me is_____"; "One of the things I wish you understood about me is_____"; "One of the things I wish I understood about you is_____"; "Sometimes I feel turned on when you _____"; "Sometimes I feel hurt when you_____"; "Sometimes I feel happy when you_____"; "If I were willing to let you hear the music inside of me_____."

Perhaps the simplest of all beginnings is "If you could hear what I cannot say_____." Sometimes endings such as the following emerge:

you would know the love inside of me struggling to find a voice.

you would know that when I'm cruel, it's because I'm afraid of losing you.

I'd have to admit my needs and wants.

you would know that sometimes I feel like a child.

you would know that when I'm remote, it's because I don't know what to say or do.

you would see I'm shy.

you would know me.

I would know myself.

I'd have to admit my feelings.

you would hear hello.

maybe we would be ready to be in love.

Three
Sabotaging Love

For many years Jean complained of unhappiness in her marriage because her husband, Paul, was so closed emotionally.

"He won't talk about his feelings," she said. "And he hardly listens if I try to talk about mine. To Paul, emotions are a foreign language. I'm frustrated and starved for intimacy." Finally, Paul consented to accompany Jean for counseling. In a short while, Paul began taking his first tentative steps to opening up—shyly, hesitantly, but courageously. Then an interesting development took place. Jean began interrupting his first timid efforts, changing the subject, belittling his expressions, challenging and correcting him, almost as if her territory were being invaded. The predictable result was that Paul retreated into the shell from which he had been struggling to emerge.

"I don't understand," Paul said miserably. "It's as if she's doing everything possible to prevent me from being the very way she's been crying for."

When Linda and Jeff were having an affair, they both felt their sexual relationship was deeply gratifying; they seemed ideally compatible. But shortly after they married, Linda's interest seemed to drop radically; when they did make love she was barely responsive, and no longer appeared interested in her own orgasms. At the same time she became more and more irritable, like a woman who was sexually frustrated. Jeff did his best to remain sensitive and caring, but nothing worked.

"It's as if she won't allow herself to be happy," he said. "As if she won't allow either of us to be happy. I don't know how to break through."

By the third year of their marriage, Phillip began to feel that Ann had only two emotions: anger and depression. When she was angry, she resorted to ridicule, bewildering and contradictory complaints, and remarks that seemed calculated to hurt. When she was depressed, she often became guilty, apologetic, and passive. In either state Phillip saw her withdrawing from him more and more—and was helpless to understand why. In response, he too began to withdraw; he felt inadequate and defeated. When Ann learned of his affair with an office worker, her first reaction was to become hysterical and enraged; soon that gave way to feelings of self-blame and despair.

"What's the use?" she said. "This is what happens in marriage. I saw the same thing with my mother and father."

When Jean, Linda, and Ann first married, their conscious intention was to be happy. If asked, they certainly would have denied any plan to sabotage their relationship with their respective husbands. And yet, each fell into a pattern of behavior that threatened marital tragedy.

It is useful to understand the how and why, because any one of us may find some aspect of ourselves in the psychology of these three women. Any one of us may at times do things to sabotage our most important relationship.

As a psychotherapist and marriage counselor I see many instances of women and men simultaneously struggling for happiness, marital or otherwise, and taking actions that make their aspirations unattainable. Indeed, one of the first questions I ask any individual to consider is: What is my role in bringing about or at least contributing to the very suffering of which I complain?

At one time or another in our life, that is the question all of us need to ask ourselves.

Later, after we have looked at these three couples more closely and better understand what relationship self-sabotaging means, I will suggest how you can assess *your* behavior in this area, and thereby learn whether you might be undermining your relationship with someone you love.

"I don't know how you can imply that I might be contributing to Paul's emotional repression," Jean protested when she and Paul came to see me. "I admit I sometimes get excited and interrupt when he's trying to tell me something. Don't I have a right to have feelings, too? If he's learning to be open with his emotions, does that mean I have to be closed with mine?"

"I guess that's a valid point," Paul responded, looking off at some distant point in space.

"And yet," I suggested gently, "you do seem to feel that somehow Jean is making it harder for you to break out."

"I would do anything in the world that would help," Jean said impulsively, taking Paul's hand. There were tears in her eyes.

"I wonder if we could drop the idea of blame and try to understand what happens between you two," I said. "I'd like to use a sentence-completion procedure. Paul, I'd like you to look at Jean and listen to what she'll be saying without answering. Jean, I'm going to give you a sentence stem. Keep repeating it, putting a different ending on each time, without worrying whether any particular ending is true or false. If you get stuck, invent. 'One of the ways I make it difficult for you to express your feelings is————.' "

"But I *don't!*" Jean protested.

"Are you willing to try the experiment anyway?"

After a moment's hesitation, Jean plunged in. Here is what, to her astonishment, she heard herself saying:

"One of the ways I make it difficult for you to express your feelings is————."

I interrupt before you really get going.

I correct you.

I tell you not to feel what you're feeling.

I criticize your choice of words.

I get my feelings hurt.

I start arguing.

I sidetrack you in a discussion of my reactions.

I ask you why you didn't do this years earlier.

"Pause here," I said to Jean. "Any of these endings true—or are they invented?"

"They're *all* true," she replied, a little dazed.

"Okay, let's continue. Now we'll reverse. Paul, over to you. 'One of the ways you could make it easier for me to talk about my feelings is_____.' "

And facing her, Paul proceeded as follows:

"One of the ways you could make it easier for me·to talk about my feelings is_____."

by talking about your own feelings, but not when I'm in the middle of saying something.

by not always lecturing me.

by being willing to just listen.

by letting me come out at my own speed.

by not moving around when I'm talking.

by understanding that sometimes I'm very scared.

by accepting my anger.

by not telling me, "I told you so."

by not acting like my parent.

"Good," I said. "Jean, back to you. 'If I give you what you're asking for_____.' "

And Jean plunged in. "If I give you what you're asking for_____."

I'd have to give up control.

you'd begin to see that I'm not always open either.

you'd talk to me more.

I'd learn what you feel.

I wouldn't hold the monopoly on feelings any longer.

I'd sometimes be scared of what you might say.

you might start talking about my shortcomings.

Then I suggested another stem to her. "So long as you're emotionally closed_____." And she responded:

we don't focus on my problems.

I get to suffer and blame you.

I keep you off balance.

I'm one up.

I'm the authority

"My God," she said, turning to me. "Am I really saying all this?"

"I wonder if you'd be willing to accept a homework assignment. Nothing special—just listening when Paul wants to talk to you. Listening like a friend, not a reproachful parent or a too self-absorbed child. Like an equal. Find out what happens. Find out if you like the results. Find out if your marriage works better than it does now. Paul, are *you* willing to try again, to try to come out of your shell?" Paul nodded. "Jean, if you agree to try, you may find it a bit difficult at first. Even frightening, like a plunge into the unknown. But if you do persevere, I think you'll like what happens. I think Paul will, too."

They did.

"Don't you think it's natural that romance and sexual excitement fade after you're married?" Linda asked me.

"She thinks it's for teenagers," Jeff added despondently. "Except I'm thirty-five and as attracted to her as I ever was."

"Do you *never* feel strong desire for Jeff?" I asked Linda.

"Well, of course I do," she conceded, almost reluctantly.

"And what happens at such times?"

"Nothing," said Jeff.

Linda sighed. "I tell myself . . . there are other things that need doing."

When I heard this, I led them right into sentence completion. I asked Linda to face Jeff and work with the stem: "If I were to act freely on my desires for you_____." After some initial stumbling and blocking, here is how she responded:

I'd feel foolish.

I wouldn't feel grown up.

I'd feel undeserving.

"Say that again," I cut in.

I'd feel undeserving.

"Go on," I encouraged her.

I'd feel: Nothing lasts, anyway—why set yourself up to be hurt?

I'd feel frightened of when it would end.

I gave her a new stem: "The good thing about ending things myself is_____."

I don't have to wait.

I don't have to be so afraid.

I reject you before you can reject me.

Then I suggested: "I first learned love and happiness can't last when_____."

Mother told me they don't.

I saw everyone else's marriage turn bad when I was grow-ing up.

my father died and left me.

at the funeral people said, "Life is suffering."

Then I said: "By bringing my own suffering about _____."

I make everyone right.

I make my mother right.

I protect myself.

I don't have to fear being abandoned again, like when my father died.

at least there are no unexpected unpleasant surprises.

Then I said: "If I were to surrender to happiness
_____."

I would be frightened.

Jeff would be happy.

I could be sexual.

we could be the way we used to be.

Then I asked her to switch to: "If I allowed myself fully
to feel my love for Jeff_____."

I'd be ecstatic.

I'd be scared.

I'd be defying Mother's view of things.

I'd come alive.

I'd be my own person.

"Say that again," I requested

I'd be my own person.

my life would belong to me.

I'd take my chances.

maybe tragedy wouldn't strike.

we would be carving out new territory.

I said: "If I sabotage my own chances for happiness
_____."

I'll have no one but myself to blame.

I'll be a coward.

I'll lose the man I love.

I'm not going to do that anymore.

Then we began to discuss the internal messages which,
in effect, told Linda that happiness was not her destiny.

"Expectations turn into actions," I explained. "That's how self-fulfilling prophecies work."

Thereafter, the course of therapy was concerned with helping her to enliven her marriage by challenging these internal messages, and to show her how to experiment with behaviors that would defy the messages. Jeff, too, had played a part in maintaining the problem and now he had to help eliminate it, but I will not discuss that here.

For both of them, however, the essence of the successful pattern of behavior they learned consisted of *honoring* their love for each other, *honoring* their own vision of what was possible to them, and persevering in that vision through every day of their lives.

As to Linda's sentence completions, I think they speak for themselves. *Is there any part of her psychology you recognize?*

" 'They're writing songs of love, but not for me,' " said Phillip. "That seems to be Ann's theme song."

"I know I'm a rotten wife," Ann said. "I can't help it. I get these moods. Sometimes I wonder why Phillip stays with me."

"How do you feel about his affair with another woman?" I asked.

"That's over," Phillip cut in hastily.

"How do you feel about it?" I asked, looking at Ann.

"Devastated. Hurt. As if I deserve it."

"How are you planning to make Phillip pay?"

"Oh, that's behind us now."

"How?"

"What do you mean?"

"How did it get behind you?"

"Well, I—"

"Through discussion? Mutual understanding? Forgiveness? How?"

"Phillip feels awful enough," Ann protested. "Why should I try to make him feel guilty?"

"I haven't talked about guilt. But what do you do with your hurt and anger?"

"Didn't I get crazy for a while?" Ann asked, turning to Phillip.

Phillip said slowly, "I don't think that's what Dr. Branden means. Sure, you shriek at me a lot. But that's not really talking honestly about feelings. Your shrieking keeps me out, it doesn't allow me in. I know I've hurt you. I know you're angry. I wish we could talk about it. I don't want another woman. I want you. The way we were in the beginning, if that's not impossible now."

I thought of something Ann had said about her parents that suggested an avenue of exploration. Explaining how sentence completion worked, I asked Ann to begin with the stem: "If Mother saw me happily married_____." She responded as follows:

she would be hurt.

she would be angry.

she would be betrayed.

she would feel, "How can you do this to me?"

Then I proposed: "One of the ways I protect my relationship with Mother is_____"

by not having a better marriage than she did.

by making her mistakes.

by making Phillip miserable.

by making myself miserable.

Then I guided her into: "One of the ways I keep us unhappy is_____."

by never talking about what's really bothering me.

by getting angry over trivia and avoiding the real frustrations.

by not giving Phillip a chance.

by not telling him my needs.

by pretending I have no wants.

by making Phillip feel whatever he does is wrong.

by withholding sex.

by making him feel ineffective.

by maneuvering him to be like my father.

Then I proposed: "By re-creating my mother's pattern
_____."

I'm a good girl.

Mother will approve of me.

I won't have to be different.

I won't have to be on my own.

I won't have to take my own chances.

I can blame Phillip and then feel guilty.

I never have to grow up.

"If it turns out I'm not my mother and Phillip is not my father_____."

we can be happy.

I don't have to be depressed.

I don't have to swallow my feelings.

I can feel the rage I do feel about my mother.

I can risk Mother's disapproval.

Mother may not even disapprove.

she might even want me to be happy.

I'll know what matters is what I want.

"If any of what I am saying is true_____."

I can be happy.

I can enjoy sex.

I can let Phillip know if something is bothering me without attacking him.

I can give him a chance.

I can take my chances.

I can remember how we felt when we were first married.

Considerable effort was needed, in therapy, to assist Ann in attaining the level of independence necessary for a happy marriage. So long as, subconsciously, she identified her survival with her relationship with her mother (which many women do), she could not allow herself to make a better life for herself than her mother had made for herself. That was the tie that needed to be broken. But the first step was to assist her to see that the frustration and pain of her marriage had not just "happened"— it had been *created*. And for a purpose.

These three stories represent just some of the ways you can sabotage your relationship without consciously intending to and without even being conscious of what you are doing. If you wish to explore this issue in your own life, here are some basic questions to consider:

- Do you accept expressions of warmth, affection, and love from your partner openly, benevolently, and responsively? Or are you closed, withdrawn, inaccessible, elusive?
- When your partner attempts to talk to you intimately or emotionally, do you listen attentively and acceptingly? Or do you typically interrupt, change the subject, lecture, chastise, or become defensive?
- Do you make it easy or difficult for your partner to give you what you want? Do you communicate your wants clearly and graciously? Or do you demand that your partner be a mind-reader? Or do you act as if you have no wants? And when your partner tries to please you, to respond to your wants, do you allow him to do so—or do you criticize or act indifferent?
- When you and your partner are happy together, do you behave in ways that support and sustain that happiness, such as expressing appreciation for your mate's actions? Or do you become depressed, or irritable, or withdrawn, or drop undermining remarks?
- Are you more sensitive to what is right in your relationship, or to what is wrong in it? Do you express positives or only negatives?
- Do you accept your partner's love for you benevolently? Or are you inclined to "test" that love by cruel or hurtful behavior?
- Do you seek to support your partner's self-esteem? Or do you try to influence your partner's behavior by evoking guilt or self-doubt?

After you have answered these questions to the best of your honest ability, you might find it useful to invite your partner to share with you his or her agreement or disagreement with your answers. And if your partner should disagree with some of your answers, remember that you have more to learn—and to gain—by listening than you have by arguing. *One of the ways you can sabotage a relationship is by being more interested in making yourself right than in understanding what your partner is trying to tell you.*

All of us at times know unhappiness in our relationships; that is natural. The question is: Are we willing to take responsibility for recognizing what our own role might be in creating or maintaining that unhappiness? Or will we choose instead to see ourselves as helpless victims to whom life (or our partner) has dealt a rotten blow?

Happily married people do not see themselves as victims—or as martyrs.

Their first response to problems is: What can *I* do to improve or change things?

They face life actively rather than passively. And they do not look for blame; they look for solutions.

More than love is needed to make love work. Knowledge is needed. Skill is needed. Self-responsibility is needed. Attitudes that *allow* love to flourish are needed.

It is up to us.

II. Questions and Answers on Romantic Love

by Nathaniel and Devers Branden

Four
Understanding Romantic Love

In this chapter we address ourselves to a group of questions that all aim in one way or another at clarifying the meaning of romantic love and resolving some of the most prevalent misconceptions associated with it. It is a concept surrounded by false notions. When different people speak of it, they often mean very different things. So we need to be precise in our understanding of what we'll be talking about.

The concept of romantic love, as we intend the term to be understood, is presented in the first chapter. Our answers to the questions that follow are offered as further elaboration and amplification.

Q. What is the difference between "loving" someone and "being in love with" someone?

A. While we can love any number of persons, ordinarily we speak of *being in love* with only one person. We love parents, brothers and sisters, children, friends, and even pets, but usually we are in love with *a* lover.

When we love a person in the most general sense of the word "love," we see in that individual the embodiment of important values of ours, so that we associate the person in some way with our pleasure, joy, or fulfillment. We want to be with this person and feel actively concerned with his or her well-being. In the absence of such a response, we cannot call the feeling "love."

Being in love includes all of the above and more. It implies a response at the highest possible level of emotional intensity. It places the desire for interaction and involvement at the center of our emotional life. It implies the presence of a powerful sexual factor in all its excitement. It conveys the notion of having found a "soulmate." We feel a drive to organize far more of our life around this relationship than around any other. To *be in love* implies not merely love but romantic love.

We have heard the question about the difference between loving and being in love asked most often by those who are confused about their feelings for another person. They may report a deep warmth and affection but no particular spark of sexual excitement. Or there may be sexual desire and a kind of affection but no great admiration, no fascination or enchantment.

A woman complained that the thrill had gone out of her marriage, saying, "I love my husband, but I'm not *in love* with him." Then she asked, "What's the difference, anyway?" She shared many values with her husband, genuinely cared about his welfare, and enjoyed much of their time together. But she did not miss him when he was away on business trips, she found other men far more stimulating as sexual prospects, and she felt no particular need to share important thoughts and feelings with him. She perceived him as existing largely at the periphery of her emotional life and thus felt open to other men's attention, often wondering whether there was "something better" out there. When Devers pointed this out, the woman asked, "But isn't that what happens in every marriage, sooner or later? Isn't this how every love affair ends up?" We shall deal with this question later, but for now we answer briefly: *no*.

Q. **What is the difference between infatuation and romantic love?**

A. In the context of relationships, infatuation means an intense attraction to another arising from our focusing on one or two aspects of the other as if those aspects represented the whole. I see a beautiful face, for example, and assume it is the image of a beautiful soul. I see how kindly this person treats me and assume we share significant affinities. I discover we share important values in one area and expand this area to include the whole sphere of life.

When people are lonely, when they are bored, when they are insecure and low in self-esteem, when they are struggling to overcome rejection, they are especially prone to infatuation. Sometimes they are susceptible because this new person is treating them better than anyone has in the past.

Not that level-headed people never experience infatuation; they may. But they are more likely to be aware that this condition, even if briefly enjoyable, is not romantic love.

To love a human being is to know and love his or her *person*. Romantic love, in the mature sense, requires the ability and willingness to see our partner as he or she is, with shortcomings as well as virtues. We shall return to this theme in discussing the psychological requirements of romantic love in the next chapter.

If we are confused about whether our feelings are infatuation or love, it is useful to ask some questions. How much do I really know about this person? How full a list of this person's assets and shortcomings am I able, and willing, to make? Do I *admire* this individual, or am I just sexually excited by him or her? What do we have in common—and what makes me think so? An impulse to rush past these questions is reason enough to suspect infatuation.

It is not necessarily irrational to have a fling on the basis of infatuation, providing we are clear about our feelings and providing I deceive neither myself nor the other person. But to *marry* on the basis of infatuation—or to make any other kind of serious commitment—is to invite consequences that are all too predictable.

Q. How do I know when I'm in love?

A. Romantic love represents the integration of three factors:
1) a strong sense of affinity, a sense of being "soulmates"
2) the presence of admiration

3) strong sexual attraction

In our view, when these three factors exist simultaneously within a person in his or her response to another, that is the condition we call "being in love."

Q. Why do people say, "Love is blind"? Is it true?

A. Sometimes men and women experience a strong sexual attraction for each other, conclude that they are in love, and proceed to live together or marry on the basis of their sexual attraction. They ignore the fact that they have few values or interests in common, have little or no appreciation of each other as persons, are bound to each other predominantly by dependency, have incompatible personalities and temperaments, and, in fact, have little or no real interest in each other. When they "discover" these facts, the relationship often falls apart. Then someone says, "Love is blind." But are such relationships love? We do not think so.

Even when two people are genuinely in love, they may focus in the early phases of a relationship on pleasurable affinities (shared values) and ignore differences (conflicting temperaments or goals), which may later prove to be antagonistic rather than complementary. Love is not blind, but we may not want to see aspects of our partner's character or behavior that could place the relationship in jeopardy. We may choose not to see or hear what is plainly available. It is a disastrous error to tell ourselves "All that will change," or "I will change it after I am married."

Perhaps it is more accurate to say that love occasionally pretends to be blind.

At the same time we should recognize that romantic love provides us with a unique power of sight. We are unlikely ever to know another human being as well as we know the person we are in love with. When we are not in love, the fascination is not there, so the attention is not there, the absorption is not there. Contrary to the notion that "love is blind," love can be the most powerful of all magnifying glasses, allowing us to see what otherwise remains invisible.

Q. "Romantic love" evokes associations of valentines, violins and soft music, and knights in shining armor. Aren't we too sophisticated for that today?

A. It is unfortunate that a few popular symbols of what people like to call "romance" have replaced the psychological reality of romantic love. We need to think more deeply than that. Valentines and violins have nothing to do with the essential meaning of love between man and woman.

And no, if we want to speak of sophistication, we are not too sophisticated today. We are not sophisticated enough.

The first time Devers heard this question raised, she remarked, "The error is already evident in the use of the word 'sophistication.' In this context, it's a frivolous word."

"Sophistication," in the modern world, is often the last refuge of people who are simply frightened of passion, devotion, and commmitment.

Many people are so naive as to believe that if they surround themselves with the trappings of "romance"—if they plant themselves in a glamorous restaurant with soft lights and music—something magical will happen to their relationship. They sit there staring at each other helplessly, waiting for the ambiance to work a miracle. It never does.

Externals can be very pleasant, but they are not the core of romantic love. The core lies within the mind of the individual man and woman. It is there or nowhere.

"Being romantic" means *treating the relationship as important*, behaving in ways that underscore its importance. Flowers can be a lovely gift, or a meaningless gesture. There are people who know how to be romantic in a hovel; there are people who do not know how to be romantic in a palace.

As for the image of the knight in shining armor, it is an ambiguous symbol. It could represent a woman's longing for a man she can admire. It could also represent the immature wish for someone coming to rescue her, coming to make the world safe for her. As such, it is more a projection of adolescent insecurity than a projection of mature love. From the male perspective, it could represent a man's desire to achieve an admirable soul and to be so perceived by the woman he loves. But it could also represent the craving of a man to play hero for a "weak and helpless" female. We see romantic love as a relationship between independent equals, not between a waif and a rescuer, or a child and a parent.

Q. Why is love so important? Can't we live without it?

A. People all over the world live without romantic love and always have. Other things being equal, they do not live as happily.

There is certainly no duty to seek romantic love. If there is any obligation involved, it is only to our own possibilities for life, and only if we so choose.

Romantic love answers to very real human needs, and fulfilling those needs makes us feel more energetic, more complete, and more capable of joy in living. We feel safe in saying that anyone who has been in love, even briefly, will recognize the validity of this statement.

Recently a highly successful businessman said to us, "I don't know whether we need romantic love or not. All I know is, I've had it and I lost it and I feel empty. I'm proud of what I've achieved, but other achievements don't make up for what's missing."

Q. Is romantic love for everyone?

A. In one sense, we want to say yes. In another sense, no.

As a *potential*, providing we have met other needs (self-esteem, for example) and have achieved an appropriate level of maturity, romantic love *is* for everyone. But millions of men and women grow to adulthood with so many unresolved emotional problems, such impoverished self-esteem, so much self-alienation, that their efforts at love fail inevitably—if it occurs to them to seek out love at all.

We have met people who are completely unprepared for our concept of love. They have nothing in their own experience to help them understand it. They tend to perceive other human beings as sources of security or danger, sexual satisfaction or frustration, help or hindrance, convenience or inconvenience, but never as ends in themselves. Romantic love is not for them.

For now at least, those who know how to love and how to sustain love are definitely a minority. But this is a reason, not to ignore or discount them, but to study and better understand them. What they have, we want for ourselves as well.

If we may permit ourselves a prophecy: we believe that, over the next decades, as individualism and individuality become better understood within cultures throughout the world, more and more people are going to become conscious of and long for the experience of romantic love. We think it is the wave of the future.

Q. Is there one "ultimately right" person for each of us?

A. If we are in a relationship that is intensely happy and has been so for some time, our perfectly natural tendency is to think of our partner as "the one and only." But a realistic consideration will suggest to us that there are other people in the world, even if we never meet them, with whom we might be happy.

True enough, we would not be happy in quite the same way. Every relationship is unique. Every love affair is a private universe. But the odds would be hopelessly against us, and life would be truly malevolent, if there were only one person in the whole world with whom we could have a joyful relationship.

A successful relationship between a man and a woman rests on fundamental similarities between them, and on complementary differences. Harmony in love requires a partner with whom we enjoy essential affinities in values and in basic outlook on life. But the excitement we also hope to find requires that there be some differences in personality development, in skills, in style of being and doing—complementary differences, obviously, not antagonistic ones. This special combination is necessary to make two people "right" for each other.

One of the pleasures of love is to experience a sense-of-life affinity—"He (she) sees and feels about life as I do." A sense-of-life affinity encompasses a basic similarity in how we perceive life, how we respond to its challenges, what we see as its possibilities and rewards, how we feel about its dangers, what kind of survival strategies we develop.

Given this sense-of-life affinity, the right attitude toward love, and an appropriate level of maturity and self-esteem, a number of people could certainly satisfy us romantically. Whether or not we will be fortunate enough to meet them is another question.

We suspect that as an individual becomes highly evolved, highly realized, and attains a greater capacity for love, the number of people who could present themselves as potential "soulmates" declines. But this is hardly the dilemma of most men and women.

Indeed, many who insist on a "one and only" who is out there somewhere or is unavailable are rationalizing their fear of failure. Rather than saying "I don't believe anyone could love me" or "I'm afraid of being hurt," they say, "I don't know how to find him (or her)." Or, "Unfortunately, he (she) is already married." Such statements may be true, but they are often self-deceiving.

It is useful to remember that likes attract, not opposites. Opposites, on the fundamental level, repel. Couples described as "opposites" are sometimes merely people with complementary differences. We tend to fall in love with persons of approximately the same level of self-esteem, maturity, intelligence, and attractiveness as ourselves. When there are differences, there are usually compensating factors: for example, a good-looking man attracted to a rather plain woman who surpasses him in education and social self-possession. If, therefore, we see someone daydreaming of that "one and only"— clearly his or her superior in just about every conceivable respect—while avoiding real love in the real world, then we understand we are seeing a person in retreat from the challenges of life.

Q. Is it possible to be in love with two people at the same time?

A. In human relationships almost anything is "possible."

*   *   *

In principle, yes, someone can be in love with two people at the same time. But in our observation it is very difficult to love two people with *equal intensity* over a period of time. Briefly: yes. Long-range: doubtful. Such is the conclusion forced upon us. by our experience with men and women who have believed themselves to be in love with two people.

Usually it is a married person having an extramarital affair who will query us on this. There is no doubt but that for a while the individual feels him or herself to be enamored of both the spouse and the lover. Passion does not continue, however, to flow equally in both directions. Sooner or later one relationship almost always yields to the other; one is "comfortable"; the other is "intense."

Sometimes neither is all that intense, and the individual is *half* in love with two persons, not fully in love with either. This is among the most common patterns we have seen. Each relationship helps the individual tolerate the deficiencies in the other.

The circumstances of life often force us to choose, even if we are genuinely in love with two people. Love requires time, energy, attention, commitment. Our resources are not unlimited. We can only spread ourselves so thin. Whatever our initial feelings, these other demands speak against our sustaining an intense relationship with two people.

But, to say it once more, we hesitate to declare anything of this kind impossible, when no doubt there are people presently involved in three-way relationships that seem to be working to everyone's satisfaction.

Q. Don't time and familiarity wear down romantic love? Is it realistic to expect to be excited about the same person after many years?

A. It is a mistake to reduce romantic love to its first phase, in which the thrill of novelty plays a powerful role. There is an excitement that normally accompanies the happy beginning of a relationship, which must change in quality with time, but it need not become extinguished.

I shall never forget the expression on Nathaniel's face when a psychologist at a party said to him, "I am per-

fectly willing to admit there are a few couples around who
somehow manage to go on adoring each other, even after
being together for years. But how meaningful is that to
the rest of us? Don't you think it's best to think of such
people as some sort of biological mutation irrelevant to
our studies?"

It is easy enough to be cynical about man/woman relationships and to point, in justification, to all the people
who experience disenchantment. But cynicism cannot accommodate the reality of those couples who retain their
deep love for each other into old age. Theirs is a passion
different from the passion of youth, no doubt, but it is
nonetheless meaningful. It encompasses a profound sense
of connectedness and involvement forged from life problems met and resolved, crises overcome, struggles, losses,
and victories shared together. Passion renews itself in
admiration earned and earned again, enhanced by years
of mutual devotion, support, and integrity. Sexual enchantment is kept alive, not only by everything two people have shared, but also by the ability of each to keep his
or her excitement for life fresh and to see the other, each
morning, as if for the first time.

Some people explain the erosion of excitement and passion as a "fact of life," observing that men and women
behave "romantically" in the early stages of a relationship
but neglect to when they are feeling more secure, as after
marriage. And why is this? It is not in the nature of life.

Sometimes a partner abandons loving behavior because
the other has, sometimes because of the misguided notion
that once we're settled it is time to be "practical" and
"realistic." An accumulation of hurts that have not been
dealt with can undermine passion; so can the fallacious
belief that once the "challenge" of love has been successfully met, it is best to move on to other "challenges."
Sometimes it perishes because there was no real basis for
passion in the first place.

The first wisdom needed is the wisdom of knowing
whom to love. The next is knowing that love, like any
other human value, can be sustained only by action, energy, and conscious intention. Without them there can be
no reasonable hope of maintaining passion.

Knowing how to keep our excitement for another person alive is not different from knowing how to keep alive

our excitement for life. Knowing how to honor and sustain our ability to be excited is among the rarest of human achievements and, in our view, among the most admirable.

Q. Can romantic love develop during the course of a relationship that began as a friendship without sexual attraction?

A. Statistically, it is safe enough to say that sexual attraction is present almost from the very beginning in most love relationships. But this rule is not an absolute. There don't appear to be any limits on how romantic love can begin.

Two couples we know had been friends for many years. A partner in each relationship died within a relatively short time. Shortly thereafter, the surviving man and woman fell in love.

Another man and woman we know used to talk with each other as friends about dates or affairs they had with other people. Then, as a result of some subtle shift that neither had noticed, they became aware of sexual feelings which deepened into love.

But there is another side to this story. We also know a man and woman, friends for some years without sexual involvement, who decided one day to initiate an affair, on the grounds that there was no one else in the picture for either of them. They were genuinely fond of each other, and both felt lonely. It didn't work. After being comfortable with each other for many years, lovemaking turned them into strangers. The unique combination of affinities and differences necessary to ignite a love affair was missing and could not be commanded into existence. "It would have been so convenient," one of them sighed to us. Love is not controlled by convenience.

Q. Is it realistic to expect one human being to fulfill most or all of our needs?

A. First of all, we have some needs that no human being can fulfill except ourselves, such as the need for self-esteem.

* * *

Beyond that, if the question means "Is there a place in the life of a couple in love for other friends and other caring relationships," the answer is clearly yes. No one person can provide us all the gratifications and joys inherent in social existence. For instance, just as there are unique rewards in relationships with the opposite sex, so there are special forms of satisfaction to be found in relationships with members of our own sex.

When an individual lacks self-confidence, he or she may be jealous of any other relationships the partner has and may try to manipulate the partner into relinquishing them, asking "Aren't I enough?" We need to challenge the premise of such a question: namely, that if we are "enough," our partner will not desire interaction with anyone else.

If we have a solid self-esteem and know we are loved, it is natural to take pleasure in our partner's finding other human beings to appreciate. It would not be a happy state of affairs if there were only one human being in the world for each of us to enjoy. (No, this is not a sanction for extramarital relationships, a separate issue we discuss later.)

We place a terrible burden on the person we profess to love if we expect him or her to fulfill all of our needs. Sooner or later we are very likely to provoke resentment. It is a terrific hardship to carry total responsibility for another person's emotional life. Independent men and women do not approach love with such unrealistic demands.

No matter how much in love we may be, it is normal and appropriate to find other human beings we can like, respect, and admire. For a while, in the excitement of a newly developing relationship, this desire may diminish in importance and urgency. That is natural and understandable. But love as a way of life does not mean sole and exclusive focus on only one other human being.

Q. Is it true that love can be just as wonderful "the second time around"? Can feelings be equally intense twice in a lifetime? Is it possible to be deeply, deeply happy in more than one love relationship during a lifetime?

A. Yes to all of the above. But will the two relationships feel the same? Never.

*   *   *

Just as each individual is unique, so is the emotional quality of the love between two individuals. It can never be duplicated, and one should never try. Reaching back for yesterday's happiness can sabotage today's. And if we are open to today, open to the uniqueness of a new person we have encountered, then it may be possible to feel as intensely, or even more intensely, than we did in the past.

In *The Psychology of Romantic Love*, I wrote about the death of my previous wife, Patrecia, in a drowning accident, after our many years of happiness together. I wrote about the agony and chaos of the period that followed and about the very difficult circumstances under which my love for Devers, and hers for me, developed.

There were many painful feelings that had to be assimilated and worked through before I was fully able to open myself to another woman. I will not repeat what I wrote about the process of recovery or Devers's extraordinary support and courage. I needed time to accept my new happiness, to welcome the life that was returning within me, to open myself to the powerful feelings Devers evoked. I had to allow myself to feel as deeply in love as I do. Today I am experiencing the most profound and consistent joy I have ever known. I have reached a fulfillment I could not have imagined when I was younger.

Q. Why do some people seem frightened to love?

A. At many of our Intensives on *Self-Esteem and Romantic Relationships* we invite participants to talk about their fears in this area. Here are typical comments:

"Deep down, I don't feel lovable. Anyone who appeared to love me would only end up rejecting and abandoning me—so why open myself to being hurt?"

"I've been hurt and rejected so many times in the past. Why go through it again?"

"Suppose I fall in love and my feelings aren't reciprocated?"

"I'll lay myself bare to raw emotions, and then it won't last."

"I don't know anyone who's happily married. How can I hope to be any different?"

"Being open and vulnerable is too scary. Loving someone means giving that person the power to hurt you."

"If I allow myself to be happy, I feel something terrible will happen."

"Sooner or later your partner is always unfaithful. It's too painful."

"If I were to pull the plug on my wants and needs, I'd overwhelm the most loving person in the world. Better not get started."

"I'd feel like a traitor to my parents if I had a better marriage than they did."

"Love can't last. And it hurts so much when it ends."

"If I were to fall in love, I'd lose my identity. I'd be overwhelmed and controlled by the person I love."

"I'm afraid of appearing foolish."

"If I fall in love, I'll start thinking about marriage, and I don't want the financial responsibilities."

One them recurs in all these responses: the desire to experience joy is less powerful than the desire to avoid pain. This, in the end, is the downfall of most people, and not only in romantic love. An obsession with avoiding hurt restricts and impoverishes their lives.

People who are afraid of love do not necessarily avoid it. More often they seek it out and then withdraw from committing themselves all the way. They love from inside their armor. Afraid to surrender, they fail in their relationships, and they tell themselves how right they were to be afraid of love.

In the early stages of our relationship Nathaniel and I both had fears to deal with, rather different in terms of precipitating causes from those suggested above.

For a long period following Patrecia's death, Nathaniel was in a state of shock and disorientation. His love for me at times had the quality almost of panic, as if some part of him were expecting a new disaster. He would sometimes become remote and withdrawn. I recall when we were conducting an Intensive in New York City. I was to meet him in our hotel suite but was delayed by half an hour. When I arrived he was pale, distraught—and angry. He was tormented thinking something had happened to me. Allowing himself to love me meant, among other things, opening himself once again to the kind of loss he had suffered with Patrecia. Such losses are in the very nature of life. He said many times that he felt he was being tested in the most severe way, on whether he could practice what he preached: not to deny his feelings but to own them, to allow the organism to feel whatever it needed to feel in order to recover, trusting that eventually life and serenity would return. They did, through a long, difficult process.

I had my own fears. When I met Nathaniel, I was in my forties. I had never been passionately in love—not all the way, not without reservations. I had been divorced and widowed when I was young and had been single for fifteen years. I believed in the possibility of the love Nathaniel writes about, but I had never found it. I no longer thought it likely that I would. I had relationships with men I liked and respected and in some cases "had a love for," but never with anyone I could fully commit myself to. It was frightening and unfamiliar, being confronted with the living reality of my private dreams. I had been taking care of myself and knew how to think "I." I did not know if I could learn to think "we." I was afraid, at times, to believe I was as happy as I was. It was doubly difficult because I was in love with a man whose period of mourning was to last a very long time. I knew that the measure of his pain was the measure of his ability to love, and I admired him for that. Still, the waiting was not easy.

We talked about our fears, and talking saved us. We withheld nothing; we concealed nothing. We could tremble together and talk about it. I told him—and I meant it—that I was happier than I had ever been in my life. Even at the worst moments, I knew that this was what one lives for.

Q. Why does romantic love so often end in disappointment and disenchantment?

A. Perhaps, because the initial choice of partner is inappropriate. Or perhaps, because of doubts and insecurities felt by the man and woman. Or because of unrealistic expectations. Or because of their lack of knowledge and their ineffectiveness at communication. Or because they are unable to deal with normal conflicts and frictions of living together.

Sometimes a man and woman *require* the relationship to fail—one or the other or both have a self-concept that contains the injunction "You are not to be happy. You are not to succeed at love."

Sometimes one partner unrealistically imagines that marriage will alter the character of the other and learns too late that it is not the function of marriage to reform character.

Sometimes one partner stops growing. Sometimes one partner tries to arrest the other's growing.

There are many reasons why relationships fail, and it is impossible to list them all. It is more useful to explain and discuss how to succeed at love. The place to begin is an understanding of what romantic love requires of us in terms of our own psychological development. Let us turn to that subject now.

Five
Living Up to Romantic Love

We take a great step toward the possibility of romantic love when we begin to realize that "love is not enough," that the success of a relationship depends on more than the presence of certain feelings, however intense they may be.

No human value perpetuates itself automatically. We must act to sustain it. The ultimate value, life itself, clearly demands action of us, and the same is true of every value that makes life worth living, such as love and work.

In the case of work most people understand the necessity for action fairly well. No one would imagine that merely feeling "I love my work" guarantees success. Without competence and continued effort the business disappears, the career falters, the work fails. The identical principle applies to romantic love.

"Competence" may sound like a strange word to apply to loving, and yet the evidence is unmistakable that some people know more about how to love and how to sustain love than others.

We need to consider how they came by their good fortune or, more precisely, their skill. It is not an impenetrable mystery. Their "good fortune" has its roots in a set of psychological states bearing directly on love's requirements. Let us now examine what these requirements are.

Q. Whenever you discuss the psychological requirements of romantic love, you invariably mention
self-esteem first. Why is self-esteem so important?

A. As a psychological state, self-esteem is a sense of
personal efficacy and personal worth, an integration of self-confidence and self-respect. It is the conviction—or, more precisely, the experience—of being *competent*
to live and *worthy* of happiness. Self-esteem is the assurance that we can meet life's requirements and challenges.

Two earlier books, *Honoring the Self* and *The Psychology of
Self-Esteem*, provide a general treatment of the importance
of self-esteem in human life. In Biocentric therapy, we
place primary emphasis on strengthening self-esteem as a
precondition of success in life and in love. Here we shall
concentrate exclusively on how the presence or absence of
self-esteem affects our ability to love. (We speak relatively
of self-esteem, since everyone has *some* self-esteem. It is
always a matter of degree.)

To condense our position into a single statement: the
first love affair we must consummate successfully is the
love affair with ourselves. Only then are we ready for
other relationships. Now why should this be so? Part of
the answer was given in the first chapter. But there is
more to be said.

If I enjoy a fundamental sense of efficacy and worth,
and if, as a consequence, I feel lovable as a human being,
then I have a basis, or precedent, for appreciating and
loving others. I am not trapped in feelings of deficiency. I
have a surplus of life within me, an emotional "wealth"
that I can channel into loving.

Without respect for who I am and enjoyment in who I
am, I have very little to give. My sense of deficiency, of
not having anything to give, impoverishes me. I see other
people essentially as sources of approval or disapproval. I
do not appreciate people for who they are in their own
right. I am not looking for people whom I can admire and
with whom I can share the excitement and adventure of
life. My ability to love remains undeveloped, unactualized.

If I do not feel that I am lovable, it is very difficult to
believe that anyone else loves me. If I cannot accept myself, how can I accept your love for me? Your profession

of love is confusing. It confounds my self-concept, since I know I am not lovable. Your feeling for me cannot possibly be real, reliable, or lasting. It is very difficult to let love in.

Even if I consciously disown my feelings of being unlovable, even if I insist that I am wonderful, the poor self-concept remains deep within me to undermine my attempts at relationships.

I attempt love, but the base within is shot through. And in my insecurity I subvert love by demanding excessive reassurance, by venting irrational possessiveness, by making catastrophes of small frictions, by seeking to control through subservience or domination, by finding ways to reject my partner before my partner can reject me. The possibilities for sabotage are unlimited.

Examples abound of people acting against their own best interests in love. One of our clients, a man with poor self-esteem, married a woman who cared for him deeply. Nothing she could do was ever enough to make him feel loved. Endlessly he cried for more. He was insatiable. When at last she convinced him that she really loved him, he began to wonder whether he had set his own standards too low. He began to wonder whether she was good enough for him. "How can I love this woman who is inferior even to me, who has been so easily duped into loving me?"

Another client of ours, a woman with low self-esteem, felt compelled to tell the man who adored her all the ways in which other women were superior to herself. When he did not agree, she ridiculed him. It took her a year of concentrated effort, but finally she wore him down and he left her. She was hurt and astonished. She felt like an abandoned child. How could she have so misjudged him? But soon she was telling herself, "I always knew no one could love me." This is a perfect example of self-fulfilling prophecy.

A good self-esteem generates, among other things, a set of expectations. So does a poor self-esteem. In both cases we convert our expectations into reality. When I feel deserving of love, I deal with you in a confident, benevolent, and loving manner, and I receive your love. When I feel undeserving of love, I deal with you in a fearful, suspicious, and hostile manner, and you withdraw from me. My self-concept is my destiny.

Men and women of high self-esteem tend to expect success and happiness, and they proceed to create these conditions for themselves. Men and women of low self-esteem tend to expect defeat and suffering, and these people shape their lives accordingly.

There is still another aspect of self-esteem we must consider along with self-confidence, and that is self-respect: the conviction that we are worthy of happiness.

If I do not feel deserving of happiness, consciously or subconsciously, or if I have accepted the belief that happiness is somehow wrong or cannot last, how am I likely to respond when happiness comes knocking at my door in the form of romantic love? No matter how much I may have waited and cried, I will not welcome love when it arrives.

The possibility of happiness triggers anxiety. Happiness is not my fate. Joy does violence to my self-concept, since happiness is possible for some, but I am not among the chosen: "They're writing songs of love, but not for me." I don't experience the happiness as real. It never fully convinces me. Not, at any rate, as pain does, because my pain is what life is really all about.

Happiness makes me feel anxious. When we feel anxious, we attempt to reduce our anxiety. If happiness is the cause of my anxiety, the solution is to get rid of the happiness. I cannot permit myself to be distracted from the real nature of life by the temporary illusion of joy.

Not that I am forbidden to dream of happiness, aspire to happiness, yearn for happiness. So long as joy remains out of reach, so long as it remains a distant longing, I can accept it.

One woman came for therapy in anguish because, she said, she could not understand why her marriage was failing. She had been taught as a little girl that a desire for happiness is selfish—which is true—and that virtuous people are not selfish—which is false. (We shall take up the whole question of selfishness and its appropriateness shortly.) To be concerned with the self at all, she had been taught, is evil, whereas to serve others is the essence of virtue. She saw her mother subordinate herself over years to her "duty" in a marriage devoid of joy or satisfaction.

On a subconscious level the daughter felt driven to re-create her mother's pattern to secure her mother's love. As it happened, she married a man with greater gifts for participating in a marriage than her father's. She had to work harder to produce the defeat her subconscious self needed, quietly belittling her husband and playing the martyr. "It really doesn't matter that you don't earn as good a salary as most of my friends' husbands do. Let them have their fancy clothes. Last year's dress is good enough for me." She professed bewilderment about why her marriage was unfulfilling; she even chose to enter therapy. She wanted to know: "Why are my husband and I unhappy?" We invited her to consider whether or not she felt she could be comfortable with happiness. After realizing with dismay that she couldn't, she took the first step toward interrupting her pattern of self-sabotage.

This is why the questions "Do I feel that I am lovable?" and "Do I feel I deserve to be happy?" must precede all others. Self-esteem is crucial to romantic love.

Q. Isn't there the risk that I will turn self-love into arrogance and overestimate my abilities?

A. Not if we are talking about authentic self-esteem, not if we are talking about genuine self-acceptance and joy in being alive.

Arrogance, boastfulness, and the overestimation of our abilities result from inadequate self-esteem. People of high self-esteem do not have to prove their worth to other people, or flaunt it, or exaggerate it. Several studies disclose that persons of high self-esteem assess their talents and abilities more realistically than persons of low self-esteem; the latter tend either to underestimate or overestimate what they are able to do.

So we are talking about compensation for feelings of inadequacy, the result not of too much self-esteem but of too little.

We discussed this question with a very self-confident, very happily married man of our acquaintance, who remarked, "I was thinking recently about all the things I love about my wife, and I realized that one of the things I love most is her ego. I have a strong ego myself, and I couldn't bear to be married to a woman with a weak one. I'd always be worried about overwhelming her. It's wonderful never to have to think about that. Her self-confidence and assurance make me feel free to be myself." Clearly he was not talking about arrogance or phony pretensions of superiority.

A well-known study conducted several decades ago by Abraham Maslow points in a similar direction. Maslow asked a group of women, who had achieved high self-esteem scores on a previous test, to arrange in order of priority the qualities they found most desirable in a mate. Self-assurance, self-assertiveness, and self-confidence headed the list. Women of somewhat lower self-esteem taking the same test ranked such qualities as kindness and gentleness highest.

To contribute to a person's self-esteem is to contribute to his or her ability to love. When parents treat a child with respect, when they acknowledge the child's dignity as a human being, when they encourage autonomy, when they delight in the child's delight in his or her own being, they help their child lay a magnificent foundation for future success in love.

Q. **What can we do to help if the person we love really doesn't have good self-esteem?**

A. Let us begin by acknowledging that there are limits to what we can do. We cannot be a psychotherapist to a person we are romantically involved with.

But we can always relate to that person from our own vision of his or her worth and value, providing an experience of total acceptance and respect.

We can consistently speak and react with genuinely felt confidence in our partner's ability to change and grow.

We can learn to listen to our partner's expression of feelings, even when those feelings are self-doubt and insecurity. And we can listen without indulging any impulse to lecture, argue, sermonize, or reform, because we understand that fully owning and experiencing unwanted feelings is the first step toward transcending them.

We can recognize that sometimes our partner may use self-disparaging remarks to manipulate us into disagreeing and paying compliments. We can refuse to participate in that game.

It can be very difficult to go on believing in another person when that person seems not to believe in him or herself. One of the greatest gifts we can offer is our refusal to buy a person's negative self-concept, seeing through it to the deeper, stronger self. We cannot always succeed. We can only try.

Successes, when they do occur, can be dramatic and inspiring. After participating in our Intensive on *Self-Esteem and the Art of Being*, one man wrote: "I went home and said to my lover, 'Let's talk about the ways each of us allows self-doubts to sabotage our relationship.' I volunteered to go first. I got a large note pad and showed her one way of using your sentence-completion technique. I wrote at the top of the page, 'One of the ways I sabotage our relationship_____'; then, as rapidly as I could, I wrote fifteen endings to that sentence. She gasped when she read them. 'Do you know all that?' she asked. I thought she might collapse with shock. 'Here,' I said, giving her the pad, 'you try it. Write as fast as you can. Don't worry whether any particular ending is literally true or false. Say things that are crazy. That will help to get you going. Later we can talk about what fits and what doesn't.' She could only produce seven endings, but every one of them was on target. We were laughing, but there were tears in our eyes. That night was a beginning for us, letting go of our destructive routines."

Q. How mature do we both have to be to make a success of romantic love?

A. "Maturity" and "immaturity" describe success or failure in an individual's biological, intellectual, and psychological evolution to an adult stage of development. With regard to intimate relationships, certain aspects of psychological maturity are especially important:

The development of a healthy level of self-esteem.

The development of autonomy. With a capacity for self-reliance and self-regulation, we are able to face our partner as an independent equal. We do not look to another person to create our self-esteem or the meaning of our life.

The development of our own set of values, so that we know what is important to us, what we care about, what is dispensable and what is indispensable. We are able to select a partner with some degree of realism.

The development of internal resources, so that we are not bowled over by the normal difficulties, obstacles, and frictions of life in general and of a relationship in particular. We can respond to challenges with confidence, optimism, and determination.

Too many men and women grow to adulthood biologically while remaining children psychologically. They expect others to assume responsibility for their existence, especially their emotional life. They wait for others to make them happy. They imagine "the right person" can provide them with feelings of self-worth, can spare them the necessity of independence, can help them evade the immutable fact of their ultimate aloneness. And they feel hurt, resentful, and depressed when others fail to live up to their expectations.

Many men and women carry into adulthood so much "unfinished business" from childhood, so many unresolved conflicts, that they enter the arena of adult love with terrible handicaps. And yet they are blind to their own incapacities, crying for love to perform a miracle. When the miracle does not happen, they blame love. Or they blame their partner.

"I can't understand how any grown-up person can talk seriously about romantic love," said an embittered divorcée of thirty-five, still trapped in the problems of a four-year-old girl. She had been trying vainly all her life to win affection from a cold, unresponsive father. She was shocked and disappointed when, soon after marriage, she realized that her husband, too, had emotional needs; she had imagined that she only had to be aware of her own. "Anyway," she added, "men don't know how to love."

Often two "grownups" marry with the tacit agreement that one will play child and one will play parent. Neither is comfortable relating adult to adult. It is as if one had said to the other, "I will be helpless, needy, dependent, a taker rather than a giver, and in exchange you can enjoy feeling superior." It is as if the other had said, "I will play the strong, supportive parent figure, the responsible one, the one who carries the burdens for both of us, the martyr at times, and you can enjoy feeling safe." Inside the "child" is a disowned adult, who will sooner or later cry out for expression. Inside the "parent" is a disowned child, who will sometimes cry out over unmet needs. Conflicts are inevitable. The one playing helpless will protest, "Stop treating me like an infant!" And the one playing tower of strength will protest, "Why should all the burdens be mine? Can't you ever carry your own weight?"

There are females who feel comfortable as a mother or as a child but not as a woman. There are males who feel comfortable as a father or as a child but not as a man. And they have a genius for finding each other. Then they conspire to produce their own kind of tormented nursery, calling it a "marriage" or a "relationship."

Psychologists often explain the failure of a relationship in terms of the couple's "unrealistic expectations." Unrealistic expectations can result in disaster, undeniably. But we need not abandon the dream of romantic love as unrealistic, if we recognize that it is an adventure for adults, not for children. It *demands* realism.

Let us clarify our understanding of what constitutes adulthood. To be an adult does not mean abandoning the child's part of our personality but integrating it as we grow in self-responsibility and autonomy. Without in any way contradicting what we have just said, we affirm that there is a child in each of us and that the child is to be loved, respected, and treasured, not denied or repudiated. Mature men and women can love the child in their partner, can delight in nurturing the child, because the child is not all there is. The child is part of the adult they love.

A paradox emerges here. If we insist on remaining a child, the child is forever frustrated, the child's needs are forever unmet. If we can accept the responsibilities of adulthood, if we are willing and able to grow up, then we can become ready for a love affair in which the child within is nurtured.

Q. What do you mean by nurturing?

A. Nurturing is acting to sustain the life and growth of another person.

Thus understood, nurturing is clearly significant to any love relationship. It should not be confused with "mothering," which is merely one form of nurturing, appropriate in particular circumstances, but not the essence of the concept. (Sometimes grown men are a little afraid to permit themselves to be nurtured because they mistakenly associate it with being mothered, or else they are reluctant to nurture because they mistakenly associate it with mothering.)

Ideally, nurturing is a reciprocal process. If we can see only our own needs and not the needs of our partner, we relate as a child to a parent, not as an equal to an equal. In romantic love, independent equals do not drain or exploit each other; they nurture each other. Mutual nurturing is one of the characteristics of happy relationships.

To nurture another human being is to accept him or her unreservedly, to respect his or her sovereignty, to support his or her growth toward self-actualization, and to *care* about his or her thoughts, feelings, and wants. It is to create an environment in which a person can flourish.

To nurture is to love not only our partner's strength but also his or her fragility, not only that within our partner which is powerful but also that which is delicate, not only that which is grown up, but also that which is young.

In no sense, however, does this imply tolerating or encouraging behavior that is destructive to our partner or to ourselves. It does not mean putting up with everything at the expense of our own well-being. It does not mean surrendering our judgment or our sanity. But it does mean giving support when support is possible and appropriate.

There are moments when all of us want to abandon the responsibility of adulthood, want to be stroked, pampered, cared for almost as a child, and there is no implication of immaturity in this. It is merely part of being human. And when our partner gives us this form of nurturing, we feel loved.

To be nurtured, then, is to experience that I am cared for. Not to be nurtured is to be deprived of the experience that I am cared for.

Furthermore, if I do not respond to my need to be nurtured, I am unlikely to provide nurturing to the person I love. If I cannot accept the child in myself, I am unlikely to accept the child in you.

I can best express my love for you by nurturing you and by allowing you to nurture me, with a willingness to give and to receive.

Frustration arising from inadequate nurturing seems to be one of the most common complaints of couples, yet it is often difficult for them to talk about. They often feel uncomfortable acknowledging such a need.

Sometimes men and women who are married and in love with their mates fall into affairs with other people, longing not so much for excitement as for nurturing. The need for nurturing is a powerful one, whether or not we recognize it as such.

Often partners have difficulty saying, "I just want you to hold me and cuddle me for a few minutes, without sex." Or, "Sometimes I would love you to bring home flowers. I don't need them, but they would make me feel cared for." Or, "I would like you to hold me, if I'm weeping or unhappy, without your feeling there is anything special you have to do." Or, "I would love it, when I'm feeling down, if you would just look at me and let your smile say you believe in me and you know I'll land on my feet."

In our therapy and couple counseling sessions, we help couples learn the nurturing process. We may have them sit facing each other for a two-person sentence-completion exercise. One person listens attentively while the other does a string of ten or fifteen sentence completions, beginning with "One of the things I want from you and am hesitant to ask for is_____." The idea is to finish the sentence several times as rapidly as possible with whatever comes to mind. Then the process is reversed; the partner who had been listening now does his or her own string of sentence completions. We then encourage the couple to explore whether or not each would be willing to provide what the other wants and, if there are barriers, whether they can be overcome. If they are willing to cooperate, the couple can begin their apprenticeship in the art of nurturing.

I want to acknowledge that a great deal of what I understand of this subject I have learned from Devers. She is by far the most nurturing human being I have ever encountered. It was she who made me aware of the importance of including a discussion of nurturing in *The Psychology of Romantic Love*. I recall that early in our relationship I had been inconsiderate in some matter. Devers said to me, "I know that you are a very kind, generous, and loving man. But a lot of your kindness is impulse. It happens or doesn't happen, according to the mood of the moment. There is such a thing as learning the discipline of kindness." For me, that phrase, "the discipline of kindness," expresses something profoundly useful in mastering the art of nurturing.

Q. Why do women seem to know innately how to nurture better than men?

A. In all the cultures we know of, females are raised to regard some forms of nurturing as essential to their femininity. In our culture, little girls receive dolls, tea sets, and other toys and games that teach *taking care of.*

Males are not generally exposed to any comparable emphasis on the value of nurturing. They learn more about the value of work. Indeed, many males perceive nurturing as somehow incompatible with manhood.

Some evolutionary biologists believe that there is a genetic basis for the fact that nurturing seems to come more naturally to women than to men, that the issue is not simply one of cultural training. Even if this is true, even if women are constituted to learn nurturing more readily, that does not change the fact that both sexes need nurturing and need it from each other. If a man does not know how to nurture, he is limited in his effectiveness at love. Men need to learn to perceive nurturing as a normal expression of love, not of femininity.

We tell men, "Everything you want from a woman, a woman wants from you." Men who have difficulty accepting this, men who can perceive themselves only as the recipients of nurturing, have never fully emancipated themselves from the relationship of a son to his mother, which is hardly an ideal model for romantic love.

Q. Doesn't selfishness destroy romantic love?

A. It would be closer to the truth to say that *selflessness*, the absence of self, destroys love. As was already seen in our discussion of self-esteem, persons with deficient egos are badly hampered in their efforts to build satisfying relationships.

We regard selfishness, rationally understood, as necessary to our well-being. But let us consider what selfishness means, since it is surrounded by confusion.

To be selfish is to be concerned with our own interests. When we speak of selfishness, we mean honoring the needs, wants, and values of the self, honoring our own life. We mean having the courage to stand by our own convictions (which are an expression of the self) and to fight for our own happiness (which is a celebration of the self).

If this is to be regarded as evil, then life itself must be regarded as evil, because an organism that does not honor its own interests cannot survive. (For more on this, read the discussion on the ethics of self-interest in *Honoring the Self*.)

By "selfishness," we do *not* mean disregarding the rights of others or sacrificing others to our own goals. Or exploiting people. Or seeing nothing but our concerns of the moment. Or being blind to everyone else's concerns. Indeed, we consider such policies self-destructive, and self-destruction is not in our self-interest. It is irrational. If, for example, a man continually neglects a wife he loves—goes off to a party, leaving her ill at home and unattended—and if she leaves him and he then is devastated and miserable, we might say that he was "selfish." But it would be truer to say he had a fool's notion of his self-interest.

In love, the self is celebrated, not denied, abandoned, or sacrificed. What I love is the embodiment of my values in another person, which is hardly an expression of self-abnegation or selflessness.

To love *selfishly* does not mean to be indifferent to the needs or interests of our partner. When we love, our concept of self-interest embraces the well-being of our partner. This is the great compliment of love: to declare to another human being that his or her happiness is of *selfish* importance to ourselves. Do we wish to believe that for our partner the relationship is an act of self-denial and self-sacrifice? Do we want to be told that our happiness is *not* of selfish interest to our partner?

To quote from *The Psychology of Romantic Love:*

> To help us understand this, let us ask ourselves whether we want our lover to caress us *un*selfishly, with no personal gratification in the doing, or do we want our lover to caress us because it is a joy and a pleasure for him or her to do so? And let us ask ourselves whether we want our partner to spend time with us, alone together, and to experience the doing as an *act of self-sacrifice.* Or do we want our partner to experience such time as glory? And if it is glory that we want our partner to feel, if we want our partner to experience joy in our presence, excitement, ardor, passion, fascination, delight, then let us stop talking of "selfless love" as a noble ideal.

Even in the most intimate and loving of relationships, where we care deeply about our partner's happiness, we still need to respect our own needs and wants. No one denies that compromise and accommodation are necessary in every relationship. Sometimes I do things to please you that I may not especially feel like doing. Sometimes I will place your immediate concerns above my own. To label such behaviors as sacrifices is to poison their meaning as expressions of love. If too often I ignore my own needs and wants in order to please you, I commit a crime against both of us: against myself, because of the treason to my own values; against you, because I allow you to become someone I will resent.

As we have already indicated, there are persons so deficient in maturity, so narrow in their vision of their own interests, that they do not understand the sharing and nurturing so essential to romantic love. But enjoining such people to be less "selfish" will accomplish nothing. They need to learn, not to set aside their own interests, but to expand their understanding of where their interests lie.

Q. What is the difference between compromise and sacrifice?

A. A compromise is an agreement reached as a result of mutual concessions.

If I want to spend our two-week vacation in New York City and my partner wants to spend it in Chicago, and we agree to spend a week in each city, we have compromised. If I sometimes spend time with my partner's family when I'm not in the mood to, and my partner sometimes spends time with my family when not in the mood to, this again is compromise, the kind of adjustment we need to make in just about any relationship at one time or another.

To give a personal example, Devers and I have about the same taste in movies, but each of us has preferences not shared by the other. I am more partial to science fiction, while Devers has a passion for movies about horses. Occasionally we go to movies alone, but since we enjoy going with each other whenever possible, we have negotiated the following procedure: if there is no movie we are both *equally* eager to see, then we take turns selecting the movie we will go to, each accommodating the other.

This principle, of course, applies to more than movies. It is a way of life. We are two separate and unique individuals, and our inclinations and preferences cannot always be perfectly matched. We do not "keep score." But we approach differences on the premise that we *want* to accommodate each other whenever we can do so without major discomfort (and sometimes even then).

No surrender of moral principles or personal integrity is involved in compromise, no act of self-destruction. Sacrifice, on the other hand, literally involves self-destruction. Its first meaning in any dictionary is the surrender of a precious value to a deity, such as an immolated victim.

Sacrifice in everyday life means the surrender of a precious value in the name of duty, against what the sacrificer perceives to be his or her own self-interest. If, for example, a wife insists that her husband continue in a high-paying job he detests, in order to keep her in luxuries, she is demanding a sacrifice from him. If a husband demands that his wife set aside a career to devote herself entirely to him, placing his happiness above her own, he is asking for a sacrifice.

Whether or not a particular act should be called a sacrifice depends, of course, on our values. Any act becomes a sacrifice when we feel we have surrendered a higher value to a lesser one (for example, giving up our integrity to avoid upsetting a partner). In exchanging a lesser value for a higher one, we feel we have gained by the act (for example, giving up my vacation plans in order to spend the money on the best medical attention for my ailing spouse. If I were to call it "sacrifice," what would I be saying about our relationship?).

So while compromise and accommodation are essential, sacrifice is dangerous to a relationship. We need sensitivity and judgment to tell us when we've crossed the line between compromise and sacrifice. If our support of a relationship leaves us always feeling angry, hurt, or impoverished, we are probably not supporting the relationship at all but committing treason against ourselves.

When we try to assert our own rights, we may be accused of "selfishness." We should not be afraid of this word. The accusation of "selfishness" is often a manipulative response to perfectly appropriate acts of self-assertion.

A marriage counseling client said to me, "Any time I suggest to my husband that I have needs or wants of my own, any time I express desires that inconvenience him or the kids, he tells me, 'Don't be selfish.' What a sweet racket that is!" She had come to therapy after her guilt had turned into rage. Stumbling through bewilderment, she felt her warmth, tenderness, and love for her family evaporating, leaving a residue of bitter duty. As she learned to take proper care of herself, to respect her own needs and wants, her love for her family returned, and she saw that her husband was also lost, that he too felt like an object of sacrifice with no rights of his own. After joining her in therapy, he learned greater respect for her needs as he learned greater respect for his own. Together they came to appreciate that love is not for victims.

Whoever teaches that love is most beautifully expressed by sacrifice understands neither love nor sacrifice, or else is no friend of love.

Q. **How can I surrender to love and still preserve my independence and sense of personal identity? Is there not an unavoidable conflict here?**

A. We do not deny that in any relationship each party must make a number of adjustments. A process of learning is involved in shifting from "I" to "we." We do challenge the notion that this shift entails any loss of independence or personal identity. If it did, we would question whether love was worth it.

A woman once asked this question at an Intensive, and rather than answering directly, Nathaniel invited her to participate in an exercise. He asked her to face the group and do a series of sentence completions, beginning with "When I speak of losing my independence, what I really mean is_____." Here are the sentence endings she rapidly came up with:

I'll have to do whatever the man wants.

my needs won't count anymore.

I'll have to turn into a selfless servant like my mother.

giving up anything just to keep him.

I'll be so scared of rejection I'll sell out.

I'll have to admit I have needs.

I'll give someone the power to hurt me.

I'll have to accommodate my lifestyle to his.

No answer of ours could have been as penetrating as the answers she provided herself. The knowledge was already within her. The technique of sentence completion allowed her to gain access to it.

Surrendering to love does not, in the nature of things, mean surrendering our convictions, values, integrity, or mind. It does not mean selling our soul to keep love. Yet to this woman it meant exactly that. Why? Her responses indicate that for a long time she had been disowning a need for love. The need was so urgent that she was in danger of giving herself away entirely if she ever succumbed to it. She paid a miser's price for her "independence," denying herself to everyone, including herself.

In order to start her toward a resolution, Nathaniel followed with a second exercise. He asked her to repeat a particular sentence again and again, taking a deep breath each time before saying it, testing how it felt: "I really would like to experience love . . . and perhaps I don't have to sell my soul to get it." Nathaniel did not ask her to agree or disagree with the sentence, merely to experience saying it aloud to a large number of people. Each time she said the sentence, her body relaxed more; a smile grew tentatively into radiant amusement. "Has your question been answered?" Nathaniel asked. "Yes," she laughed.

In our experience, the more self-confident men and women are, the more enthusiastic they are in surrendering to love. And the less self-actualized they are, the more frightened they are of surrendering to love. Independence is actually a prerequisite of love, not a barrier. To worry about losing myself in love suggests that my sense of personal identity is rather fragile in the first place.

When we fall in love, we experience another human being as enormously important to us, enormously important to our personal happiness. We allow that person to enter the private world within us, which no one else ever enters or perhaps even knows about. We allow that person to matter at the deepest level of our being. Surrender is involved, but not a surrender *to* the other person; we surrender ourselves to our feelings *for* the other person. Without that surrender, love is incomplete.

It is a fallacy to tell myself, "I must be who my partner wants me to be." That would be a betrayal of self and also of the partner, because it implies faking. It implies deception and manipulation. Sooner or later I will resent my partner for not seeing the self I have chosen to conceal. Sooner or later my partner will resent me for not being the person I pretended to be. Lies do not work. Deception and phoniness are not practical. Unfortunately, the world is full of unhappy couples who believe otherwise.

As a postscript, it is perhaps worth mentioning that if it is an error to assume that we will lose our identity in a relationship, it is no less disastrous an error to hope to find our identity in a relationship. Immature people imagine that "love" can fill a vacuum of identity. Love is for people who already have identities. Love is for people who know who they are.

If I do not yet know who I am, if I do not experience myself as having an identity, whom are you doing to fall in love with? What do I expect you to respond to?

It seems appropriate to conclude with a quotation from *The Pscyhology of Romantic Love:* "First, a self—then, a possibility: the exquisite joy of one self encountering another."

Q. **Why do I always seem to be attracted to partners I clearly can't be happy with?**

A. Let us begin by remembering what we said in the previous chapter about the problem of fearing happiness. Sometimes we believe, subconsciously, that we are not supposed to be happy, that we do not deserve it, or that something terrible will happen to us if we are happy. To be happy means we are immoral. And we organize our love life so that we make happiness impossible for ourselves even while professing, on a conscious level, to desire happiness.

We see ourselves as a martyr perhaps, re-creating the life story of our mother or father, and martyrdom requires that someone make us suffer. When we find our leading man or lady, our persecutor, we describe our response as "love."

We may be afraid of the challenges of love, afraid of testing ourselves, afraid to learn whether or not we are able to keep another person's devotion. To avoid anxiety and uncertainty, we precipitate the worst, all the while bemoaning our choice or partner.

Sometimes we are afraid to abandon our defenses, being convinced that to be open is to be hurt. So we select a person who *will* hurt us, thereby justifying our anxiety and our defenses. We do not have to change or grow. We have proved ourselves right. The world is full of people who would rather be "right" than happy.

If we experienced considerable rejection as children,

being rejected may have been built into our self-concept. "I am a person destined to be rejected." Under the influence of this subconscious programming, we look for people to reject us, to let us down, betray us, abandon us, as Mother or Father did, and bewail the way the people treat us after we've chosen them.

More than one of these attitudes can co-exist in the same person. A woman came to me for therapy and said, "Devers, I always fall for men that are either married or have emotional problems. I always end up giving. Taking care of them. The married men claim not to love their wives and to care for me, and yet I feel rejected and used."

A mirror can be a marvelous aid to self-discovery. I sat her in front of a mirror in my office and told her that the reflection was her present self, Barbara, the adult. The person looking into the mirror was Barbie, age five, who was in the room with me. I encouraged her to deepen her breathing as little Barbie watched the reflection of grown up Barbara, and then I said, "How fortunate that you can look and see the woman you are going to become. This is a magic mirror that allows you to peek into the future." Tears rolled down Barbie's face, and when I asked her why, she pointed to the grownup in the mirror. "She looks so sad and frightened."

I asked Barbie to do some sentence completions for the stem "Mother gave *us* a view of men as_____." She replied with such endings as "cold; not there; busy; impatient; no feelings; only caring about what they wanted." When I asked her to work with another stem, "One of the ways *we* stay in control is_____," she replied: "pick men we know won't be good to us; play games; never get involved all the way; set ourselves up to be treated badly." When she was given the stem "Until Daddy gives *us* what we want_____," she replied, "we're not going to be happy; we won't grow up; we'll keep falling for men who don't know how to love; we'll keep trying to get what we want from creeps; we'll stay clear of men who expect us to be adult women." The stem "One of the ways I (Barbie) keep you (Barbara) safe is_____" led to endings such as "keeping you on the sidelines of relationships; selecting men with whom you can know the end at the beginning; keeping you with the types you're already familiar with;

letting it all be a game." The stem "If we were to be
happier in love than Mother was_____" led to "she'd
never forgive us; she'd be hurt; she'd be jealous; she
wouldn't love us anymore."

Not everyone's problems are as complex, fortunately.
This woman needed psychotherapy to work through the
many barriers that stood in her way.

Readers whose blocks and conflicts are not as severe
and who would like to begin exploring this question on
their own may find this exercise useful. Take a notebook
and write "The good thing about being attracted to people who will make me unhappy is_____ ." Then, as
quickly as possible and with as little censorship as possible, without worrying about literal truth or falsehood,
write ten or fifteen endings. As a variation, write "The
bad thing about being with a person with whom I could
be happy is_____," again listing ten or fifteen endings
(ignore the impulse to protest that there is nothing bad
about being with such a person). Try these as well:

> When I'm with a person who treats me well_____
>
> If I were to find myself enjoying a relationship_____
>
> If it ever turns out that being in love doesn't mean I have
> to be miserable_____

If you do these sentence completions with true spontaneity, you may have some surprises in store for you. You
may even find yourself smiling. Enlightenment just may
wedge one foot in the door.

Q. Why am I so often attracted to people who are
almost certainly unattainable?

A. Our answer to the preceding question applies here.
We will just add one or two comments.

Being attracted to a person we cannot have is very safe.
As with the question about a "one and only," we face no
challenge, we expend no effort, we overcome no anxieties. We can drift in a cloud of self-deceptions.

Anyone might meet a very attractive individual who is
happily married or otherwise unavailable and generate a

few pleasant fantasies about him or her. There is no harm in this. It is only harmful as a way of life. If we are attracted only to people who are unattainable, we have to look at our fear of intimacy with a real person in the here and now. We have to consider whether or not we fear rejection—or fear happiness. And if we wish to grow, we have to be willing to accept our anxieties, experience them, and move through them.

In addition to the sentence completions suggested in our preceding answer, here are others that are useful to experiment with:

If I were to find myself attracted to someone who was available_____

The good thing about being attracted to someone who is unattainable is_____

The bad thing about being attracted to someone who is attainable is_____

Don't rehearse answers. Don't try to reason it out. Allow endings to flow spontaneously from the subconscious mind with as little obstruction or self-criticism as possible. Be willing to say *anything*. Afterward, decide what is true and what is false.

Consider it an exercise in deepening self-awareness. Sentence completion tends to interrupt habitual, mechanical patterns of response—turning the lights on. It is far less easy to behave self-destructively when we see precisely what we are doing and why. Moreover, as we learn not only to recognize but also to own and experience our feelings, we become "unstuck," no longer quite so bound by past programming. And we are likely to be more open to experimenting with new behavior—dating people who *are* available, who *do* treat us well. New territory opens to us.

Q. Is there any "cure" for my tendency to idealize my lover and then feel disappointed when he or she does not live up to my expectations?

A. A good way to begin is admitting that we may be avoiding signals that get in the way of our fantasies because we want to be in love. If we can fully recognize how much we want things to be a certain way, we free ourselves to see clearly when they are not.

If we have this tendency to idealize, it is not useful to berate or reproach ourselves for it. Adding guilt merely makes the problem more difficult to solve. We can respond instead with compassion for our longing and for the loneliness from which it may have sprung, and then we can take a deep breath and ask ourselves, "Now what are the facts about this person to whom I am attracted?"

It is often useful to put our thoughts on paper. First, make a list of all the traits of your partner that you like. Avoid sweeping generalizations; the more specific you can be, the better. Make a list of any traits you do not like, enjoy, or respect. If you feel resistance at this point, sentence completion can help:

*One of the things I don't enjoy about him (her) is*_____

*One of the ways I wish he (she) were different is*_____

*One of the things that bothers me about him (her) is*_____

*One of the things that sometimes annoys me about him (her) is*_____

When a woman asked at one of our Intensives about the tendency to idealize, Devers had her work with a sentence stem that illuminates still another aspect of this issue: "The good thing about idealizing the man in my life is_____." The woman responded with "maybe he'll do the same for me; maybe he won't notice my shortcomings either; maybe he'll think I'm perfect, too."

When we are willing to be honest about our own shortcomings, we are more comfortable about perceiving shortcomings in our partner. If I can love myself without denying my shortcomings, I can love you without evading yours. Then our love can happen in reality. And neither of us will have to resent the other for not living up to a fantasy.

Q. Do you think it's a good idea to have a number of relationships or affairs so that I can better choose a partner for life?

A. According to statistics, a man who marries before he is twenty-five faces an 80 percent chance that his marriage will end in divorce. With or without experience in relationships, early marriages are very risky ventures. Few of us are equipped in our early twenties to make a lifetime commitment to another person.

Since every relationship is a potential source of self-discovery and, therefore, of maturation, some experience in relationships or affairs prior to marriage gives us a better opportunity to learn who we are, what we want, what is most important to us. Thus it gives us a better chance of choosing a life partner wisely.

People who marry without prior experience often begin to wonder in their later years what they have missed. They begin to feel restless and dissatisfied with their marriage, and divorce is the common result. With those who have satisfied their curiosity and who are not still wondering what is "out there," this particular problem arises less frequently.

Of course there is absolutely no guarantee that a given individual will learn from his or her past experience. Some of the most "experienced" men and women we know are also the most blind when it comes to love and marriage. We are thinking of a man of our acquaintance who recently married for the fourth time. Apart from his marriages, he is the "graduate" of innumerable affairs. A highly successful businessman, he had little nurture from his parents, who subtly communicated (his father in particular) that he would probably "not amount to much." His two brothers, who became "professional men," were the favorites. He is almost invariably drawn to women a good deal younger than himself, who take from him but rarely give in return. He "fathers" them, spoils them. They are impressed by his success and utterly oblivious to his emotional needs. He exhausts himself trying to entertain them, showers them with gifts, asks for nothing in return, and is chronically depressed. He cries for help, entering psychotherapy every once in a while but never staying longer than a few sessions. In the past ten years, he has gone through perhaps a dozen different psychotherapists.

The point is, experience per se guarantees nothing. The

question is whether or not a person thinks about his or her experience and learns from it. The statistics available suggest that people who marry with *no* previous experience in relationships and people who marry with a *great deal* of experience are unlikely to remain with their marriage partner.

The fact that some experience is good does not mean that a great deal of experience is better, from the point of view of choosing a life partner.

Perhaps we can best answer this way: experience cannot guarantee your choosing wisely, but lack of experience endangers your chances of choosing wisely and well.

Q. You speak of how important mutual self-disclosure is to a good relationship. Why can't more couples do this? Why is it to difficult?

A. Through mutual self-disclosure a couple share their feelings, thoughts, fantasies, memories, concerns, and aspirations. It is a two-way process of *self*-disclosure correlated to an interest in the disclosures of the *other*. The process of mutual self-disclosure goes to the heart of what is meant by two people "sharing a life."

Unfortunately, most of us are raised and educated in ways that make the practice of mutual self-disclosure difficult. We learn very early to deny what we feel, to pretend, to wear a mask, and eventually we lose contact with our inner self. We become *unconscious* of our inner self—in the name of "adjustment" to the world around us.

Our elders encourage us to disown fear, anger, and pain, because such feelings make them uncomfortable. Often they don't know how to respond when the pretense of family harmony is shattered. We are also encouraged to hide (and eventually extinguish) our excitement. It gets on their nerves. It makes our elders unpleasantly aware of what they have surrendered long ago. It disrupts routine.

Emotionally remote and inhibited parents tend to raise emotionally remote and inhibited children, not only through their explicit communications, but also by their own behavior, which proclaims to the child what is proper, appropriate, socially acceptable.

Since so much in childhood is frightening, bewildering, and frustrating, we learn emotional repression as a defense mechanism, as a way of making life more tolerable. We learn all too quickly how to avoid the nightmare. In order to survive, we learn to "play dead."

"Playing dead" is so common that we generally find it a normal and desirable state of affairs. Too often psychiatrists join parents and teachers in advising, "Don't be too happy, don't be too sad, don't be too excited—that's the formula for a well-adjusted life." In fact, it is the formula for psychic numbing and self-alienation. It is the formula for self-rejection and self-estrangement. In the most profound sense, it is antilife.

And it is antilove, because love requires openness, vitality, spontaneity, passion, vulnerability. Small wonder that the average couple finds mutual self-disclosure so difficult. They have been educated against it since the day they were born.

So much of the joy of love has to do with showing and sharing who we are. Self-disclosure enhances the experiences of psychological visibility, and it nourishes loves. Support and validation by our partner are impossible without self-disclosure, and so, in turn, is growth.

If we are free to know honestly what we feel and to experience it, then we can share our inner life. But we cannot share if we do not know ourselves. If we are forbidden to know or afraid to know, if we have learned *unconsciousness of the self*, then we are crippled for genuine intimacy, which means that we are crippled for romantic love.

In working with couples who wish to move through this barrier, we almost invariably suggest the "experiment in intimacy" described in *The Psychology of Romantic Love*. In essence, they agree to spend a day together, twelve hours, entirely alone. No books, no television, no telephone calls, no distractions of any kind. If they have children, they call a sitter. They are committed to remaining in the same room with each other, except for meal breaks and bathroom visits. They further agree that no matter what the other might say, neither will leave the room refusing to talk. They can sit for several hours in total and absolute silence if they like, but they must remain together. And there must be no physical violence.

We have found that if two people love each other but do not know how to communicate effectively, a twelve-hour session at least once a month produces radical changes in the relationship. They discover skills in communication they did not even dream they possessed.

A couple conducting this experiment for the first time will usually feel stiff and self-conscious during the first hour or two. They may joke or become irritated. But almost always they begin to communicate. Perhaps one partner talks about something that has angered him or her. Perhaps a quarrel develops. In another hour or two, the situation may reverse itself with a growing closeness and a new intimacy. Very often they make love. Afterward they are generally cheerful. But it may be only three o'clock in the afternoon.

One of them, out of nervousness, frequently proposes that the experiment has worked so why don't they go off to the movies or take a drive or visit friends or *do something*. If they stay with their original commitment, which of course we urge them to do, they soon move down to a much deeper level of contact and intimacy than the earlier one, and the area of communication begins to expand. Ignored or disowned emotions rise to the surface of awareness. Often couples share feelings they have never discussed, dreams and longings they have never revealed. They discover things in themselves and their partner that they never saw. They are free during this twelve-hour session to talk about anything, *providing it is personal*. No talk of business, the children's schoolwork, redecorating the living room. They must talk about themselves or each other or the relationship.

Having placed themselves in a situation where all other sources of stimulation are absent, they have only themselves, and they begin to learn the meaning of intimacy. Although every couple's experience is different in important ways, there is almost always a gradual deepening of feeling. They give up "playing dead."

Another process we use in assisting couples to open up emotionally is the two-person sentence-completion exercise. Usually we introduce the couple to the process during a psychotherapy session. Then the man and woman continue at home on their own.

They sit facing each other. One is the silently attentive

listener, the other is the speaker. They reverse roles when it feels like the right moment. Suppose *A* is the listener and *B* the speaker. *B* might begin with a sentence stem such as "One of the things I'd like you to know about me is————," repeating the stem with a different ending ten or fifteen times. Then it is *A*'s turn with the same stem, if the moment is right. During the exercise, there is no discussion, no comment on each other's endings, no arguing. *B* might then go on with:

Ever since I was a child————

Sometimes I feel hurt when————

One of the things I wish you understood about me is————

Sometimes I feel sexually excited when————

Sometimes I feel happy when————

If I were willing to let you hear the music inside of me————

If it feels appropriate, *A* goes through the same set of sentence completions (couples generally learn to improvise their own stems). Often we advise couples to use a tape recorder so they can refer later to precisely what they said, since they defer all discussion until after the exercise.

It is almost impossible to convey in print the power of the sentence-completion exercise as a technique for breaking through barriers of repression. Throughout this book we will mention situations in which the technique can be useful. We urge readers to experiment and decide for themselves whether it can contribute both to self-awareness and to effective communication. Since *The Disowned Self* is addressed explicitly to the problem of self-estrangement, it is particularly useful to read as an aid in developing comfort and ease with self-disclosure.

Q. How important to the success of romantic love are the man's and woman's attitudes toward sex? And how important is sexual compatibility?

A. Since the presence of a powerful sexual element is one of the defining characteristics of romantic love, as contrasted with other kinds of love, a man's and woman's attitude toward sex and their ability to enjoy sex with each other naturally play a powerful role in determining the quality of their relationship. Sexual frustration and incompatibility are among the most painful sources of friction.

Romantic love requires a set of attitudes that make erotic fulfillment possible. These attitudes will be reflected in answers to such questions as the following:

To what extent am I aware of myself as a sexual entity?

What is my view of sex and of its significance in human life?

How do I feel about my own body? (This last does not mean, *How do I appraise my body esthetically?* but rather, *Do I experience my body as a value, as a source of pleasure?*)

How do I view the opposite sex?

How do I feel about the body of the opposite sex?

How do I feel about the sexual encounter of male and female?

What is the level of my ability to act and respond freely in this encounter?

More than in any other realm, our total personality tends to find expression in sex. Several studies suggest that, other things being equal, the higher the level of our general self-esteem, the more likely it is that we will respond in a healthy and affirmative way to our own sexuality and to sex in general.

An affirmative response to our sexual nature is one of the most important preconditions of success in romantic love.

With regard to the questions listed above, this means we are disposed to experience sex as an expression of the self rather than as something alien, darkly incomprehensible, sinful, or dirty. We have a positive and self-valuing feeling about our own body and an enthusiastic appreciation of the body of the other, which together embody a capacity for freedom, spontaneity, and delight in the sexual encounter.

Through the giving and receiving of sexual pleasure,

lovers continually reaffirm that they are a source of joy to each other. Joy is a nutrient of love: it makes love grow. On the other hand, it is very difficult not to interpret sexual neglect as rejection or abandonment, no matter what the partner's protestations of devotion.

This is one of the reasons why, when there is a disparity between the sex drive of a man and woman who have a good relationship, the less desirous one does everything in his or her power to be available to the other—not as a duty or an act of self-sacrifice, but as an act of love (generally as the result of a conscious decision). We can take joy in our partner's pleasure even during times when we are not intensely oriented toward pleasure ourselves. Of course we must always reserve the right to say no at times, but it is a right that wise lovers exercise as infrequently as possible (except, perhaps, when there are very deep problems demanding resolution).

No, sex is not all there is to romantic love, but can one imagine fulfilled romantic love without it? Perhaps under very unusual, very tragic circumstances, but never as a preferred way of life. Sex at its highest potential is an exquisite celebration of love. Even in the later years of life, when frequency of sexual intercourse may be diminished, the act remains a precious form of connectedness replaceable by no other.

Often problems of so-called sexual incompatibility are in fact problems of emotional incompatibility, manifested sexually. Failures of communication outside the bedroom can cause the best of sexual relationships to deteriorate eventually. Unresolved emotional problems often generate unresolved sexual problems, just as unresolved sexual problems often generate unresolved emotional problems. The destructive patterns thus set up are self-perpetuating.

Men and women who wish to protect their relationship do not ignore danger signals. They treat problems as important—not making catastrophes of them, but realizing that they need solutions, because the decision to suffer in silence generally ends in deterioration of the relationship.

A woman in therapy remarked, "My marriage was so marvelous in every other way, I tried to tell myself our rotten sex life didn't matter. I thought I could live with my frustrations. Sure, I could live, but I was finding more and more fault with my husband's behavior, jumping at him over trivia. And I was withdrawing more and more, living inside, sharing less of myself in a thousand subtle ways. Five years of things getting worse and worse before it occurred to me that we should seek professional help."

In the overwhelming majority of cases, sexual difficulties between men and women are resolvable, but only if they are willing to admit the existence of the problem and take appropriate action. We will have more to say about what constitutes appropriate action later in the book.

One final word. Passion is not a prerogative of youth. Discussing the subject of romantic love with groups of older people throughout the country, we have heard men and women in their sixties and seventies say to us more than once, "Please tell the world that we are still sexual beings, that we have sexual needs, and that passion still has meaning for us." We know today beyond any shadow of a doubt that sex can remain an enjoyable and important expression between men and women well into old age.

Q. **What if we recognize that our attitudes are not ideal, and yet we are in relationships and we want them to work?**

A. We would create a very false picture of reality if we left the impression that individuals master all the psychological requirements of romantic love first and then participate in a relationship.

It is through being part of a relationship and struggling with its problems that we grow. A love relationship is a unique opportunity to work on ourselves, to progress along the path of our personal evolution by meeting the challenges that love poses.

In the following chapters we shall address concrete instances of just this opportunity.

Six

Communicating Our Emotions

If we are free to create an atmosphere in which our partner will feel free to express feelings and emotions, we must learn to create it for ourselves. If we have learned to lecture and reproach ourselves for "inappropriate" feelings, we almost certainly will treat others the same way. We will lecture and reproach our partner, we will lecture and reproach our children. "I never had a right to my emotions. Why should you have a right to yours?" We will encourage the person we love to practice the same self-disowning, the same self-repudiation, that we practice. "I play dead. Why can't you?" By treating each other as they treat themselves, two perfectly well-intentioned human beings can undermine and eventually destroy their happiness. Working on a relationship always begins, therefore, with working on ourselves.

One of our central goals in this chapter is to show how a couple can open up blocked lines of communication by simultaneously supporting the relationship and their own persons. Men and women in love want to communicate but often don't know how. Let us proceed, therefore, to look at the "how."

We want to mention that there is inevitably some overlapping of the questions raised as well as the strategies we propose. Some repetitions are unavoidable. But even when we seem to be recommending almost the identical strategy in two different situations, its goal or purpose is different in some way. The same words can achieve differing effects in differing circumstances.

It would be an error to perceive the strategies as manipulative or superficial. Our point is not that the strategy itself will always work the deeper change desired but that it will at least change the old patterns of communication that haven't been effective. Regard them as initiating strategies to start up movement in a new direction.

Further, when we suggest dialogue that we have found useful, we do not mean it to be copied literally. The words are a vehicle to convey an attitude and a spirit. We hope our readers will infuse the spirit into their own communications.

Q. I hear so much talk today about the importance of communication. What precisely is communication and what blocks it?

A. Communication is a process by which individuals exchange meanings through a common system of symbols. The symbols may be a written or spoken language, physical gestures, or other actions significant to the person receiving the communication. An act that conveys a message to someone.

If I want you to pass the salt, I can say, "Please pass the salt." If you hand it to me, this is an instance of successful communication. I can also gesture toward the salt shaker. If you hand it to me, this also is an instance of successful communication. Obviously the communications that present difficulties for us in intimate relationships are of a far more complex nature, but we have here the essence of communication. The communication is successful when it elicits the response desired.

The essence needs to be refined, of course: "response desired" does not necessarily mean an affirmative response, but it does mean an appropriate response. The purpose of communication is to elicit a reaction to the content of the communication. My attempt at communication is never successful until you react to the content of what I have said. When I ask if you would like to go to the movies, I can accept yes or no or an infinite number of responses in between. But an answer of "I wonder if you're allowed to feed elephants at the zoo" would leave me in doubt as to whether you had even heard me. A more pertinent example: I may tell my partner that I desire her beyond all other women. If she continues to view me with distrust, I have failed to get my message across. My partner is telling me in deed that I have failed to communicate in word.

But communication consists of far more than what I say. For example, the tone of my voice, my facial expressions, gestures, and behavior—do they support my statements? This may be an important question to ask myself, if I find my attempts at communication less than successful.

Communications sometimes fail because they are not congruent with feelings or behavior. My words do not match the emotions I express or the way I act. If I tell you I love you while looking bored and distracted, you are unlikely to believe me. If I tell you I really want to spend time with you alone and yet always arrange our social life to include other people, again you will have difficulty believing me. Incongruent communication points to some conflict or ambivalence within the communicator that needs to be confronted, clarified, and resolved.

Sometimes communications fail because they are too indirect. "I want to tell you about something exciting that happened to me" is an example of a direct communication. An indirect way to communicate the same message: "Anything interesting happen to you today?" (I am hoping you will ask the same question of me so I can tell you my story. This may work or it may not.)

We are often reluctant to ask directly for what we want. But our means of asking may be so indirect that we fail to accomplish our purpose. I want to go away with my partner for the weekend so we can spend some time alone together, enjoying each other, talking, walking, and making love. I say to my partner in an almost reproachful tone of voice, "You don't look too good. I think you need a rest." When my partner shrugs, "I feel fine," I am left hurt and my partner may be left a bit annoyed. This illustrates one of the most common patterns of bad communication between couples.

Indirect communication is not necessarily undesirable. It is only undesirable when it does not accomplish its purpose. If I leave on your dinner plate two airline tickets to a city you have been eager to visit, and you respond with delight, indirect communication works!

The moral of the story is "Pay attention to whether or not communications succeed." If they do, fine. If they don't, try something different.

One of our favorite stories, told by a woman at one of our Intensives, illustrates this principle. Whenever she tried to talk with her husband about matters of importance to her, he went on reading his book (he was apparently an inveterate reader), insisting that he could listen and read simultaneously. She reasoned with him, argued, begged, she even shrieked—nothing worked. When she tried to share her experiences with him the first night of the Intensive, he assured her he was listening and went on reading. In despair she stopped talking and went to bed. On the second day of the Intensive we talked about the pointlessness of persisting in ineffective communication patterns. We stressed the importance of being willing to experiment with alternatives that are compatible with one's values, character, and integrity.

That night she went home from the Intensive feeling high from the day's work, greeted her husband cheerfully—he was sitting in a chair reading—and went into the kitchen to make herself a cup of tea. This behavior was a marked departure from her standard policy of bombarding him with chatter the moment she arrived home. She had decided not to fight his book any longer and not to demand that he live up to her expectations. When she returned to the living room with her tea, he looked up from his book and asked, "How was your day?" This was a departure from his standard procedure, a response to the change in hers. She flashed him a smile and said, "Terrific!" as she moved toward the stairs. He put down his book. "Tell me about it."

She shared this story on the third morning of the Intensive, enraptured. "I thought I would keep my sentences short and simple and see what happened," she laughed. "I didn't say anything I didn't feel, mean, or intend. But it was different from what I usually do. He kept asking for more!"

Q. For a long time I've realized that both my partner and I have been retreating from any real communication on the emotional level. I am wondering what the long-range effects are likely to be.

A. We feel safe in saying that such a relationship must become more and more mechanical, if it continues at all. Such a relationship suffers an energy drain. It loses life as the man and woman become more and more alienated from each other.

Sometimes extramarital affairs originate in just such estrangement and frustration, almost, one might say, in a human organisms's natural drive toward some experience of being alive.

But even in the absence of outside affairs, two people who remain together but avoid letting each other know what they feel are hurt, angry, and lonely. They find ways to cause fresh pain to each other.

There is less and less to talk about, less and less to share. In all probability, sex wanes sooner or later in such a pattern. Machines do not have exciting sex lives.

None of us who value our relationships can afford to "retreat from communication on an emotional level."

Q. Why do we often find communication so difficult, especially when we are in love?

A. Deeper feelings usually distinguish the communication between people who are in love from communication between people in less intense relationships—at least some of the time. These deeper feelings may bring confusion and discomfort when they upset the ordinary routines of our daily life or threaten our sense of control.

If I am confused about my thoughts and feelings, if I am unclear as to what I am experiencing or what I want my partner to know, then I cannot express myself well.

When the simple fact of my being overwhelmed by my emotions causes difficulty in communications, I need to describe my feelings at length rather than try to race past them. Otherwise, I may become not only unclear but incoherent.

The first step toward a solution in such a case is to acknowledge my confusion and not to pretend to clarity. I can say to my partner, "I know that I'm not too clear right now. Please be patient with me while I try, as best I can, to describe what I'm aware of and let's see where that might lead."

If, beyond that simple confusion, I am out of touch with my emotions, denying my needs and wants, and if I attempt to communicate without setting forth honestly what I am experiencing internally, I cannot possibly express anything that will satisfy you or me. Very likely I will go off on a tangent leaving both of us feeling helpless, bewildered, and frustrated. Back up, take a deep breath; let's try to describe the experience as we are conscious of it without intellectualizing or psychologizing, asking our partner for the right to think aloud without having to defend or justify each and every sentence. This is a freedom that wise lovers give each other.

If I am afraid of how you will respond, afraid that you won't understand and that you will be hurt or resentful, my mind may jam up when I begin to speak. I may say everything except what I most need to say, which is that I have these fears, whether well-founded or not. So our efforts at communication may lead straight to estrangement. Whenever we feel the presence of such fear, we should be able to say to our partner, "There are things I feel the need to tell you, thoughts and feelings I want to share with you, and I am aware of my anxiety about your reaction. My fantasies of your exploding at me are inhibiting my ability to express myself."

Acknowledging our fear accomplishes two things. First, it allows us to relax a little, since we don't have to pretend about what we are feeling. Second, it increases the probability that our partner will listen acceptingly to whatever we are struggling to express, because we are trusting our partner.

Sometimes the accumulation of grievances interrupts my present train of thought. I try to stick to the point but I feel myself pulled into the past. From my partner's point of view, I am cluttering up our discussion with references to incidents long ago that don't bear in any obvious way on the present. So I need to make a further decision: either confine myself to the present or acknowledge to my partner my need to talk about incidents that are past but still powerfully relevant to me. Again, it is very helpful to describe my state to my partner and ask for a genuine effort at understanding.

It takes time. Communication can break down because I feel I do not have enough time to explain. I may have been preparing to discuss some important matter with my partner when he or she says, "Okay, we have half an hour. What's on your mind?" The clock is like a gun aimed at my head; I cannot think. Therefore, I cannot speak effectively. Rather than try, it is far better to describe my feelings and ask for another time when we can speak at greater leisure.

Obviously, none of the difficulties we are describing here are confined to people in love. If they appear to come up most frequently in love relationships, it is because, as we have already indicated, we are most likely to be speaking from deep emotions in such relationships. Fears and blocks are that much more likely to sabotage our efforts.

If I see that my partner is struggling to tell me something and the message isn't getting through, often I can be helpful by saying, "Stop. Take a deep breath. Forget about the subject under discussion. Just describe to me what you're feeling right now in as much detail as you can." We have found that such an approach has an almost magical power between two people who love each other, even when they feel cut off.

Communication may break down for a different reason entirely: my partner and I are operating from different assumptions without realizing it. Again, this can happen in any relationship, not just a love relationship. To take a literal example of "different assumptions": a breakdown in communication, hilarious in retrospect, occurred between Devers and me while we were working on one of the early questions in this book. Somehow the wording of the question in her notes was different from mine, but it was close enough so that the disparity was not grossly apparent. When she read her answer to the question, I thought she had gone totally off the track. When I read her my answer, she thought I had failed even to understand the question. The conversation became, shall we say, heated.

Even when Devers read the question aloud in exasperation, I kept hearing the version in my own notes. After an hour, when we were utterly frustrated and exhausted, we decided to analyze the question word by word. *Then* we noticed the difference in our respective versions.

We were aware of our feelings, all right, and we didn't hesitate about communicating them, but we became so lost in our own frustration that we unwittingly fell into the role of adversaries. We didn't think quickly enough to say, "Wait a minute. This isn't going anywhere. We seem to be operating from some different premises. Let's try to figure out what they might be."

To give a more serious and tragic example: A woman we know believed for years that her husband had married her only because she was pregnant. He, on the other hand, knew he had married her because he was deeply in love. She was continually picking quarrels, ridiculing him, so that he felt she did not love him. She knew how much he loved her and was behaving this way only to hurt him, or so he thought, because she was not in love anymore. It went on for years. Both of them being highly explosive people, they never got to the assumptions underlying their mutual torment. Whether or not they have retained enough love, good will, and rationality to overcome their problems in communication remains uncertain as of this writing. Without the willingness to explore those underlying assumptions, their marriage is doomed.

Q. Why do I so often find it difficult to express love? Can I "learn" to tell someone I love him or her?

A. This is a painful problem for an extraordinarily large number of people: the feeling of love coupled with discomfort or anxiety over expressing it.

The booming success of the greeting card industry is, in part, a sign of this problem. With each year that passes, more people purchase second-hand messages of love—letting the cards do the talking for them—because they want to express caring but do not know how or are afraid to try.

Expressing love is often difficult for the same reason that seeking love is difficult. Fear: I will be rejected; my feelings won't be reciprocated; I will be abandoned. The implicit premise is that if I don't express my feelings in words, it won't hurt so much if I don't receive the response I desire.

Then there is the fear of showing any feelings at all, the fear of self-disclosure of any kind, resulting from years of emotional repression. In other words, the problem of self-disowning and self-alienation.

Furthermore, I may have grown up in a home where I never had any opportunity to see love expressed (or worse still, saw only expressions of anger, bitterness, fear). My parents showed no affection toward each other so I had no role models. Later, I never discovered the language of feelings on my own (or from other sources, such as books, movies, and other people). Part of me remains a child, waiting for someone to come and show me the way; part of me remains trapped back in those early years when emotions were a foreign language no one spoke.

Some of us are afraid of words. They have a reality that makes us anxious. We are more comfortable expressing our love through actions, such as bringing gifts, or being kind and thoughtful. Action is communication and can be beautiful communication. In fact, words are rarely enough by themselves. And yet, without words, our experience of being loved would feel incomplete. Words have a power nothing else can quite match. If words did not have this power, people would not be so afraid of them. The reason we avoid words is precisely the reason we should strive to give them voice.

Some people, of course, have a superficial ease with words but are still frightened of words that express deep and intimate feelings. These are the very words we want to learn to be comfortable with.

I can give you a gift, leaving you to infer that I care for you. Still, it is gratifying to be told. It is sad if two people genuinely love each other and yet one or both find it difficult to look into the other's eyes and say, "I love you."

How do we break through to expressions of love? We take a deep breath, we acknowledge our fear—and then we do it.

We will probably begin shyly, awkwardly, self-consciously. We can live with that. So can our partner. Learning doesn't happen in an instant. We need practice and experience. Probably our partner will see that we are trying to break through a barrier and appreciate our struggle. The willingness to persevere is itself an expression of love.

Q. Isn't there something artificial about learning "appropriate communication"? Won't I lose the spontaneity of natural expression?

A. We are not born knowing how to communicate effectively. We are not born knowing how to elicit the responses we desire. Effective communication is a learned art.

Some of our attempts at communication work and some don't. If our "natural" and "spontaneous" communications aren't succeeding, we have a choice. We can go on feeling frustrated and perhaps blame the other party, or we can learn to communicate more effectively.

To understand this approach, consider for a moment the art of psychotherapy, from which we have learned much of what we know about communication.

Good psychotherapists recognize that a client who feels heard and understood responds better so they learn the act of active listening: they learn to offer appropriate feedback, which shows appreciation of what the client has said, and to control any "natural" impulse to interrupt and lecture. A good psychotherapist must also listen to a client's intention, not only to the literal words, and respond to the feeling behind the words to get better results, so he or she discards any "natural" inclination to take words at face value. A good psychotherapist understands that treating the person who comes for help with respect creates a context of mutual dignity, thus enhancing the client's self-esteem and contributing to the solution of the problem. So he or she overrides any "spontaneous" inclination to explode with "How can you be so foolish?" or "You're really hopeless!" Following simple rules of effective communication does not hamper the therapist's individuality or opportunity for self-expression (in any sense that matters), but it does promote the success of the therapy. Many men and women feel more

comfortable talking to a psychotherapist than to their partner precisely because the therapist understands and prac-
tices these principles of communication.

As the late child psychologist Haim Ginott observed
many years ago, "Why should such knowledge be the
private preserve of professionals? Why should such knowledge and skills not be made available to everyone?" (We
regard Dr. Ginott as one of the great teachers of effective
communication, and we enthusiastically recommend his
books, not only to parents and teachers, but to everyone
interested in caring relationships; his books appear in our
bibliography.)

When we first learn new communication skills (such as
active listening, giving appropriate feedback, acknowledging feelings, maintaining eye contact), we sometimes feel
they are artificial, mechanical. We feel self-conscious in
using them. With practice, they integrate themselves into
our own way of speaking, and then they feel natural. This
is the pattern of acquiring any new skill.

By the same token, when we see our partner coming to
grips with a new and potentially more effective way of
speaking, it is hardly helpful to reproach him or her for
talking in a way that sounds "unnatural."

New ways of behaving may feel "unnatural" for a while,
both to you and your partner. But then you may have
been complaining about the "natural" for years.

Q. How can I help my partner to be less afraid of
expressing emotions?

A. A woman asked this question at an Intensive, and
since her husband was present, Nathaniel proposed that they participate in a sentence-completion
exercise.

He had the couple sit facing each other and surprised
the woman by asking her to begin with the sentence stem
"One of the ways I make it difficult for you to express
your feelings is_____." He chose this opening because
we know from experience that the problem of a silent
husband is usually a collaborative problem.

To her astonishment (and almost everyone else's), she

proceeded with admirable candor to keep repeating the stem with such endings as:

I interrupt you as soon as you begin to talk.

I correct you.

I tell you you shouldn't be feeling what you're feeling.

I criticize your choice of words.

I get my feelings hurt.

I start arguing.

I sidetrack us into a discussion of my reactions.

I ask you why you didn't do this years earlier.

I pressure you to admit you're glad you've learned at last how to talk about emotions!

Nathaniel asked her to pause and sit silently for a moment while each of them experienced their feelings without words, taking some time to absorb what she had said.

There was an expression of exhausted sadness on the man's face. "My God," his wife whispered to him, acknowledging the meaning of her statements. He responded with a slow, patient smile that seemed to be meant for the two of them.

Nathaniel asked the husband to work with the stem "One of the ways you could help me to talk about my feelings is_____." The man responded with:

by talking about your own feelings, but not when I'm in the middle of saying something.

by setting a better example.

by not always haranguing and harassing.

by not always lecturing me.

by listening when I try to talk about something that hurts me.

by acting like you're really interested.

by letting me come out at my own speed.

by understanding that I am very scared.

by allowing me my angers.

by not moving around when I'm trying to talk.

by not drowning me in your words.

by not acting like you're my parent.

by understanding that often I don't need an answer from you, I just need to struggle and stumble at my own pace.

by not telling me, "I told you so."

Example is the most powerful form of teaching. If I want you to be open with your feelings, I need to be open with mine. If I want you to learn simplicity and honesty, I need to know I have learned them myself.

And if I want you to talk about your feelings, I need to learn how to listen to feelings.

There are many ways we can help a person who is struggling to express emotions, or struggling to avoid expressing them. We can say, "You look a little sad. Is it something you want to talk about?" Or, "You seem angry. What's happened to upset you?" Or, "You look like you're churning inside right now. Do you feel like talking about it?" Or, "It's wonderful to see you so excited. Tell me about it."

We must be patient throughout the exploration process. Rarely do people respond to our first attempts the way we'd like them to. But if and when they do struggle to communicate, we must be careful not to sabotage their efforts.

Why would we sabotage our partner's efforts to speak freely? Why would we obstruct the very behavior that we have been asking for?

If I am the only one who talks about my feelings, then I am the "authority" on feelings. As my partner learns to be comfortable with expressing emotions and the balance of our relationship begins to shift, I no longer enjoy a monopoly. I may start hearing about feelings I am not comfortable with. Or my partner may learn to recognize that there's plenty I have not been saying about my own emotions and call me on it. Unconsciously, I may subvert my partner's escape from the prison of repression, even while I am crying for more emotional communication.

We have already said that we cannot be a psychotherapist to someone with whom we are romantically involved. This does not mean we cannot help our partner to grow. And I can be of greatest help by cultivating in myself those traits and qualities I want to nurture in my partner.

Q. My partner is adept at creating the illusion of listening while his (her) mind is really somewhere else. How do I deal with this?

A. Ask your partner, "Are you willing to discuss this matter with me now?" If the response is no, ask for a time that would be acceptable. If the response is yes but your partner's mind still appears to drift off, ask "What do you think about what I have been saying? What are your feelings about this?" In other words, we advise the same strategy as for the partner who listens silently and doesn't respond. Some of our clients and students have found these approaches useful in stimulating communication:

I have the impression I don't have your full attention. Perhaps I'm mistaken. Can you tell me how you understand what I've been saying?

I have the impression you're finding it difficult to listen to me. If I am right, would you tell me about it?

I wonder if you're feeling some resentment right now that's making it difficult for you to listen.

Sometimes, when you listen silently like this and look a little absentminded, I imagine you're feeling angry and don't want to talk about it. Is that true?

Would you be willing for me to tape record our discussion so I could play it back later and really think about what we've said? (It's very difficult to remain absentminded in a recorded conversation, and the purpose here is to interrupt a habitual response, which switching on a tape recorder certainly does. We're aware that some people may be taken aback by this strategy, but it is powerfully effective.)

Q. My partner's most common response when I express hurt or anger is to express his (her) own hurt or anger without responding to mine. I never feel heard or satisfied when he (she) becomes defensive, and no issue ever gets resolved. What can I do?

A. No matter how appropriately and carefully we express our anger, our partner may feel attacked and become defensive, possibly because of childhood experiences with excessive criticism.

The first step is to reach an agreement that there is indeed a problem. Say, for instance, "I think it's important to protect our relationship against unresolved hurts. Here is my experience of what happens when I try to talk about something bothering me. Instead of dealing with what I say, you start shouting about some defect of mine." Give a specific example or two. (It may even be necessary, with your partner's consent, to tape record a discussion/quarrel before your partner will be convinced.) Always invite your partner to participate in the solution. "How do you think we should handle this?" Or you might try: "I understand that what I want to tell you is upsetting. What would make it easier for you to respond so that we can reach a resolution?"

In other words, avoid falling into an adversary relationship with your partner. Keep asking, "What are *your* ideas? How do *you* think we can resolve this best? How would *you* like me to respond when you need to talk about something troubling you?" Encourage a detailed answer. Almost always, your partner wants the same attention that you want, so this emphasis on his or her feelings actually helps your partner to understand your perspective.

"It's pretty hard," one husband remarked, "to go on being defensive after I've told my wife that I would really appreciate it if she would just listen, without making alibis or counterattacking, when I talk about something she does that irritates me." He grinned. "Looks like I trapped myself."

Another man was deeply touched when his partner said to him, "The thing I want most is to protect my love for you. I never want to feel numb. I never want to feel dead inside. So I need to tell you when I am hurting or angry. That's one of the ways I take care of our relationship."

A woman who had come with her lover for couple counseling said, "It got easier after I learned a little trick to use whenever my partner complained about something bothering him. I would look at him and I would tell myself silently, 'You are not my mother. You are not telling me I am a bad girl.' It sounds funny, telling yourself that your lover isn't your mother, but that's how I learned to hear him and stay with him when he got angry, instead of getting angry back."

Q. When I tell my partner I am hurt or angry about something he (she) has done or not done, I hear that I am criticizing, blaming, and refusing to take responsibility for my own emotions and I end up feeling outmaneuvered. How should I respond?

A. First, consider, whether or not there is any truth in your partner's accusation.

Ask yourself, "Am I condemning my partner for failing to live up to my expectations? Do I expect my partner to make me happy? Do I take responsibility for myself in our relationship? Do I indulge in insults?"

Then ask your partner, "In what way am I blaming or criticizing? What am I saying or doing that causes you to think I don't take responsibility for my own emotions? What would *you* like me to do when I'm feeling hurt or angry?"

Sometimes it is relevant to ask, "Do you want me to be so 'independent' that your behavior would not affect me? What if you didn't affect me emotionally at all; would you think I loved you?"

In one of our therapy groups we worked with a couple for whom this issue constituted a central problem. Often, when the woman attempted to discuss some aspect of the relationship that troubled her, the man would accuse her of refusing to take responsibility for her own life, and since she did believe in taking responsibility, she was generally left feeling frustrated and conned.

Actually it was the man who avoided responsibility. He would insist that he loved her, then withdraw into indifference. He would talk about the importance of marriage and then insist that he needed his freedom to date other women. And when she became bewildered, he said *she* had an emotional problem. Her disorientation was in fact a thoroughly logical and predictable response.

She began to challenge him in just the way we suggested in the preceding questions. She asked him how, specifically, he would like her to feel and behave when he acted as he did. He began to understand that only her unquestioning and uncomplaining compliance with his every mood would satisfy him. He was hardly prepared to demand this explicitly, so he gave up expecting it. And he ceased to look upon her as overly critical.

Q. Listening to you discuss communication, I get the impression that you attach great importance to empathy and compassion. How do they relate to effective communication?

A. Empathy is the capacity to imagine oneself as another, to participate in another's feelings or ideas. Compassion is the sympathetic consciousness of another's distress and is linked to a desire to alleviate it.

My ability to express both empathy and compassion implies that I have some access to my own feelings. Insofar as I am emotionally blocked, empathy and compassion are very difficult for me. And we have already begun to see how blocked feelings get in the way of communication.

We cannot treat the emotions of another better than we treat our own. If I am cut off from my own emotions, I will find it extraordinarily difficult to respond appropriately to yours. If you attempt to speak to me about your feelings, saying, "I'm hurt, disturbed, or angry about something," I cannot understand you or respond to you without referring (usually subconsciously) to my own experience of such states. This is one of the reasons why we place so much emphasis on listening to our own feelings and on encouraging our partner to listen to his or hers. Listening with love and acceptance can enhance our partner's ability to experience his or her own emotions, which in turn deepens both our capacities for empathy and compassion.

My partner is worried about an impending surgical op-

eration. With empathy, I read the signs of concern, take
my partner in my arms, and say, "It's really rough, isn't
it?" I don't need to have once faced that problem myself
to understand how it must feel; I can know, at least
approximately.

My partner is filled with delight over some success at
work. With empathy, I listen to my partner's report, recognize the joy underlying the words, smile, and say enthusiastically, "It's lovely to feel brilliant, isn't it?" Or, "I
love seeing you this happy." Without empathy, I mutter
"Uh-huh," leaving my partner feeling frustrated and
invisible.

Whereas empathy pertains to our ability to participate
in the thought or feeling of another, happy or sad, compassion pertains specifically to suffering—pain, anger, frustration, helplessness, bewilderment, grief—and this requires
special discussion with respect to love.

There are times in any relationship when one partner or
the other is in emotional difficulty and needs the opportunity to talk about it, to be heard, understood, and cared
for. If I attempt to tell you of my hurts and you don't
participate in them, I will feel thwarted, whatever your
words. To put it another way, we will not experience
successful communication.

On the other hand, to feel compassion for a person I
love does not mean to become so overwhelmed by his or
her feelings that I lose all objectivity. Compassion com-
bines with an element of objectivity or detachment; otherwise, especially in the case of pain, my own feelings may
even inundate yours. A client of ours complained that
every time she attempted to share suffering with her husband, he broke into tears, becoming so upset and agitated
that she was unable to continue speaking. The capacity
for some measure of detachment is a requirement of successful communication and love.

A cautionary note: most people do not enjoy being told
"I know exactly what you're feeling." Chances are we
don't know exactly what another person is feeling. Better
to ask questions, better to encourage our partner to talk
and describe feelings, better to practice active listening
and learn to be sensitive to what our partner wants and
needs from us.

Empathy is not an ability that we either possess or don't

possess. It can be learned. We can practice imagining how we would feel in a given situation if we were our partner. The most important step is the decision to try.

Making my partner's feelings real to myself is not a matter of an hour or an evening; it's a way of life. And yet, without it, what happens to love?

Q. If I ever express suffering, my partner's distress becomes so acute I feel unable to continue. What can I do?

A. This is a good example of the issue just discussed: compassion needs to be combined sometimes with a capacity for detachment.

We will assume, for the purposes of our answer, that your communication is honest and nonabusive.

Begin by describing the problem to your partner. Explain its effect on you. Explain that you feel interrupted, distracted, short-circuited in your own efforts to express your feelings. Ask your partner if he or she feels able to listen to you without interjecting feelings of such intensity that they prevent you from continuing.

In effect, say to your partner, "If I feel that my pain will knock you over, how can I feel free to express pain in your presence? How can I express unhappiness if you switch the conversation to yours?"

Sometimes we use the sentence-completion technique to explore this problem. "When I see my partner suffering———" has brought out such endings as:

I feel guilty.

I feel blamed.

I feel I have to do something.

I feel inadequate as a man (woman).

my self-worth plummets.

I start thinking about my own hurts.

When we switch to "The good thing about interjecting my own pain into the situation is———," we get such endings as:

I don't have to deal with her (him).

she (he) starts feeling sorry for me.

I get to talk about myself.

I don't have to deal with her (his) emotions.

she'll (he'll) stop talking.

We need the ability to feel compassion for the pain of someone we love without becoming swamped by it, drowned in it, or otherwise knocked off center so that we can't help our lover. There is a discipline here that we can learn—that we must learn.

By way of leading your partner to this understanding, ask benevolently, "How would you feel if the situation were reversed, so that when you showed distress I fell apart?"

When both of you are feeling distress and an urgent need to express it, the appropriate batting order for the occasion is this: the partner who initiated a communication of distress is up first.

Just as we may need to learn expression, so we may need to learn containment. Just as we may need to learn when to speak, so we may need to learn when to remain silent. Each has its place in life and in romantic love.

Q. Whenever I raise a difficult or painful subject, my partner's typical response is to leave the room. How do I deal with this?

A. Begin by explaining to your partner how hurtful this behavior is and ask whether it is intended to evoke hurt or anger in you. Ask your partner to imagine how you will feel if you are never allowed to express negative feelings. Ask your partner to specify under what conditions he or she would be willing to remain in the room when you are expressing negative feelings.

Ask whether your partner wants you to conclude that he or she does not care if you are in pain. As always, keep engaging your partner in the search for a solution.

We know a woman who had this problem and whose every effort to resolve it failed. She was packing her bag when he came home one afternoon. She said, "I know how hard it is on you when I'm struggling with something painful. So I am moving out for a few days until I feel better."

"Wait a minute," he said. "This is ridiculous. You don't have to move out. Sit down and tell me what's wrong."

Does her strategy sound drastic? Not when she had exhausted every other resource. In our view, her final strategy is not nearly so appalling as his leaving her no alternative.

We know a man who had this problem with his lover. She would flee the room and fling herself on the bed, as they do in old-fashioned movies. His good-natured efforts to persuade her to drop this policy availed him nothing. One day he did not follow her and try to make things right. Instead, he went for a long walk. When he returned two hours later, she cried real tears. She swore she would never do it again. There was only one relapse. During a quarrel months later she began to run out of the room but stopped abruptly when she heard him say, "See you later." He cured her without psychotherapy.

We do not serve our relationship well by cooperating in patterns that subvert it. We serve ourselves and our relationship if we refuse to cooperate, shattering harmful patterns to create new and better ones.

Q. Why is it so often difficult to express desire simply, clearly, and straightforwardly?

A. There is an exercise we often use in the Intensive on *Self-Esteem and the Art of Being* that bears on this question.

After the class has broken up into small groups, each person does a string of sentence completions from the stem "One of the things I want and don't know how to ask for is_____." After everyone has had the opportunity to express the frustration of his (her) various desires in personal relationships, we introduce a new stem: "One of the ways I make it difficult for people to give me what I want is_____":

I don't say what I want.

I pretend I don't want anything.

I don't allow myself to know what I want.

I'm never there when people try to give me what I want.

I act as if I don't need anything.

I pretend no one has anything of value to offer me.

I disparage whatever people attempt to give me.

I keep myself unavailable.

I run from kindness.

I expect people to know what I want without my telling them.

I imply that whatever they give me is not satisfactory.

I give and give and give and make of my giving a solid wall no one can get through.

When we shift to "The scary thing about expressing what I want honestly is_____," typical responses are:

no one may care.

I may not get it.

I may discover my partner's indifference.

I'll have to admit I have needs.

I'll open myself to being hurt.

I'll be too vulnerable.

no one has ever cared about my needs.

it makes you too naked.

not getting it would hurt too much.

Sometimes we follow this with "If I were to be more straightforward about what I want_____." We hear such endings as:

I might get it.

I might not feel such resentment.

I could relax more.

People would know me.

I think my marriage might work.

I could stop feeling so hurt.

I might get hurt more.

There might be hope.

I sure would be different from the rest of my family.

perhaps other people wouldn't respond as my parents did.

maybe my partner would care.

maybe I could have a relationship.

I could come out of hiding and show my mate who I am.

I would be more willing to hear what my partner wants.

I would be kinder.

I think I could love more.

We think these responses speak largely for themselves. Many of us, when we were young, did not experience having our wants and desires taken very seriously, which is very often one of the frustrations of being a child. We receive many messages that amount to: "Your wants don't count." Many of us grew up believing our wants would never matter to anyone except ourselves. We internalized the messages we received from our elders. In some cases, we struggled to make our wants not matter even to ourselves, so the pain of others' indifference wouldn't be so acute.

If I never express my wants (or if I can teach myself not even to know what they are), I never have to find out whether or not you will care, I never have to risk being hurt. That, in a single sentence, is the essence of the problem.

When we fall in love, we do not automatically regain (or even gain for the first time) confidence in expressing our wants. More often, we carry the problem with us into our relationship.

This should not be, for part of love is caring deeply about the wants of the person we love. And communicating that we care. Another part of love is trusting our partner enough to communicate our own wants.

There are no guarantees that someone who loves us will always satisfy our wants. But we will certainly achieve more satisfaction than if we keep our desires a secret. To express our wants may not guarantee fulfillment, but to suppress them does guarantee frustration.

What if we are afraid? We acknowledge the fear to ourselves and to our partner. We describe our apprehension simply and honestly. Then we communicate our desires. We must not let ourselves be stopped by the fear of being hurt. That is unworthy of people who love.

Q. Why is it so often difficult for my partner and me to express anger or resentment? And once we start, won't we run the risk of hurting each other emotionally? Could the solution be worse than the problem?

A. To begin with, when we were children, anger, especially anger against our parents, was usually *the* forbidden emotion. "If I were to show my mother my anger, she would not love me. If I were to show my father my anger, he would kill me." So often, at a conscious or subconscious level, the expression of anger is associated with either loss of love or with terrifying retaliation.

Further, many of us were taught that good people are never angry; resentment, we were encouraged to believe, points to our own deficiencies. Our self-esteem may have become tied to being above anger or resentment.

The truth is that there are circumstances under which anger and resentment are perfectly normal emotions. When we deny and repress them, our fear of our own outrage grows worse. The seething urge to erupt, after years of holding ourselves in check, grows more and more frightening to us. It can become associated in our fantasies with going crazy.

In therapy, under safe and controlled conditions, we help clients explore the extremes of their anger, not only because of the direct benefits of emotional release, but also because it is important to discover that anger does not mean irrationality (let alone uncontrollable destructiveness or madness).

In expressing my anger at you, neither insults nor blows are necessary. Indeed, they are usually the result of denying anger too long.

The expression of anger always means "I don't like what is happening. I don't like the way I am being treated. There is something here that does violence to me." Underneath there is self-assertion, protecting my rights, my dignity, my values. And many of us are afraid of self-assertion. We may feel, "Who am I to stick up for myself? Who am I to protest ill treatment?" So once again we are led back to the important issue of self-esteem.

A married woman complained in a psychotherapy group about her mother-in-law: "Whenever my mother-in-law comes to visit, she talks only to her son, acts like I'm not present, barely acknowledges me, never asks me questions, never engages me in conversation. It makes me so angry."

"And what do you do?" I (Nathaniel) asked.

"I don't do anything. I swallow. Oh, if only I weren't so timid! If only I weren't such a coward! If only I weren't afraid of showing anger!"

"Well, then, what would you do?" I asked.

"I would tell her_____." She groped for words helplessly. "I would tell her, 'You're so mean, you're so inconsiderate, you're really a rotten, contemptible person, a horrible person, a nasty human being, you don't care who you hurt.' I might even call her a witch—I don't know—something terrible like that."

"I'd like to try a small experiment. Close your eyes and just listen for a moment, please. I'd like you to imagine how you would feel if you were to respond quite differently. Suppose you were to say to your mother-in-law, in an ordinary tone of voice, something like this: 'I would like to look forward to your visits here. I would like to be able to enjoy your visits to our home. But when I see that you talk only to your son and ignore me, when I see that you barely acknowledge my existence, I find it impossible to enjoy your presence or to look forward to your visits.' How does the thought of saying that make you feel?"

"Oh, that would be much more frightening! And much harder for me to say. That's worse than anything I was thinking of."

"Oh, really, why?" I pointed out that I had not raised my voice. "I didn't say anything abusive or insulting."

She astonished me by the perceptiveness of her answer: "Yes, but you see, in my version, with all the insults, the focus is on her. I'm not talking about myself. I'm talking about her. That's safer. In your version, the focus is on me, on my feelings. To say what you said, I'd have to act as if my own feelings counted."

Precisely.

I encouraged the woman to speak to her mother-in-law more or less in the manner I indicated. She tried it. To her surprise, her mother-in-law was utterly shocked and more than a little intimidated. The mother-in-law became almost pathetically solicitous. The son began to feel neglected.

Our thinking about anger and resentment should not remain simply on the level of emotion itself. We need to go deeper, to think of self-assertion as a willingness to honor our own needs, wants, and dignity and an unwillingness to be treated with disrespect.

And the same principle applies even more intensely to lovers. The most important question is not whether or not we feel free to shout. It is whether we speak up at all when we object to how we are being dealt with. Speaking up can be learned only through practice. Sometimes we will speak up quietly, sometimes angrily. But the point is to speak—while avoiding attacks on the personal worth of the other person.

I can be angry at something you have said or failed to say, I can describe disappointment, dismay, fury, I can tell you what I would like you to do or stop doing, and I can do it without telling you that you are a worthless human being, that your intention was to hurt me, or that you are just like my last husband or wife. I do not need to attack your self-esteem.

It is not anger that is harmful in relationships but the moralizing, psychologizing, and attacks on the other person's self-esteem that too often accompany expressions of anger. It is these that we need to learn to let go of.

Insult and scorn invite defensiveness and counterattack. If I tell you that I am angry because you never show up for a date on time, we can deal with that situation. But if I tell you that you never show up for a date on time because you are a rotten and uncaring person, you have to defend yourself. It is much easier and more constructive to deal with your habitual lateness.

Undeniably, learning the appropriate expression of anger—Haim Ginott calls it "anger without insult"—requires discipline. Too often we reach for words we know will hurt. This is an impulse we need to control if we do not wish to damage our relationship.

While learning the art of "anger without insult," it is useful to ask ourselves, "Is my purpose to hurt and humiliate my partner to inspire change?" If my purpose is to induce change, then insults can only be subversive to this purpose.

We are friends with a man in Lake Arrowhead, now in his sixties, who has been married for many years. One day he gave us his Three Rules for a Happy Marriage. We like his rules well enough to share them with you here.

Whoever is angry gets to speak first.

The one who is angry gets to have his or her full say, without interruption or argument, while the other listens attentively. Only when the angry partner has finished does the other respond.

Never go to bed angry.

"Sometimes," our friend told us, "that meant my wife and I stayed up all night. But generally the system works. We finally reach a point where sleep matters to us more than our anger, so we find a solution."

When we told this story at an Intensive, a man said, "But I get upset and agitated when she gets angry at me." Devers called out from across the room, "The good thing about getting upset and agitated is＿＿＿，" and the man responded, "It keeps my wife from getting angry!"

We owe it to our mate to listen to anger—which may include loud anger—without insisting that we are about to fall apart because our nerves can't stand it. No one likes noisy anger as a steady diet, but an occasional raised voice is hardly a crime. We are not too delicate to listen. If we are that delicate, it is worth wondering whether we are really old enough to be in a relationship.

Q. How should I respond when, in the midst of an argument, my partner reproaches me about the past?

A. We can all agree that ideally we should confine ourselves to what is bothering us right now. Hearing reproaches about the past makes it harder for us to respond to the problem that has arisen in the present. Yet bringing in the past is one of the most common tactics in a quarrel. Why?

We bring up old issues now because we did not speak up then. When we are sufficiently angry, we want to get everything off our chest.

Even if we did speak up then, we never felt that our partner dealt satisfactorily with what was bothering us, so our grievances are still there. Any new slight sets them off once more.

Sometimes we are angry today about just one more instance in a long line of behavior that bothers us, and we bring up the past because all the behavior represents the same principle. It has to end somewhere.

Here are statements that our clients and students find useful when wrestling with this problem:

I understand that you're bothered by unfinished business between us, but right now your talking about that makes it very difficult for me to respond to the problem of today. Could we agree to talk about those other issues at another time? First let's try to deal with what's irritating you right now.

It's hard for me to concentrate on what's just happened and understand your viewpoint when you keep bringing up matters I thought were resolved years ago. I feel mentally divided and don't know what to respond to, the past or present.

And for those who find themselves always reintroducing past grievances:

*I know I'm throwing a lot at you at once. Just listen and
let me get all this off my chest, and then we can try to
figure out what to do.*

*I don't expect you to respond to all of these issues at once.
I'm trying to show you a pattern. It's the pattern that
worries me, not any particular event. Do you get the basic
idea I'm driving at?*

*I'm going to write down a list of things I don't feel we
have dealt with. After you have read it on your own, let's
get together and talk about what each of us thinks should
be done.*

As we said at the beginning of this chapter, we want to
teach an attitude, not provide you with a script. Genuine
concern will resolve the problem raised in this question as
parroting never can.

If we deal with problems as they arise and if each
partner takes responsibility for checking that the other is
satisfied by the solutions to the problems, the impulse to
bring up the past is far less likely to arise.

Q. **When my partner is hurt or angry, it seems that
no response is right. What's the solution?**

A. Sometimes no response of ours seems right because we are responding too soon. What our partner needs is just to go on talking, being listened to and
understood. Our response should be quiet attentiveness.

Since many of us struggle with the feeling that perhaps
no one really cares about our pain, we often need more
than anything else to feel that we are heard, to feel that
the listener is with us both physically and mentally. This
experience can be worth more than a dozen explanations
or apologies.

It may help to say something like "I can see that you're
hurt (or angry or upset) right now. How can I help?"
Or, "My responses don't seem to satisfy you. I can see
that you're very upset. Please tell me what I can do for
you."

We need to remember that the response that might

work for us might not work for our partner. Therein lies the value of asking. To ask is to show that we care. That by itself can be healing.

Q. I have a strong tendency to interrupt my partner with apologies, reassurances, counterarguments, proposed solutions, distracting digressions, love talk, or whatever—all of which my partner tells me is acutely frustrating and stymieing. How can I help my partner feel heard?

A. We have already indicated how important active listening is to successful communication. Appropriate listening can be fully as important as appropriate speaking.

This is especially true when the speaker is dealing with pain. The opportunity to talk about pain can be an intrinsically healing experience.

I recall the period when I was still in an acute stage of mourning after the death of Patrecia. I would talk for very long periods of time about the shock, anguish, and sometimes anger I felt over her death. I needed to relive the night of her accident many times. I needed to tell Devers the same stories about my relationship with Patrecia many times. It would have been difficult for me if Devers cut me off by saying, "I'm so sorry" or "Everything will be all right." Reassurances of that kind get in the way of the healing process.

By giving me an opportunity to talk as long as I needed to, to ramble, to move from one subject to another in ways she couldn't always follow, Devers gave me an incomparable gift: an environment for my recovery.

In less tragic circumstances, there are still times when each of us needs to speak aloud, to vent feelings, to express sorrows or longings or angers, and we may not be able to do so with exquisite clarity. We may need to stumble along the way, and the most beautiful gift we can receive from someone who loves us is just being there to help us along, to allow this process to happen, to ask enough questions to keep us going, perhaps to give us a little shove if we get stuck, and to step out of our way when we are progressing.

Sometimes we need to tell the person we love how he or she has hurt us, and the same principle of assisting the weary traveler applies. Often the only solution needed is the opportunity to talk and feel heard. We want a sense that the listener understands us and hears.

Hearing and understanding are easier when we feel comfortable in expressing our feelings. If we are not comfortable, listening to our partner for any length of time can make us distinctly uncomfortable, and under the guise of trying to cheer our partner up, we can communicate indirectly, "Please stop talking. You're making me uncomfortable."

This is an error we are especially prone to make if our partner is talking about pain in our relationship. The impulse to interrupt or distract our partner from his or her feelings can be very powerful. It takes discipline to learn to say, "I can see that you're really hurting. Is there more you want to tell me?"

How can you help your partner to feel heard? Perhaps by reading aloud our answers to this question, by expressing these thoughts in your own words, and by actively listening to your partner.

Q. Is there a value in talking about my pain when there's nothing to be done, when action can't change anything?

A. Let us reiterate why the answer to this question is yes. Through the act of describing our pain, we give ourselves the opportunity to experience it, to assimilate it, eventually to be free of it. The same principle applies not only to extreme cases, such as mourning, divorce, or a broken love affair, but to countless smaller occasions of pain. It helps when you can say to someone who cares, "I really regret not getting that promotion." Or, "I'm really worried about having that gall bladder operation."

Lori, one of my daughters by a previous marriage, was ill a while back and the diagnosis of her condition took some time to determine. While waiting, I was haunted by certain ominous possibilities. I did not share with Nathaniel the extent of my concern. Sensing that something was wrong, he would ask, "What's troubling you?" I would reply that I was concerned about Lori, without showing the magnitude of my anxiety. My behavior was erratic and bewildering to him at times. Since I knew he was working very hard, I did not wish to burden him. There was nothing to be done until we received the medical report anyway. I became more and more depressed and remote from Nathaniel.

Finally, I broke down. I wept, I talked about my fears for the worst. He listened and held me, and I felt stronger and more serene. I still did not know the results of the tests: all the terrifying possibilities still existed, and yet I felt clearer, steadier, better prepared for whatever we might have to face.

Fortunately, the tests were negative and Lori regained her health. Did talking help during the period when there was nothing to be done? It helped enormously.

Four of the most loving words in the world are: "Tell me about it."

Q. Can I overdo this talking about my pain?

A. Of course—if the sole purpose of such talk is to avoid action that might remedy the situation, to evoke guilt in the listener, or to manipulate the listener.

To quote from *The Disowned Self:*

To face one's painful emotions, to experience them fully, to acknowledge them, to listen to the message they contain concerning one's frustrations, and perhaps to describe in words what one is feeling, requires courage and honesty; it is not an exercise in self-indulgence. To be self-pitying is to make no effort to deal with one's suffering or to understand it, to complain of it while seeking to avoid confronting it, and to indulge in thoughts or utterances about the cruelty of life, the futility of struggle, the hopelessness of one's predicament, the unfairness of fate, and so forth. To say, "*Right now* I am feeling hopeless," is not self-pity; to say, "My situation *is* hopeless," *is* (usually) self-pity. In the first instance, one is describing a feeling; in the second, one is making a statement of alleged fact. Descriptions of feelings, however painful, can be therapeutic; statements of alleged facts about life or the world, motivated solely by one's painful emotions of the moment, generally are self-destructive. In the first case, one takes responsibility—the responsibility of awareness; in the second case, one abandons responsibility and surrenders to passivity. This is a distinction of the most vital importance.

There is a world of difference between saying "I am in pain and I need to talk about it" and saying "I am in pain and there's nothing I can do, and the world is rotten, and anyway it's your fault, and you'd better be feeling sorry for me, and you'd better be feeling guilty, and you'd better be prepared to do something."

Some of us cling to our pain as an excuse for inactivity. We cling because we think of ourselves as a martyr—pitiable, tragic, and unlovable.

Q. **My partner and I are strongly attracted to each other sexually, and often disagreements get put on the shelf when one of us initiates lovemaking. Sex can be a form of communication, but can't it sometimes be the wrong form?**

A. Certainly. Sex, as the question itself implies, can be an evasive or manipulative device for getting our partner to forget his or her grievances.

On the other hand, anger can be a stimulant, and it's not all that unusual for people in love to move from quarreling to lovemaking. The question is what happens afterward? If sex brings people closer and they make a renewed effort to solve their disagreement, no harm is done; quite the contrary.

But if they proceed to forget about the disagreement, or if only one of them does, and they make no further attempt to go back and resolve the blowup, then sex does not serve the relationship; it gets in the way. The partner who raised the initial grievance will eventually accumulate resentment and may also shut down sexually.

Like a bank loan, ignored grievances are sooner or later

called in for collection. As some philosopher might have put it: "There is a time for talking and there is a time for sex; there is a time for sex *with* talking and there is a time for sex *without* talking; and there is a time for talking without sex."

Q. **Must I always verbalize my feelings before I can hope for an acknowledgement from my partner? For example, with the tears in my eyes plainly visible, my partner says nothing until I say something like "I'm in a bad way." Seeing also fits into communication, doesn't it?**

A. Seeing is indeed a vital element in communicating— just as not seeing can be a vital element in not communicating.

What I don't see, I don't have to deal with. If I am unaware of my partner's emotional state, I don't have to respond. I can remain safely in neutral. This is, perhaps, the most common reason for failing to see the obvious.

It is clearly desirable to be responsive to signals from as many different senses as possible—sight, hearing, touch— especially when the signals come from someone we love.

It is undeniably true, however, that some people are more oriented toward hearing, while others are more oriented toward seeing. Some respond more readily to the statement "I'm in pain" than to the sight of tears. For others it is just the opposite.

A woman in therapy learned to ask, "What do you see on my face?" When her partner answered, "Tears," she replied, "Then it's not easy for me to understand your silence." No reproaches. They had begun to communicate.

Sometimes she would ask, "What do you see on my face?" He would answer, "I don't know."

"Guess."

"Anger?"

She replied, "Right." Often we know more than we admit.

A woman client complained to Devers that her husband was oblivious to her feelings unless she spelled them out. Not that the woman objected to communicating her feelings verbally. She did so often. She did not demand that he be a mind reader. Still, at times she was bewildered by his extraordinary blindness.

Devers suggested something absurd, and it worked. She proposed to the woman that when she got home she put a smudge, a lipstick smear, an ink mark, or something on her face and that she do the same every day shortly before her husband arrived home. If he didn't notice it, she was to say nothing. After a few days, he began looking at her more closely and finally asked, "What's that on your face?" She replied as she had been instructed to: "Show me what you're seeing." He took her to the mirror, pointed out the smudge, and she removed it. She continued this program for two weeks, during which time her husband was always looking at her face to see what might be there. He began to notice and ask about things besides the smudge. Whenever he stopped asking, she put a smudge on her face, near the eyes when she was feeling sad, near the mouth when she was feeling angry.

"You're playing a game with me," he said.

"Yes."

"It's working."

Having acknowledged that seeing is a vital element in communication, we feel the need to introduce a caution before concluding.

Some of us are afraid to put our feelings into words. We are unwilling to take responsibility for expressing what we feel. We expect our partner to just know, to see without being told. We are hurt if our partner fails to be a good mind reader. Our partner typically responds with guilt and resentment. This is a pattern to be guarded against.

All our senses have a role to play in effective communication, and exclusive reliance on only one sense is almost always a mistake on the part of both sender and receiver.

Q. Why is it so difficult for most men to acknowledge being afraid or in pain?

A. This has to do with the way males are commonly raised in our culture. "Men don't show fear. Men don't cry."

Males are indoctrinated with a concept of masculinity which proscribes pain and fear as shameful and unworthy. These are the first two emotions young males are encouraged to suppress, deny, conceal, disown. Frequently taught since childhood to ignore body signals of pain or discomfort, to push on no matter what they are feeling, many of these prime specimens of manhood die of heart attacks after years of disregarding signs of danger. (In emergency situations, the ability to override signals of exhaustion has survival value, but as a way of life, it is a way of death.)

In romantic love this concept is significant because it condemns feelings as a sign of weakness. Many articles have been written about "the silent husband," the man who almost never talks about his feelings and is virtually helpless when confronted with his wife's feelings. The equation of manhood with emotional self-alienation is disastrous for romantic love.

In our Intensive on *Self-Esteem and the Art of Being,* we demonstrate how people manifest their blocked emotions physically: the mouth pulled down in suppressed anger, the breathing stopped with fear, the shoulders set to bear too many burdens in lethal resignation. Not long ago a woman who had taken this Intensive told us, "It took me about six months of persistence to teach my husband how to recognize when he was in a bad way. In the past, when I told him outright that he was exhausted or in pain, he usually met me with a denial. I learned to say, 'Your forehead is so furrowed. I wonder what's worrying you.' Or, 'Those are the shoulders of a tired man. Come and sit down and let me massage your neck.' Or, 'I see hurt in your eyes. Can I just hold you? You don't have to talk, if you don't feel like it.' Slowly, tentatively, and then happily, he began to melt. He said he felt so naked, so transparent to me. It made him feel he could no longer escape his own feelings, as if the knowledge that someone else was seeing him made it impossible for him not to see himself. Now he talks openly, without prompting, about whatever is bothering him. The greatest reward of my life came on the day when he said to me, 'I think I'm going to live longer, because of you.'"

When we told this story at an Intensive recently, a man stood up and said, "In support of what you're talking about, I want to acknowledge publicly that the greatest gift my wife ever gave me was teaching me that it's okay to say 'I'm scared. I'm afraid.' It did not make me weaker. It made me stronger. Learning to tell the truth always makes you stronger."

For many men it requires an act of true independence to break free of cultural stereotypes and say, "I'm alive and I feel."

Q. How do I make my partner feel visible, appreciated, loved?

A. If I do not know you, I cannot make you feel visible. If I do not know what it is about you that delights me, I cannot make you feel appreciated. If I am unaware of what it is about you that I love, I can never make you feel completely loved.

The art of making another person feel visible begins with seeing and hearing, the two basic means by which we understand another human being. If I am to make you feel visible, appreciated, loved, I must see and know what I am seeing; I must hear and know what I am hearing.

With couples who have difficulty expressing their awareness and their feelings, we find sentence completion marvelously effective.

*One of the things I appreciate about you is*____
*One of the things I most enjoy about you is*____
*One of the things I love about you is*____

Sometimes we recommend a simple awareness exercise:

*One of the things I am aware of about you is*____
*One of the things I imagine about you is*____
*One of the things I know about you that you may not know I know is*____

If we enjoy the way our partner moves, if we delight in a particular expression in our partner's eyes, if we appreciate our partner's thoughts, choices, decisions, actions, we can learn to communicate our admiration. And doing so is the process by which we make our partner feel visible, appreciated, and loved.

It is virtually impossible for a couple to spend too much time talking about the things they like and enjoy in each other. We cannot think of any behavior as powerful in keeping love alive.

In our personal experience and in that of many couples with whom we have discussed this question, there are more and more things to talk about as a relationship progresses. Understanding goes deeper, awareness of the other expands, more and more colors come to light. The self is a vast continent, and no two people ever live long enough to explore each other fully, especially since each of us is always in process of becoming.

There is far more to making another person feel visible than paying compliments. If I am complimented for traits I do not experience in myself, I am more likely to feel confused than visible or appreciated. If a man were to say to me, "The thing I love most about you is your sweetness," I would not feel gratified. I do not know whether I am sweet or not, but I do know that it is not my most important characteristic. We want to be responded to in ways that are congruent with our self-concept, in ways that enrich our self-concept.

On the other hand, I might never have considered that a boy and a vulnerable teenager co-exist wihin me. My partner, seeing and responding to these other aspects naturally, spontaneously, and lovingly, puts me in deeper touch with who I am and enlarges my self-awareness.

Speaking of seeing, we can hardly overestimate the importance of the eyes in communicating visibility. They can tell you that I find you endlessly fascinating, that I enjoy watching and listening to you, that I take pleasure sometimes in contemplating your movements, that I see you are excited, sad, tired, or sexually aroused, that I admire what you just said or did or that I think you are kidding yourself, that you are in need of tenderness at this moment, or that I am hearing a meaning that goes deeper than your words and helping you by my expression to become aware of it. Their expressive possibilities are endless.

Let your eyes be windows, not doors. Allow your awareness to flow through your eyes. A couple happily in love will know how to talk with their eyes.

Seven
Intimacy and Sex

Through intimacy we seek to satisfy the yearning romantic love generates in us: the desire to connect spiritually and physically, emotionally and sensually, to know and be known, to be naked in soul as well as in body with another.

The Bible speaks of a man "knowing" a woman, meaning that he has experienced her sexually. The act of sex is so clearly an act of intimacy that the expression "to be intimate with" is sometimes used as a synonym for sexual contact.

We have already observed that sex is not the only form of intimacy or of "knowing." Everything we have said about visibility, mutual self-disclosure, and communication bears on the issue of intimacy, for intimacy requires that two people be willing to respond at the deepest levels of their being.

And yet, in a consideration of intimacy, the image of sexual union stands us in good stead, symbolizing the joy of two beings who exult in and seek contact with their own and each other's nakedness, in willing and eager vulnerability. Spiritually no less than physically, this is the meaning of intimacy.

Since we have already said a good deal about intimacy in its nonsexual aspects, we will focus in this chapter principally on its sexual dimension, on the confusions, problems, and barriers that people in love sometimes experience.

It is an uncomfortable topic for many people, activating fears of vulnerability and rejection. At times people had trouble asking their questions directly. Often we had to guess at the real nature of the inquiry and judge from the response whether or not we had guessed correctly.

We are aware that the questions in this chapter do not flow into each other quite as smoothly as in the preceding chapters, nor do they always seem directly related to romantic love. And yet these are the questions presented to us most frequently. We have adhered to our questioners' concerns as a first principle of selection. The questions lack some continuity, but they convey authentically the painful confusion that so often surrounds attempts to integrate intimacy, sex, and romantic love.

Q. **Is intimacy really all that important? Can't I just enjoy love and affection and good sex?**

A. Intimacy is important if we are to experience fully the potential of romantic love. In intimacy we keep breaking down barriers to mutual self-disclosure. To be intimate with another person as a way of life means reaching always deeper into the self, becoming more and more vulnerable, sharing more and more of our essence with the person we love.

I can certainly limit contact, disclosure, and sharing to the superficial levels of the self by talking only about daily activities and concerns and never going deeper into feelings, thoughts, and aspirations. But in doing so I limit the possibilities of love, I limit the growth of love, I limit the world that love can disclose to me. That is the way most people live: playing it safe, taking very few risks, living only on the surface of their lives.

When I show you how I feel about you, and you respond in a way that creates a resonance in our minds and bodies, we achieve intimacy. Telling you of my anxieties, my dreams, or my passions and hearing you respond from the same depth is the experience of intimacy.

Intimacy is not a fixed quality in a relationship; it takes different forms, depending on both the circumstances and the people involved. For example, a man and a woman, each married to someone else, meet and feel strongly attracted to each other. After overcoming great internal resistance, they allow their hands to touch in a moment of exquisite and electrifying intimacy. They feel as if they have allowed their hearts to touch. Another man and woman may experience their most intense moments of intimacy after sex, when they hold each other and look into each other's eyes. After many years of marriage, a man may one day tell his wife about some painful or humiliating experience from long ago. As she listens with love, acceptance, and understanding, each feels a deeper sense of intimacy in their relationship.

To avoid intimacy is to avoid feeling deeply, to avoid connecting deeply with the person we love. Love is not superficial, and that is why intimacy is important. If our goal is set beyond merely playing at life and love, but experiencing them fully, intimacy is crucial.

After his participation in an Intensive on *Self-Esteem and Romantic Relationships*, a man wrote to us: "It seems to me, in retrospect, that I did not know what love is when I was playing it cool with my girlfriend. You know, lots of laughs and lots of sex. I was scared to get into why I felt for her as I do or to really tell her about myself. When she tried to talk intimately, I would change the subject, make a joke, try to get our minds on sex, just get away from deep feelings. After I cried at the Intensive, she and I went out to lunch and *talked* about the things that made me cry. It was like a light going on, and suddenly I understood what love is."

Q. **Isn't intimacy something that naturally goes with having sex together?**

A. Sex can be an exquisite expression of intimacy, but it can also be a way of avoiding intimacy.

Sex can express feelings of love, but it can also be used to avoid feelings of love.

Sex obviously involves physical intimacy. As for emotional intimacy, we can use our sexual feelings and those of our partner to defend ourselves against other feelings, which might take us deeper into ourselves than we feel comfortable going at the moment. We therefore flee into safe territory: "I'm beginning to feel too much—quick, let's make love."

The point is that we shouldn't equate intimacy with sex. Sometimes talking is far more intimate. Sometimes looking at each other without words can be more intimate than sex.

Q. How can I help my partner to overcome his (her) fear of intimacy?

A. Go first in risking self-expression and self-disclosure, and do it in a way that demonstrates your confidence in your partner. Show your partner that you are not afraid to trust.

Or show that you can be trusted. Be sensitive to your partner's shyness, and recognize that he or she may say very important things initially in a casual or offhand manner. You can help your partner when he or she takes the first tentative steps by responding to the essence of the communication, to the underlying intention. An invitation to intimacy rarely comes in a formal announcement.

For example, a reticent, inhibited man might mutter, "Kind of had fun at work today." He may be bursting to tell you about some important achievement of his or some important recognition he received but may not know how to go about it. Don't be deceived by the casualness. Say, "Really? Tell me about it."

We avoid intimacy because we are afraid of being vulnerable, afraid of our feelings, afraid of our partner, afraid of being out of control. We fear being rejected or losing face, in our own eyes as well as our partner's.

If you have laid your own fears to rest, you may still need patience and benevolence toward your partner. A single encounter is rarely enough to build trust.

Sometimes couples find themselves more prepared to talk intimately when they are naked, as if in taking off their clothes they shed other defenses as well. Knowing this, we ask couples to practice spending time together, naked, talking, by themselves. Frequently they interrupt the talk with sex, but then they talk again, and nakedness seems to facilitate the couple's efforts toward candor.

Couples find that in these circumstances they feel free

to say things they would not say at any other time. They gradually become more comfortable, extending their freedom to other ordinary activities, such as walking together, having dinner, or just sitting together.

One woman said to us, "It's interesting sitting together, naked and talking, and sometimes postponing sex. It's as if we're using the buildup of sexual energy to knock down walls in each of us. We end up saying even more intimate things. We don't allow sex to divert our attention or discharge the intensity that develops between us. I mean, not for a while anyway, not until we're really connected on a verbal and emotional level. Then sex is incredible. Postponing can be dynamite. We get the courage to say all kinds of things. After a while, talking gets easier, not just when we're naked."

Q. My partner and I experience the joys of intimacy and emotional closeness during or immediately before sex, but what can I do to help my partner remain intimate after sex?

A. We recommend that you begin by asking your partner this very question: "Is there anything I can do that would make you want to go on talking and remain intimate after sex?" Not that talking is the only form of intimacy; falling asleep in each other's arms can be a very intimate act. Yet there is a tendency to withdraw into the self immediately following sex, and this is the issue to which we are addressing ourselves.

When a couple came in for counseling about this problem, we suggested that the wife, who normally cleaned the kitchen after dinner while the children watched television, should retire with her husband to the bedroom instead, after making a Do Not Disturb announcement to the children. They made love, they talked, and often they went on talking while the wife *and* husband cleaned the kitchen later. They began to look for other opportunities in their regular routine for more private time together. Sex and intimacy need not be the very last priority of the day.

Fatigue may not be the only problem. Sex is a powerful but transient force, temporarily breaking down barriers of inhibition and repression. When the sexual drive is satisfied, the walls often go up again.

A man in one of our therapy groups complained of this problem. We asked him to work with the sentence stem "The scary thing about staying in touch with my partner after sex is_____." His endings included:

I feel too exposed.

I feel raw.

I feel vulnerable and helpless.

my defenses are down.

she can see me.

I'll feel how important she is to me.

We suggested that he look at his partner when they had made love the next time and say, "If I don't fall asleep right now _____." It helped him tell her what he had avoided telling her before:

I can tell you how good that felt.

I can tell you how I liked being close to you.

I can tell you that being close to you scares me.

I can tell you I want to run sometimes.

I can let you know I'm glad I'm not running away now.

I can tell you how much you mean to me.

I can admit how much I need you.

I can admit how scared I am that you might leave me.

Intimate talk followed naturally for both of them. Whenever he would lapse back into old habits, his partner would give him a sentence stem, "If I were to stay connected with you now_____." Gradually, as he developed a capacity for sustaining intimacy, he found that he no longer hastened to avoid his feelings by going to sleep.

Q. What is the relation of sex to romantic love?

A. Since that issue was discussed in some detail in *The Psychology of Romantic Love*, we will confine our answer here to a few essentials.

Sex and love, though related, are different. We can have gratifying sexual experiences without love. On the other hand, romantic love is always involved with a desire for sexual union. And the most intense sexual experiences almost always occur as an expression of love.

Sex involves an act of self-celebration. When we feel love of ourselves and in harmony with ourselves, then sex is a natural and spontaneous expression of our feelings for our partner, for ourselves, and for our existence. In sex we desire the freedom to be spontaneous, to be emotionally open, to assert our right to pleasure in our own being. In romantic love, the person we most desire sexually would be the person with whom we feel most free, the person we consciously or subconsciously regard as our appropriate psychological mirror, the person who reflects our deepest view of self and of life. Sex in romantic love is thus a celebrating of self, a celebration of two selves, and a celebration of life.

Success in romantic love reflects the integration of sexuality into selfhood. This means that our sexuality is not experienced as being at war with other cardinal values of the self; we are attracted to a person who embodies qualities we *admire*.

In love we do not feel a split between mind and body, between spirit and flesh, between admiration and passion. We are not divided against ourselves, so we do not struggle to prove our worth or prove anything. We are free to enjoy our own being, to enjoy the state of being alive, to enjoy and appreciate our partner.

Persons with inadequate self-esteem experience the relation of sex to love very differently, particularly when they are troubled by feelings of guilt about sex. They are incapable of feeling passion toward a person they admire because they do not admire themselves. A truly admirable partner would be degraded by the passion of a contemptible person like me—so they feel. They disconnect their sexual desires from their own values, especially their "higher" values. In the profoundest sense possible, they fail to integrate sex, love, and self.

In one of our therapy groups a woman said that while she had enjoyed oral sex with past lovers, whom she held in no particular esteem, the thought of oral sex with her husband was repulsive to her. "It would be degrading to him," she said, even as she admitted that he desired it eagerly. She was afraid he would lose respect for her if he found out she enjoyed it, as though her pleasure was a dark, secret side of herself to be concealed from the one person she most admired.

When addressing ourselves to such problems in therapy, we concentrate on the individual's self-esteem, teaching and encouraging self-awareness, self-acceptance, and responsibility to oneself. When self-esteem expands, difficulties of this kind tend to diminish.

We also approach such difficulties from another angle, the individual's attitude toward sex. We don't argue for a more positive attitude, but rather assist the individual in expressing the more positive attitude she or he already possesses and is afraid to acknowledge. For instance, we might use the following cue: "If I were to admit how much I really enjoy sex_____." Typical endings:

I'd breathe a lot easier.

I could love my partner more.

I couldn't face Mother.

Father would go crazy.

I wouldn't be a good little girl anymore.

I'd stop torturing myself.

I'd stop torturing my mate.

I might enjoy it even more.

Such insights clear the way for the individual's increasing acceptance of his or her positive sexual feelings.

Inside, each one of us already knows that sex is a normal human pleasure, a normal act of self-expression, and that it can be a tender act of caring for another. Such knowledge can be submerged in a desire to keep the good opinion and love of authority figures, such as parents, who may have conveyed that sex is dirty, shameful, ugly, or evil. A sex problem may turn out to be a problem of personal autonomy, of inadequate separation and individuation. (This phenomenon is explored from different perspectives in *The Psychology of Romantic Love, The Disowned Self, Breaking Free,* and *The Psychology of Self-Esteem*.) Self-awareness and self-acceptance are the first two steps toward personal growth and the first two steps toward understanding the relation of sex and romantic love.

Q. Can a good romantic relationship co-exist with a poor sexual one?

A. Sex is such a powerfully significant expression of love and intimacy that the long-term effects of a poor sexual relationship almost certainly take their toll on the overall quality of the romantic relationship. Not that love necessarily dies—it doesn't always—but it is hard to imagine that some form of estrangement or alienation would not develop between the man and woman.

We do not wish to imply that estrangement or alienation inevitably must follow if, for instance, temporary impotence or illness interrupts a couple's sex life for a time. A couple sometimes must join ranks against such adversities in ways that actually bring them closer. In such cases they have the wisdom not to allow the difficulty to manipulate them into an adversary relationship. The other values that bind them may be so powerful and so satisfying that they are able to live with their frustration. It all depends on the strength of those other values and on the importance each attaches to sex.

If "a poor sexual relationship" means that one or both parties are unhappy, frustrated, unfulfilled, then that unhappiness must have its effects on the relationship, whether or not it survives.

Assuming good health in both partners, we do not see any reason why an otherwise satisfying romantic relationship has to remain sexually frustrating. A couple we know adored and admired each other, delighted in each other's company, but did not have a particularly satisfying sexual relationship. While other forms of intimacy came fairly easily to them, sexual intimacy was hindered by certain unhappy experiences in childhood. When they perceived that the lack of satisfying sexual contact, despite their best efforts, was slowly eroding the joy in their marriage, they came for counseling. Fortunately, they responded well to therapy, learning to be freer about their own sexual needs and more responsive to each other's. Whether or not their relationship could have sustained itself otherwise, we are unprepared to say.

Q. Can a good sexual relationship be sustained over time in the absence of love?

A. This depends on what you mean by "a good sexual relationship."

A woman who was having an affair with a man she did not love once told us: "Sex with him is fantastic, and yet part of me, a very important part, is untouched by it all, and sometimes I just don't care that sex with him is great." While she and her partner were well-adjusted sexually, the lack of significant emotional involvement made sex unexciting for her, even when it was satisfying in a technical sense.

Enthusiasm wanes in most sexual relationships, even "good" ones, when there is no meaningful connection with the partner. Each begins to sense that there is more to sex and more to life than they are experiencing. Too much of the self remains unshared and unexpressed, too much of the self remains invisible.

If a sexual relationship "without love" did remain deeply satisfying over a long period of time, we would wonder whether the two people felt more for each other than they were conscious of or willing to admit. However, there are doubtless instances where people are content to sustain a good sexual relationship over a long period of time without feeling the need for any deeper involvement. They look elsewhere for the satisfaction of their other needs.

Q. Assuming healthy self-esteem and genuine love between a man and a woman, what elements would you say are most important for a happy sex life?

A. Apart from what we have already discussed, the number one factor is a willingness to communicate clearly and straightforwardly. To do so we must first take responsibility for learning the likes and dislikes of our partner and take responsibility for communicating our own likes and dislikes. Without honesty and openness, real communication is impossible.

Another important factor is trust in our partner: trust that our partner cares about our feelings, trust that he or she will not hurt us intentionally, trust that our partner cares about our sexual happiness. Trust gives us the freedom to be uninhibited, to express our wants and needs, to allow ourselves to be visible at a more intimate level with our partner than with anyone else.

It is worth remembering that one of the goals of sexual activity, aside from the intrinsic pleasure involved, is to feel close to our partner. After sex we should feel better about ourselves and the person we are with. This is what it means to have "a happy sex life." The couples who stand the best chance of achieving this goal are those who are secure in their mutual commitment to erotic and emotional fulfillment.

We might add one other factor, a certain lightness of spirit and attitude. We do not mean "lightness" in any sense that denies the seriousness of our sexual feelings or minimizes intensity. If we remember that making love is for *pleasure*, for *enjoyment*, and even at times for *fun*, then laughter and playfulness can be a valuable dimension of our sexual experience. Many couples approach sex with an inhibiting seriousness.

By way of illustrating what we mean by lightness of spirit, I will just mention an occasion when Nathaniel believed we had finished making love while I was entertaining the notion that perhaps we hadn't. Borrowing one of the tools I sometimes use in therapy, a Snoopy hand-puppet (I will not attempt to explain), I improvised a new use for it in bed that neither of us had contemplated before. Laughter can be erotically re-energizing—laughing at ourselves, laughing in delight at being alive.

Q. Is it normal for there to be sexual highs and lows in a happy love relationship?

A. It is hard to think of a single aspect of life which is not characterized by highs and lows, and sex is no exception.

No relationship is uniformly amorous from beginning to end. In addition, the man and woman may be at different phases of the cycle of sexual feeling within the relationship. On any particular occasion, one person may be feeling more amorous than the other. This range of feeling is entirely normal.

Apart from biological rhythms, there are any number of other factors which can influence sexual desire, such as health, drugs, involvement with work, involvement with children, involvement with other family members, even changes in the climate. It is a mistake to read ominous meanings into such normal fluctuations. They are an intrinsic part of life and love.

All of us can recognize that we do not feel equally sexual every day. Sometimes we desire sex two or three times in a single twenty-four-hour period, and sometimes we may go for a week or two rarely thinking of sex. If we recognize such fluctuations in ourselves, we can learn to recognize them in our partner without taking them as evidence of a crisis in the relationship.

"I used to worry that sometimes I wanted sex when my husband didn't," a woman in therapy remarked, "until one day I noticed that it was equally true to say that sometimes he wanted sex when I wasn't especially in the mood. Of course that's not to say that I can't put him in the mood when he isn't already inclined, or that he can't put me in the mood, or even that we can't accommodate each other without being all that much in the mood, but fluctuations definitely occur and I've stopped worrying about them. I can't imagine always being on a sexual high anyway. Change seems necessary to feel excited and alive. If we're at a low, we know it won't last. A high will come along a little later. Even if I don't always understand the rhythms operating inside myself or my husband, I know that everything in life operates by some kind of rhythm— the sun, the moon, and the tides—so we've learned to make the best of wherever we are right now, knowing that high or low, good or bad, change is inevitable."

Q. In making sure our relationship lasts, how concerned should I be with pleasing my partner sexually?

A. Mature love presupposes a desire for the happiness and well-being of a person we love and a wish to contribute to that happiness and well-being. This concern does not mean we take total responsibility for the other person. Ultimately, we can be responsible only for ourselves.

The principle applies to love in general and to sex as a particular. I am interested in my partner's pleasure, I want to know what my partner enjoys, and I want my partner to have a happy experience in bed with me. But do I assume total responsibility for my partner's sexual happiness? I do not. A partner who is overconcerned with pleasing is not an independent equal.

Sexual happiness is best served by a healthy, good-natured, loving selfishness, guided but not dominated by an active concern for the satisfaction of the partner.

This attitude excludes the psychology of both the compulsive pleaser and the compulsive performer, the man or woman who sees sex not as an opportunity for self-expression, pleasure, and the sharing of love but as a means of proving personal worth. In different ways the pleaser and the performer are both alienated sexually. Both are motivated by insecurity and self-doubt. Both are less concerned with enjoyment than with being perceived as "a good girl" or "a good boy."

Sometimes a man or a woman will complain, "I feel my partner is too concerned with me rather than with his (her) own pleasure. I find that inhibiting. I want the freedom to be involved in my own pleasure, and I want my partner to have the same freedom."

In a happy sexual relationship we move back and forth between focusing on our own pleasure and focusing on that of our partner, and we do it so swiftly, so subtly, so frequently, that there is often little awareness of where we leave off and our partner begins.

To answer the question succinctly: yes, we want our partner to experience pleasure with us, but we are not in bed primarily to service our partner.

Some of us may be overconcerned, some of us may be too little concerned with pleasing our partner. How to find out if we belong in either category? The simplest way is to discuss the matter with our partner, to invite our partner to share his or her impressions of us in this regard. Two well-intentioned and honest people can assuredly find the middle ground.

Q. How can I express a particular desire in sex without evoking insecurities and self-doubt in my partner?

A. One way is to encourage your partner to express his or her own desires, saying in effect, "I hope you'll tell me what feels good for you. I won't always know, but I'd love it if you'd signal me, ask in words, or let me know in some way whatever gives you the most pleasure."

Once again, the value of exemplifying the behavior we would like to elicit from our partner can hardly be overestimated.

When making such requests, learn to use the word *and* rather than *but* whenever possible. Notice the difference between saying "I love what you're doing *and* I wish you would press harder," as opposed to "I love what you're doing *but* I wish you would press harder." The second version carries a subtle rebuke.

Further, when your partner does things you enjoy, make sure he or she knows it. "I love what you're doing right now." "That's perfect; don't change a thing." "It's fantastic when you do that."

Finally, look for opportunities to ask and express pleasure at the same time. "I feel marvelous lying here with you. I love the way your hands touch me. I would love to feel your mouth on my breasts right now." Compare: "Don't you like kissing my breasts?"

Again: "My idea of heaven is lying with your head on my shoulder and your hands between my legs. Would you just shift the weight a little bit to the left?" Compare: "You're hurting me."

Attitude here is of the highest importance. If I express what I want in a confident, loving, and trusting manner,

conveying my belief that you want to please me, chances
are you will respond appropriately. If I convey that you
are a disappointment to me, or that I do not believe you
care about my pleasure one way or the other, chances are
you will withdraw, become resentful, hurt, defensive.

One final word: Just as men and women have the right
to do whatever provides mutual pleasure, so they have
the right to decline to participate in any sexual act they
experience as unpleasant. In sex, as in every other aspect
of life, tastes and preferences differ and should be respected. For example, some women enjoy swallowing se-
men following oral sex, some do not. Some men are
comfortable with oral sex while the woman is menstruat-
ing, some are not. There is no right or wrong here and no
point in confusing preferences and moral judgments. And
certainly we would be making a mistake if we judged our
partner's love for us by the willingness or unwillingness
to participate in a particular act.

Q. Do you make any distinction between healthy
sexual behavior and unhealthy sexual behavior?

A. We prefer to think in terms of desirable sexual
behavior and undesirable sexual behavior. It seems
doubtful that "healthy" and "unhealthy" apply in this
context, except metaphorically.

Sexual behavior that stimulates enjoyment without in-
flicting harm on either party is desirable. Sexual behavior
that is experienced as a violation, that exploits or damages
another human being or risks physical injury, is undesirable
and wrong.

Orgasm attained by any mutually enjoyable means—
fellatio, cunnilingus, masturbation, or whatever your ingenuity can create—falls within the range of appropriate
and desirable sexual behavior. So does any sexual activity
that is mutually enjoyable, whether it leads to orgasm or
not.

Some men and women may be so inhibited by their
upbringing that they are uncomfortable with any act other
than intercourse, although they may desire more variety.
For such people we recommend the sex books listed in
our bibliography to open their eyes and to encourage

them to experiment. Some couples find their sexuality enhanced by erotic films. We are in favor of whatever facilitates freedom, self-acceptance, and self-expression.

Q. **What about sexual fantasies? Do they help or hurt a romantic relationship?**

A. Many men and women fantasize at least some of the time during sex, while others rarely or never do, and neither the presence nor absence of fantasies is a cause for concern.

Undeniably, fantasies can be a source of stimulation. Because of fatigue, illness, lack of sufficient emotional contact with the partner, or because of a passing mood, we may desire that extra stimulation for full sexual arousal and responsiveness—without any implication that we do not love our partner or that our partner is not capable of arousing us. Indeed, our partner may be the beneficiary of our fantasies.

If someone is able to enjoy sex only by fantasizing about people other than his or her partner, then there is clearly a problem in the relationship. (Fantasies do not in themselves hurt a relationship.)

Many couples enjoy sharing their fantasies in bed, sometimes acting them out. They may pretend, for example, to be making love while still strangers, or they may exaggerate the dominance of one partner over the other. Such experiences can enrich and enliven a relationship with delight and excitement.

Q. **Do you recommend experimenting with different techniques of lovemaking in order to keep sex (and, therefore, our relationship) exciting?**

A. This question does not lend itself to a yes-or-no answer. While we believe couples should experiment in their lovemaking, we do not believe that varying techniques by itself will keep a sexual relationship exciting.

Boredom and excitement have far more to do with the attitudes and psychologies of individual lovers than with exotic techniques of lovemaking. We know many men and women who have experimented with every position and every kind of partner and have lived out a good many fantasies, and they have become more and more bored with their sex lives, less and less capable of any real involvement.

Boredom is a result of living on the surface of awareness, acting out routines that have ceased to have meaning. Excitement is a result of spontaneity, freshness of perception, intimacy of contact, openness of communication, and willingness to share ourselves without defenses. More than anything else, to say it once again, excitement is a consequence of communication.

Variety in lovemaking can happen naturally. We are not always in the same mood. We are not always at the same energy level. Our amorous impulses are not always equally strong. Our feelings in a particular sexual encounter can fluctuate in dozens of possible directions: on one occasion we may desire gentleness and tenderness; on another, a passionate connection bordering on violence. We may wish to dominate or to submit. We may want our lovemaking to extend for hours; we may want to take or be taken quickly. We may want our partner to lie passively while we do everything; we may want to surrender in delicious helplessness. We may be in the mood to cover every inch of our partner's body with our tongue; we may be in the mood for instant penetration.

All such feelings are normal, and if we are not acting out some notion of how sex is supposed to be, we will move naturally, as the mood of a given occasion dictates, across a wide spectrum of sexual behavior. The only rule—if you want to call it that—is to allow the act of sex to express how you and your partner feel at the moment.

Sometimes a couple will press us for specific advice "to get them started" in expanding their approach to lovemaking. Devers favors the following scenario, and couples who feel somehow stuck and mechanical in their sexual relationship generally respond well to it.

Draw a bubble bath and get in the tub together. All lights off except for candles. Two glasses of wine or some beverage on the edge of the tub. Sit facing each other. Sip the drink slowly, talk, caress and stroke each other. Wash each other's bodies. Take your time. Dry each other off

with soft towels. Make contact with every part of your
partner's body. Then . . . let things happen naturally.

This particular scenario has proven useful not only for
couples who wish to loosen up and enhance the excitement
of their lovemaking but also for men and women who feel
anxiety about sex (a woman, for example, who complains
of inadequate foreplay or a man who ejaculates too quickly).
We find this an effective and universal therapy.

Q. I was raised in a strict religious tradition that left
me with a lot of guilt about sex. I wonder sometimes how my love relationships have been affected.

A. A sense of guilt is inherently detrimental to any
love relationship.

If we regard sex as evil or tainted, then our sexuality is
severed from the rest of our values and person. It cannot
be integrated with love, benevolence, or admiration. Our
capacity for sexual enjoyment and self-assertion with a
partner we regard highly is very likely to be crippled.

Sexually, we are sometimes drawn to people we think
poorly of since only they are fitting partners for "that evil
act." If sex is evil, and if we are evil for wanting it, then
we need appropriate companions in evil.

We recall a woman who came to Devers for counseling.
She had been married eleven years, had never had a
satisfactory sex life with a husband she deeply respected,
and was distressed to see him withdrawing from her more
and more.

Standing her in front of a full-length mirror, Devers
asked her to study her reflection as if she were looking at
a stranger. She was to notice the stranger's posture, facial
expressions, and movements. Devers put on a disco tape
and asked her to dance in front of the mirror. Shy, reluctant at first, the woman began to move a little, dance a
little, timidly and awkwardly, while watching her reflection.

When Devers asked her to describe what she was seeing,
the woman replied, "Someone who is very stiff and self-
conscious. She stands and moves with her shoulders turned
in. Bad posture, all sort of folded up. Her head and body
move in opposite ways, uncoordinated."

Devers asked her to relax her shoulders, relax her body,

get centered and balanced, and then she asked the woman to describe her reflection again: "She looks proud of her body. Not embarrassed that she has breasts. She is more sensual. Sexual. Different. Not me. Is that me?"

Devers followed up with sentence completions:

"If I were proud of my body_____:"

I'd have to realize I'm a woman.

Mother would accuse me of flaunting myself sexually.

the church would condemn me.

I would look like I enjoy sex.

Father would be shocked and upset.

I'd feel guilty.

I'd be punished.

they'd call me sinful.

I would be a bad person.

Tears were rolling down her cheeks. She looked sad, frightened, and intrigued all at once. She said, a little sheepishly, "On the other hand, this feels good." To erase her negative programming about sex, she had to challenge parental authority; she had to say goodbye to Mother and Father in order to increase her independence and self-esteem.

There is no way to list all the possible consequences of antisexual religious indoctrination. Such a list would range from impotence and frigidity to self-destruction.

The doctrinal condemnation of sex as unclean has generated the good girl/bad girl syndrome, a distinction between the woman one admires and the woman one desires. The dichotomy has by no means disappeared in our society. It has led many a man to contract a disastrously unhappy marriage, for himself and for his partner. Believing that one does not marry a bad (that is, sexual) woman, and that one does not offend a good (that is, nonsexual) woman with one's depraved desires, many men select a woman they feel no passion for to be their wife and the mother of their children. They turn to someone less "admirable" for the gratification of their "lower nature."

Q. My husband suffers from the good woman/bad woman syndrome: good women aren't interested in sex; bad women enjoy sex. He wants to be married to a good woman, and he wants to have a happy sex life, and I would like not to go crazy. What can I do?

A. This is not an easy question to answer in general terms, since so much depends on the individual personalities of the man and woman involved, as well as on the particular reasons a man may have succumbed to this syndrome.

We would wonder, first of all, why the two people didn't confront the problem prior to marriage. We would have to consider the possibility that the woman shared her husband's attitude to some extent and played into his belief system from the start, rebelling against it only later.

To some men, sleeping with a "good woman" is tantamount, unconsciously and symbolically, to sleeping with Mother. In severe cases, a conflict of that kind requires psychotherapy or marriage counseling. On one occasion, at an Intensive, Nathaniel was able to set a confused husband straight rather quickly. With the wife present, Nathaniel asked the husband, "Do you consider her a good woman?"

"Definitely," the man replied.

"Terrific," said Nathaniel. "Will you come up to the front of the room and face everyone, please? Now there's a sentence I'd like you to say to the whole room. Just notice how it feels to say, 'My wife is a good woman—and I can't stand the thought that she should find me sexually desirable!'"

The man repeated the statement, louder and louder each time. He began shyly, rose to conviction, and ended sheepishly, more than a little humorously. He turned to Nathaniel: "What I'm saying is insane!"

"It's what you seem to think," Nathaniel replied. "How do you feel saying it aloud?"

"I feel ridiculous. The idea is preposterous. It doesn't make any sense!"

"I agree," Nathaniel replied.

Nathaniel asked the man to sit facing his wife for a

sentence-completion exercise: "If I can ever stop seeing you as my mother_____:"

I can see you as a human being.

I can love you.

I can enjoy having sex with you.

I won't hate you.

I won't keep expecting you to condemn me.

I can be glad that you want me.

we can have a marriage.

I can admit how sexual I feel toward you.

I can enjoy your sexuality.

A few months later Nathaniel received a note from the man which said, "Thank you for allowing me to find the sexiest 'good' woman in the world!"

What can you do on your own to help your husband recognize that a good woman is also a sexual woman? You might follow Nathaniel's example. Ask your partner if he thinks you're a good woman. Tell him how "awful" you feel being a good woman and yet finding him desirable. You love touching him. You think he's the most attractive man you've ever known. *"Isn't that terrible?"*

With a little humor and a lot of patience you may open his eyes.

Q. When my partner and I first married, we had a marvelous sex life. In the past few years it has been sadly deteriorating. Sometimes it seems to me that the way we live now, with so much more stress, is really incompatible with a good sex life. Does this sound plausible?

A. Very plausible indeed There is no question but that chronic fatigue, the pressure of overwork, the strain of too many social commitments, financial worries, or career anxieties can undermine normal and happy sexual functioning. Impotence, premature ejaculation, inability of the woman to reach climax, all can be the consequences of strain.

In working with clients in psychotherapy and marriage counseling at the Biocentric Institute, we are obliged again and again to speak of the importance of leisure, relaxation, and time for intimacy in sustaining romantic love in general and sexual happiness in particular.

One couple came for therapy because of the man's diminishing interest in sex. He professed to be bewildered as to the reason. He insisted that he loved his wife, had no interest in other women, and couldn't understand why he seemed to have gone dead sexually.

As an experiment, we asked him to join his wife in the twelve-hour intimacy marathon described in Chapter 2. A few hours into the marathon, his sexual excitement and vigor returned. It was gone again next day when he returned home in the evening from work, and it stayed gone in the days that followed. However, the exercise had accomplished its purpose in that it allowed him to perceive the relationship between leisure and his sexual capacity.

Despite his new awareness, it was hard for him to organize more leisure time for him and his wife to spend together, because his self-esteem was heavily invested in rising to the top of his profession as rapidly as possible. Only when he saw that he and his wife were on the verge of divorce was he willing to reconsider his priorities.

We taught him how to meditate, how to relax in the midst of office pressure, and how to relax when he returned home so that his mind was clear of the concerns of the day. No sexual therapy was needed.

His body had been sending him a message: "Slow down. Your way of life is incompatible with love and marriage." As he learned to listen to his body, to set aside more time for his relationship with his wife, to take better care of himself, to allow himself more rest, leisure and recreation, his desire for sex and his ability to enjoy it returned spontaneously.

Time and intimacy are the nutrients of love. Without them, the best love can die of starvation. And so can the most exciting sexual relationship.

Q. At night, when my partner desires sex, I am too tired. In the morning, when I desire sex, my partner is preoccupied with the problems of the day. What are we to do?

A. Once again we are dealing with the question of priorities. If such a problem is to be solved, the two people have to reorganize their life so that there is some period when neither is tired or preoccupied. If they cannot adjust their schedules, the problem cannot be solved.

Reproaches are not the answer. Saying "You don't really love me" is not the answer. Complaining "You avoid me" is not the answer. Proposing a cooperative effort, "Let's think how we can reorganize our schedule so as to have more time to enjoy each other," is the beginning of the answer.

In the early stages of a relationship, couples almost always find a solution to this problem. Sexual intimacy is a sufficiently high priority to motivate them. Later, when they have established their relationship, they don't feel the same urgency, and they allow their sex life to fall into neglect, with unfortunate long-term consequences.

Some couples have solved this problem by reversing the usual order of their activities, making love after dinner, for example, and then doing the evening's chores. Others get up an hour earlier in the morning, before the activities of the day begin.

Sometimes, of course, the problem is the presence of children. If time alone together seems impossible, the relationship must suffer, and not only because of sexual frustrations. One has to *make* time.

Solutions need to be tailored to the circumstances of a particular couple's life; there are no off-the-rack answers here. What seems most urgent is your absolute determination to treat the problem as important. Do not rest until you have found some way to reorganize your time.

Q. Being recently married, I am concerned to hear so many couples complain that their sexual desire diminishes after marriage or actually turns sour. Why does it have to happen?

A. Passion does not have to fade with time. It will help if we first understand why this problem can occur.

A lot of the excitement of sex, in the initial stages of a relationship, has to do with novelty and with some uncertainty as to how the relationship will develop. But these considerations are hardly the only sources of sexual excitement, as we have already seen.

After marriage, couples often feel differently because they behave differently. They do not give each other the same time and attention they gave early in the relationship. They tend to talk less, to share fewer feelings, to ask fewer questions. They rely more and more on assumptions about the thoughts, attitudes, and emotions of their partner, not bothering to check them out because they "know" each other. The relationship becomes more and more mechanical.

The simplest and most effective remedy for this destructive pattern is fifteen minutes of communication each day: sharing thoughts and feelings and inquiring about the thoughts and feelings of the other.

Another cause of estrangement and sexual boredom is the policy of ignoring verbal and nonverbal signals of hurt, anger, and frustration. These need to be dealt with and resolved before your partner shuts down communication in order to be less vulnerable. Once that happens, sexual excitement is a thoroughly predictable casualty.

Almost everything we discussed in the preceding chapter on communicating emotions bears on the issue of keeping sexual excitement alive. It is essential to continue to communicate your appreciation and admiration for each other.

Very often couples talk more, share more, focus more on each other and on their relationship when they go away on a vacation. For a while, they rekindle their sexual flame. It isn't that vacations per se enliven sex. It is rather that we behave differently when taken out of our ordinary settings and routines. We need to think about how we can integrate more vacation behaviors into our daily living. Love and sex can die when daily living amounts to neglect.

Q. How can I encourage my partner to be more demonstrative physically? I am not referring so much to sexual demonstrativeness as to simple expressions of affection, kissing, holding hands, cuddling, hugging.

A. Assuming that the man and woman genuinely care for each other, we should first try to understand why one of them might be blocked in expressing physical affection.

We asked a man who experienced this problem to walk across a room, hold his wife's hand, and then describe what he experienced. He said, "I feel silly. Self-conscious. Unmanly." Some men identify·masculinity with sexual expression.

We asked a woman who was similarly inhibited to describe her thoughts as she imagined hugging her husband in a restaurant. She said, "People mustn't know I have sexual feelings. That's for when we're alone." Shame associated with sex can also generate problems of this kind.

Someone else said, "I don't like to give my partner that much power over me. Too much affection shows that I care too much. I'm too vulnerable, and I'd rather play it cool."

Another person said, "Whenever I get affectionate, my partner gets turned on sexually, and that's not necessarily what I have in mind, so I avoid physical contact if I'm not in the mood for sex."

Another partner said, "I'm still afraid of being rejected, so I leave the initiative to my partner. I'm willing to respond, I just don't like going first."

Another person said, "Growing up in our family, I never saw anyone touch or hug anyone. So it just seems strange to me."

If we wish our partner to become more demonstrative, we need to help him or her identify the barriers that stand in the way. The simplest strategy might be sentence completion: "The bad thing about being demonstrative physically is_____." When we are able to put our resistance to touching into words, we generally find it easier to begin letting go of that resistance—especially if we are motivated to want to let go.

Communicate to your partner that you enjoy giving *and*

receiving physical affection. Try to avoid reproaches. When you are physically affectionate in a loving, cheerful, and undemanding way, your partner may overcome his or her anxiety and melt. Express your pleasure whenever your partner takes the initiative.

We believe it is natural to enjoy physical affection. Humans need to touch and respond to touching. If we feel aversion to it, some emotional block is usually the cause.

A few of the sentence completions we hear in this connection may help some of our readers to a perspective on their feelings about being affectionate: "It would be easier for me to be physically demonstrative if_____:"

> *you would let me go at my own pace.*
>
> *I could be sure you wanted it.*
>
> *you didn't always take it as a signal for instant sex.*
>
> *I could be certain I didn't appear silly.*
>
> *I could talk first about why it bothers me.*

I want to share a story about Devers and me with anyone who is struggling over this issue. Physical affection and demonstrativeness have always come naturally to me, except in the morning. I used to leap out of bed eager to get to my desk. Early in our relationship Devers wanted me to stay in bed a little longer, holding and cuddling. I tried but sometimes felt strained and impatient. I could see that she was disappointed. I decided one day that I was going to solve the problem. I *made myself* lie in bed holding her and stroking her, simply accepting whatever strain was there. "Are you suffering?" she asked.

"Only every other moment."

"Are you feeling guilty for not being at work?" she asked.

"Not as much as I did yesterday."

It got easier and easier with each day that passed, and more and more enjoyable. It didn't take long for me to love our morning time together, which now feels as natural to me as breathing.

If we have an opportunity to nourish our relationship, and the only reason for not taking it is that we feel a little strained or awkward, one solution is to make the change, experience the discomfort, and allow it to disappear—as it almost always will.

Q. My partner sometimes talks about past relationships in far more detail than I want to hear. Is there such a thing as "too much" sexual honesty between partners?

A. Let's put it this way. There is such a thing as talking too much about matters that are no part of your current relationship, and such matters would include the characteristics and techniques of former lovers, intimacy shared with them, and so forth. When we recommend honesty of communication in relationships, we are speaking of straightforward communication that pertains to the relationship.

It can be entirely appropriate to say to your partner: "I want to know of any thought or feeling concerning our relationship that you care to share with me. But I don't feel the need to know all the details of your past relationships, and sometimes listening to them makes me uncomfortable." And if your partner should ask you for details of past relationships, you have the option of deciding whether or not you wish to respond and to what degree. Give your answer openly and benevolently.

No advice we can give here obviates the need for sensitivity, independent judgment, and common sense, as the following story demonstrates.

We had a man in one of our groups who enjoyed bringing up intimate details of past love affairs for no apparent reason. Nathaniel asked his current love, "Do you enjoy listening to all this?"

"No," she replied.

"Have you ever told him so?"

"No."

"Care to tell him right now how listening to it makes you feel?"

She turned to the man. "I feel like I'm your mother. I feel like I'm supposed to be impressed by your virility and give you a pat on the back."

He blushed, looked uncomfortable and worried.

Nathaniel said to him, "The good thing about talking about other relationships is_____."

He responded, "The good thing about talking about other relationships is that I get the idea across that other women found me desirable."

"And the good thing about that is_____."

The man looked at his lover. "And the good thing about that is maybe you'll find me more desirable."

"Don't you think I find you desirable?" The woman was stunned.

"Not always," he said.

If a partner feels driven to talk too much about past relationships, or to ask for too many details about yours, it may be necessary to look into the unmet needs behind the insistence on sexual "honesty."

Q. In premarital couples' counseling a man will ask: "What are the faults or mistakes women complain of in men's lovemaking?" A woman will ask: "What are the faults men complain of in women's lovemaking?"

A. Tastes, preferences, and complaints differ, of course, but these are the complaints we hear most frequently from women about men.

Lack of adequate attention to foreplay. Some men's notion of foreplay is restricted to a few perfunctory kisses, strokes, and rubs. In fact, satisfying foreplay begins not with physical caresses at all but with mental attention, with awareness, and often with conversation. Following that, women sometimes enjoy a long period of precoital caressing, sometimes a short period, but they always enjoy the man's consciousness, sensitivity, and presence.

An overvigorous attack on the clitoris. Some men, having learned that the clitoris is the center of erotic sensitivity in the female, proceed too quickly to direct stimulation of that highly delicate organ, not realizing that it usually does not respond well to forcefulness, roughness, violence.

Reliance on one sexual technique. What worked well with your former partner may not work as well with your present one. What matched yesterday's mood may not match today's. What felt pleasurable in one context may not feel pleasurable in another. Mechanical repetition amounts to an insensitivity to the moment, a failure to notice the partner's mood and state right now, and may undermine what began as a promising sexual relationship. No single technique is going to work every time.

Pressuring the woman to have an orgasm. Many men's sexual self-esteem is invested in their ability to bring their partner to climax, and they pressure their partner inappropriately. "Did you? Did you come? Have you come yet?" No woman wants a man to be indifferent to orgasm, but neither does she want to feel that she owes him an orgasm. Such a thought can be sexually paralyzing.

And these are the sexual complaints from men about women.

Acting as if her orgasm is the man's responsibility. Many women know very little about their own bodies and are reluctant to learn anything from their bodies about sexual climax. They believe that it is for men to possess such knowledge, not themselves. Where their own pleasure is concerned, they cling to passivity, which many men legitimately experience as a burden.

Lack of spontaneity and innovativeness. Here again we deal with the theme of passivity. Many women are educated to believe that sex is principally a man's business, so much of their own sexuality remains unawakened. They feel that sexual self-assertiveness is unfeminine or immoral, so they leave the art of pleasing a man sexually to "bad women." Guilt and fear of disapproval inhibit normal sexual expression and appropriate companionship with the man.

Failure to understand that men too need to be in the mood for sex. Many women (and many men) believe that "a real man" is always ready for sex. Women who believe that arousing a man is as easy and quick as tripping a fire alarm are likely to wait passively if a man is slow to have an erection or has difficulty sustaining it. They do not think of talking to the man lovingly at such moments, stroking and caressing him, or otherwise participating in his arousal. To make matters worse, men are often ashamed to ask for what they need and thereby miss a chance to educate the woman.

So much information about sex is available today that we are uncertain as to how many men and women require more information here. Probably more than would willingly admit it. We recommend that couples review these two lists together and discuss whether any items seem applicable.

None of these errors is difficult to correct. Little more is required than an understanding that they are errors. Some intimate and candid discussion between partners with a genuine desire to change and grow will quickly reveal where change and growth are needed.

Q. In *The Psychology of Romantic Love* you refer to a man and woman expressing their "worship" of each other through the act of sex. What is the meaning of "worship" in this sense?

A. Borrowing the language of religion, because there is no secular language that adequately describes the intensity of adoration I wanted to convey, I used "worship" to indicate an act of surrender, an unreserved act of devotion and reverence. This is how two people deeply in love sometimes experience sex.

And I wrote of worship "of each other," with no implication of superiority and inferiority, no implication of a lower-order being surrendering to a higher-order being.

"I am not a religious person, in the conventional sense," wrote a woman after finishing *The Psychology of Romantic Love*, "but the idea of 'worship' while making love has a lot of meaning for me. My husband is my idol. He moves me to ecstasy. My love and my body are only for him. I feel at peace with the world. During lovemaking, he is the world. Nothing else exists; just his body and soul, and mine. His eyes and face tell me that he feels as I do. This is not something I would ever have felt comfortable discussing, because I sense that not many people share these feelings. I can't really know. But when I read your book, I thought, 'Someone understands.' "

I was very gratified to receive that letter and other comments like it, because the statement in my book about worship expressed something I personally experience about sex in romantic love. The distinction between body and spirit breaks down; it is my wife's *person* I am making love to, and I believe "worship" is not too strong a word to describe the feeling.

Eight
Jealousy and Infidelity

When we love passionately, we tend to desire sexual exclusivity. When we love passionately, we experience sex as more than a physical act. It is not only our bodies that meet in bed but our souls. The thought of our partner sharing that response with another person is almost always painful, sometimes excruciating.

True enough, many cultures take extramarital sex for granted, but they are cultures in which marriage is not associated with intense passion. The same is true for individuals who, regardless of culture, take extramarital sex for granted.

And yet we retain the sexual aspect of our being throughout life. When we fall in love, we do not become indifferent to the attractiveness of people other than our partner, although for a while it may seem to us that the rest of the human race doesn't exist. Attractiveness generates desire. Whether or not we choose to act on the desire is another question, sometimes a difficult one, but that such a desire can arise, and almost certainly will from time to time, seems an obvious and inescapable fact of human psychology.

The most challenging trials a couple may have to face in the course of a relationship hang on this issue: the tension between the desire for exclusivity and the attraction to someone other than our partner. Men and women anguish over this conflict, divorce over it, and sometimes even kill over it. It is important and worth thinking about.

The desire for sexual exclusivity is thoroughly understandable, thoroughly normal, and is not, as some people would claim today, a manifestation of neurosis or merely a remnant of old-fashioned conditioning. On the other hand, we do not share the views that an extramarital affair, if it happens, must sound the death knell for the primary relationship. A passage from *The Psychology of Romantic Love* will set forth the essentials of our view on this issue:

> Assessing the matter realistically, it seems clear that long-term sexually exclusive relationships are far more likely to happen in the second half of life than in the first. When people fall passionately in love in their forties, they are not so likely to be still sexually inexperienced; there is a better chance that much of their sexual curiosity has been satisfied; and they are more likely to be interested in and psychologically motivated to preserving a sexually exclusive, or at least *predominantly* sexually exclusive, relationship.
>
> When people fall in love and marry in their twenties, the likelihood of their preserving that relationship, with or without sexual exclusivity, across a lifetime, is very remote. . . . In our twenties we are very unlikely to be sufficiently developed to be able to make a lifelong commitment. And even if our choice of partner is appropriate at the time, even if it is a wise, intelligent, and mature choice, the normal process of change, growth, and evolution may generate different desires and needs in later years. . . .
>
> None of the foregoing is intended to deny that there are people who marry in their twenties or thirties and do remain together, happily together and with sexual exclusivity, for as long as both of them live. What needs to be challenged, however, is the assumption that any other pattern necessarily represents a failure.

We will challenge this assumption in our answers to many of the questions in this chapter. In doing so we have been sensitive to the fact that we are approaching one of the most charged issues in man/woman relationships, one about which people feel strongly. Our purpose is not to offer glib and facile cures for either jealousy or desire for someone other than our primary partner. But we offer a perspective for both the person who experiences the jealousy and the person who has aroused this jealousy to help them preserve their romantic love. We are assuming that the two people are deeply in love and committed to each other, whether or not they are married.

Q. Isn't jealousy a normal emotion and thus an intrinsic part of love?

A. We would not label jealousy normal or abnormal. We have already indicated our belief that in passionate love there is a desire for sexual exclusivity. Some degree of pain would follow the loss of exclusivity. If one wants to call that pain jealousy, then we suppose it could be called normal. But let us look at the experience of jealousy more closely.

Webster's Third International Dictionary defines jealous as: "Intolerant of rivalry or unfaithfulness; disposed to suspect rivalry or unfaithfulness; apprehensive of the loss of another's exclusive devotion; hostility toward a rival or one believed to enjoy an advantage; vigilant in guarding a possession; distrustfully watchful."

The first thing we need to understand about jealousy is that it refers to a variety of emotional states, which are similar but not identical. It is confusing when, for example, the word to describe the pain of learning that our partner has slept with another person is the same word used to describe the frenzy of a person who is constantly seeing signs of infidelity where none in fact exists or the possessiveness of someone who cannot bear for his or her partner to find value in any other human being, male or female.

We will characterize sexual jealousy as follows: it generally involves feelings of anxiety, feelings of being threatened, fantasies of rejection or abandonment, and often rage in response to our partner's involvement (real or imagined) with another person.

Many people today insist that jealousy is intrinsically irrational and that enlightened men and women are not susceptible to it, but this is not a view we can share. Emotions are neither rational nor irrational. Human beings are rational or irrational; thought processes are rational or irrational; emotions simply *are*. We might reasonably be tempted to call jealousy irrational in one circumstance only: when it is experienced in the absence of any objective provocation; when it has no basis in external reality. Even then, of course, it is not the feeling but the distorted thinking processes, which provoke the feeling, that ought to be called irrational.

Consider the many different causes of jealousy. Some people feel jealousy because they feel deep self-doubt and live with constant anticipations of rejection and abandonment. Some experience jealousy when they see someone else receiving the consideration they wanted themselves. Jealousy may arise in a new relationship because of painful experiences in past relationships involving the partner's involvement with other people; the new partner is rightly or wrongly imagined to be repeating an old pattern. Sometimes jealousy arises because a person disowns his or her sexual interest in others and so keeps a constant watch on the partner for signs of outside sexual interest. Jealousy can be a generalized apprehension that somehow happiness always dies. Sometimes jealousy is ignited by the direct knowledge that a partner is involved with another person.

Certainly we cannot say that all of these responses are "an intrinsic part of love." We will touch upon each one of them, however, and propose ways of dealing with them, since at one time or another many people do experience some of these reactions.

Early in our relationship Devers and I had a conversation that may help to clarify some aspects of our perspective on jealousy. One day she asked me, "Are you a jealous man?"

Thinking of someone who is typically watchful, suspicious, anxious over his partner's fidelity, I answered, "No."

"If I were to remain friends with a former lover, would that trouble you?"

"No."

"An occasional lunch?"

"Fine with me."

"And if I were moderately flirtatious with other men from time to time, how would you react?"

"I'm not certain. I might feel an occasional pang or even growl a little."

"And if I were *very* flirtatious?"

"I wouldn't like it. I'd probably feel hurt and angry. I'd want to know the reason, what needs you were trying to satisfy. And I'd probably wonder how committed you are to our relationship?"

"And if I were to sleep with another man?"

"I would be very upset. I would be bewildered. I would feel pain. I would probably go through a period of anger. I don't think it would last long, but for a moment or two I might want to strike out at you in some way. In the end, above everything, I would want to know why it had happened."

"Would you leave me over it?"

"Absolutely not. I'd fight to keep you. I would feel anxious, and yet it's very hard for me to believe I wouldn't win. But it would never occur to me to just give up and walk away."

It seems clear that the more self-confident we are and the more we trust and feel loved by our partner, the less likely we are to experience jealousy in its extreme forms. None of us is above the painful feelings associated with infidelity. We can have occasional feelings of jealousy without being a jealous person.

If we rephrased the question to read "Does romantic love inevitably entail feelings of pain or fear at the prospect of loss?" then the answer is yes. But if the question means, "Is anxiety over potential rivals an inevitable part of love?" we would answer no.

Q. I don't think I am especially prone to jealousy, but I do feel somewhat possessive toward my partner. I am wondering if there is a valid distinction between rational and irrational possessiveness.

A. The concepts of jealousy and possessiveness have overlapping meanings and applications, and the disposition to either is a matter of degree. There are degrees of jealousy, as we hope our answer to the preceding question makes clear, and there are degrees of possessiveness. We do think it is valid to distinguish between rational and irrational possessiveness.

*   *   *

Pride in our choice of partner as well as pride in being our partner's choice might be called rational possessiveness. It is a feeling that my partner and I belong together, a sense that my partner's primary allegiance is to me, as mine is to my partner. Rational possessiveness has its roots in self-esteem, in admiration for our partner, and in the deep intimacy between us.

Irrational possessiveness, by contrast, has its roots in self-doubt and uncertainty as to our partner's commitment to us. People actuated by irrational possessiveness resent any interests or values in their partner that do not center on themselves. They insist that their wishes and convenience take precedence over every other consideration in their partner's life. They feel anxiety over their partner's affection for any other person, reproaching their partner for not wanting to do everything together. They want their partner to regard her or himself as their property.

It is easy enough to deceive ourselves, to rationalize our self-doubts by saying "I feel this way because I love you so much." Love is not expressed by strangulation.

The difference between the rational and irrational attitudes is clear. The first is natural in the context of romantic love. The second denies individuality and so would inevitably destroy romantic love.

Q. I have a tendency to be excessively jealous and possessive, and I am wondering how best to handle my feelings, in the interest of protecting my relationship with my partner.

A. When men and women are jealous, they respond with anger, accusations, tears, and name calling: "You are rotten!" "You're a whore!" "I'll kill you if you ever look at him again!" "How can you do this to me? Don't you care about my feelings?" "If you had an ounce of decency—." And so forth. Attack provokes defensiveness and counterattack, and there are screams, denials, lies, or angry silence but no communication.

People are rarely honest about their feelings when they feel jealousy. A woman who sees her husband flirting with another woman at a party, for example, is likely to become hostile, bitter, or accusing. Were she to speak to him in the following manner, however, she would be reaching out in trust rather than suddenly treating him as an enemy: "Watching you, I felt a little anxious, I felt a little scared. I began having fantasies of your running off and leaving me." In taking responsibility for her own feelings, she does her part to create a context in which they can talk about the event as friends. If her husband does not feel attacked, he does not have to defend himself. He can listen and try to be truthful about his own feelings. If there is a problem, it has become one they can face together.

When we admit to our jealousy, we can move to a deeper level of talk about anxiety, fantasies of abandonment, terror of loss, and our painful feelings become less intense or vanish altogether. Owning, experiencing, and expressing fear or pain can be almost miraculously healing.

Both partners must participate to ameliorate problems of jealousy. This requires honesty on both sides, not just from the person experiencing jealousy. If we wish to relieve our partner of jealous feelings, we must never give our partner grounds to doubt our honesty. That is absolutely essential. And further, we must never ignore or refuse to deal with our partner's painful feelings. Jealousy hurts. No one appreciates having his pain ignored, ridiculed, or dismissed.

If, in the example given above, the husband was attracted to the other woman, it is far kinder to acknowledge this truthfully. If he denies a fact which his wife perceives clearly, he only deepens her anxiety and distrust. Then, inevitably, her jealousy worsens. Often we will hear a wife say, "It's not that my husband is sometimes turned on by other women that bothers me. I can handle that. It's the fact that he won't admit it, that he always lies about it. That drives me crazy."

The person who experiences the jealousy needs to go beneath the jealousy. If we feel jealous because our partner is sexually interested in or having an affair with another person, we need to go into the roots of the pain, feel it fully, face it, talk about it. Superficial talk about jealousy itself leads nowhere.

A couple came for counseling after many months of arguing about the husband's jealousy. All the debates were about whether or not it was reasonable for him to feel jealous. When he learned to stop talking about jealousy and to tell her of his pain, of his fear of losing her, a door opened. She heard him for the first time. She felt loved. She acknowledged her extravagant flirtation at parties and cheerfully abandoned it.

Another couple came for counseling. The man said, "We were planning to marry in a few months, but I'm having doubts because I can't stand our quarrels about other women. In my line of work I need to socialize a good deal. We go to a party, I look around the room, and I feel her eyes checking to see if I find some other woman attractive. If we're sitting in a restaurant and a woman comes over to say hello to me, I know there'll be this heavy interrogation after she walks away. Do I think she has sex appeal? Have I ever slept with her? I live in an atmosphere of constant suspicion and distrust. I feel guilty when I've done nothing to feel guilty about."

The woman said, "I hate my own responses. I know how often my father was unfaithful to my mother, and I'm still haunted by that. My first husband was unfaithful. I was devastated. I'm terrified it will happen again. I make myself crazy, and I make the man I love crazy. I become hysterical over nothing and reproach myself later."

"Do you ever find other men attractive?" Devers asked her.

"Of course. That's only natural."

"Are you ever able to accept that he can find other women attractive from time to time?"

"Easily," she said. "When we're home alone together, talking about it in the abstract. But not when there are other women around."

Nathaniel said, "I wonder how loved you feel."

She responded, "Most of the time, I think I feel very loved. He tells me he loves me ten times a day. He's very complimentary. But this is how he is when we're alone. When we're out in public, he sort of disappears, even if he's still there physically."

"Is there anything he could do," asked Nathaniel, "at parties or out socially that would help you feel more relaxed and secure?"

She thought for a moment. "Perhaps if there were more physical contact between us in those situations. An occasional touch, or a kiss, or a few intimate words. It hurts when he ignores me for an hour or two at social functions, as if I didn't exist."

The man responded with an enthusiastic yes to this proposal for putting her mind at ease. We talked with them about the importance of feeling free to acknowledge it in a relaxed and natural way when they found a man or woman attractive.

Devers asked her, "Just before you start hurling accusations, what are you feeling?"

"Frightened."

"Have you considered talking about your fear," Devers asked, "rather than leaping to jealousy, accusations, and so on?"

"That would sure be easier for me to handle," said the man.

We talked about sharing our fear, pain, and insecurity. We talked about the importance of letting our partner know that we care about such feelings. By shifting to a deeper honesty in their communications, they were able to dissolve the problem of jealousy. A few months later, we were happy to attend their wedding.

What if we feel jealousy in the absence of any discernable provocation? What if our partner has done nothing and still we feel torn by suspicion? It is possible that we have received provocation of a kind too subtle for us to register consciously. We may have received a signal on the subconscious level. On the other hand, when we deny and disown our sexual impulses because we are afraid to admit to them, we may attribute our own suppressed desires to our partner through the mechanism of projection. A person who is jealous without apparent reason may find it illuminating to ask: "Am *I* interested in outside affairs?"

Once, at an Intensive on *Self-Esteem and Romantic Relationships*, a man stood up and berated his wife for her interest in other men. Then he professed bewilderment as to why he had launched suddenly into this attack.

"I wonder if you have fantasies about other women," said Nathaniel.

A long pause. A realization: "Now that you ask . . ."

By taking responsibility for his sexual fantasies, he was able to see himself and his wife more clearly.

If we share our feelings openly, without trying to in-

duce guilt, and our partner listens with respect and responds with honesty, then we are doing our best to protect
our relationship. If we deny underlying anxiety and talk
superficially about our partner's behavior (as if that were
the only issue), or if our partner refuses to hear our pain,
then we are placing our relationship in severe jeopardy.

All of these considerations apply to the problem of
irrational possessiveness. There is the same need to acknowledge and discuss the insecurities and fears that generate it. It is futile trying to justify possessiveness in the
name of love.

It is equally futile to act on inappropriate possessiveness. We cannot allow ourselves to make demands that
effectively forbid our partner any kind of independent
existence.

If it is our partner who is excessively possessive, we
need, lovingly and benevolently, to assert our rights. "I
adore you, but I'm not willing to abandon my interests,
my friends, and my individuality in order to make myself
a mere appendage of you. If I did, there would be nothing
of me for you to love." If we do not assert our own
independence, we reinforce our partner's irrational perception of human relationships.

Q. Do you advocate sexual exclusivity in romantic
love?

A. We cannot answer with a simple yes or no. We
cannot say that we are for or against sexual exclusivity, except as a personal preference. We believe it is
unrealistic to prescribe in this matter for the whole human
race.

To quote from *The Psychology of Romantic Love:*

If the old-fashioned orthodoxy was that only sexual
exclusivity between partners is moral, appropriate,
psychologically healthy, then the new orthodoxy, in
some quarters, is that only multiple sexual relationships are moral, appropriate, psychologically healthy.
Once upon a time, if a couple came for marriage
counseling because one party desired to have an
outside affair, the consensus was that the problem

belonged to the person desiring the outside affair; today it is often considered to be the problem of the party who objects. I do not believe that this is progress. Both views assume that someone must be guilty, that there is one right pattern for everyone and that whoever is outside the pattern needs to be "fixed."

If a person does not know how to deal sensitively and intelligently with his or her lover, taking a second lover will probably not bestow such wisdom. More likely, a second lover will expand the area of incompetence. But if a person does have the sensitivity and intelligence to deal with another human being in a love relationship, then he or she may appreciate that there are no absolute rules concerning sexual exclusivity. It is always a matter of context, individual histories, personal lifestyles, and emotional needs.

There are couples who begin their relationship on the premise of sexual exclusivity, choose to drop that requirement later, and still later choose to reinstate it. Other couples follow a similar pattern of alternation from the opposite premise. Some relationships survive, some fail, whatever the pattern.

In the words of a wonderful Spanish proverb: " 'Take what you want,' said God, 'and pay for it.' "

Having discussed the subject with many friends, associates, and colleagues, we have the impression that individuals who experiment in their younger years with sexually unrestricted relationships generally favor sexual exclusivity by the time they are in their forties. They seem to desire a firm commitment, the stability and security of total dedication to one relationship. By that time, no doubt, they feel a certain boredom or disenchantment with the pursuit of sexual variety for its own sake.

As a couple, we (Devers and Nathaniel) may be strongly disposed to exclusivity, but we have too much respect for individual differences and individual needs to hand down that preference as a universal law of romantic happiness.

In this world we take what we want, and we pay for it, in sexual exclusivity and in all things.

Q. How is it possible that my partner and I can genuinely love each other and yet at times desire other sexual involvements?

A. People commonly and mistakenly assume that the basic reason for affairs (or an interest in affairs) is sexual frustration in the primary relationship. While this is sometimes the case, it is far from being a universal explanation.

Many people, for example, engage in outside affairs with partners they perceive as less attractive and less sexually exciting than their mate. They are acting on a powerful desire for novelty and variety.

A wife asks, "Is she more attractive than I am?"

"No," the man answers.

"Is she better in bed? Does she dress better? Is she a better cook?"

"No."

"Then what's the attraction?"

"She isn't you."

When people marry with little or no previous sexual experience, it is not unusual in later years for them to wonder what they may have missed, what else might be "out there." Extramarital experimentation can follow as a consequence. "I was married when I was twenty-one," a woman at an Intensive remarked. "My husband was the only man I ever slept with. One day, when I was thirty-five, I asked myself, 'Do I want to go to my grave never having made love with another man?' I loved my husband, and yet my answer to that question was no."

At any age, regardless of our past, we may seek an outside affair to relieve a staleness in our existence. Or we may seek to be consoled for some frustration, not in our primary relationship necessarily, but in our work or career.

"I've been earning my living since I was seventeen years old," a man at an Intensive told us. "I made a success of my business, I married, raised a family, had everything they say a man can want. Never for a moment have I entertained the possibility of leaving my wife. She's the most marvelous woman I've ever known. But I just got to feeling burned out after a while, bored with everything, in need of something to . . . I don't know, get my fires going again, make me feel alive. I don't know what would have happened if I had discussed it all with my wife before I did anything about it. But anyway, when I did tell my wife about the affair, she was incredible. She understood."

He was simply hungry for new stimulation, new levels of excitement.

We need to look more closely at this desire for novelty and variety, not because it isn't real, but because this simple explanation often covers over a multitude of other motives.

There is no way to list all the motives that might make us receptive to a sexual encounter outside the primary relationship, but we do want to list those that come up again and again in the course of our work.

We want to assure ourselves that we are still attractive: "A new person, seeing me for the first time, makes me feel beautiful again."

Or, in a variation, we may wish to be with someone who does not know our history, has not seen our growth, is not familiar with our faults, someone who sees us fresh: "I want to experience myself in relation to someone who knows me only as I am today, who can see me as I am now and give me a new feeling of recognition and appreciation."

When our partner hurts us, an affair can be a form of revenge or ego salvaging. Sometimes we are retaliating for an affair undertaken by our mate: "It was the only way I knew to endure the pain of her infidelity. My affair made hers less important to me."

We may be in a primary relationship with a person whose life scenario requires that we "betray" him or her. Having the affair, we may be completely unaware of having been manipulated into it. During an Intensive on *Self-Esteem and Transformation*, Nathaniel asked the participants to review their lives and ask themselves if they had ever needed their partner to "betray" them so they could suffer, feel martyred, wronged, abandoned. An astonishing number of hands went up.

Sometimes extramarital affairs grow out of loneliness, as when partners are separated from each other for some period of time: "He was traveling for six months in a play, and my job prevented me from joining him. We agreed in advance to accept that the other might have an affair."

Sometimes we meet a person who reminds us of someone we could never have had in our earlier years. When the opportunity is presented unexpectedly, the temptation may seem irresistible: "In retrospect I knew I was stupid. I slept with a fantasy. She was the kind of girl I was nuts about in high school and who wouldn't give me a second look. When this one looked at me as if I were God's gift to womankind, I was sunk."

Or we may encounter a new person who strikes chords within our being that have never been struck before. New doors open to understanding and gratification. We feel drawn to this new person on every level, including the sexual, even though the attraction may not be strong enough to separate us from our primary partner: "She was the first woman with whom I could discuss poetry. She knew ten times more than I did, and that turned me on. It was as though a whole other part of myself got unlocked. I came to feel she was someone I had to experience all the way, even though I would never leave my wife for her."

Some people are far more comfortable with sexual exclusivity than others. Some people, no matter how much they love, see decades of sexual exclusivity as impossible. We don't understand all the reasons for these differences in psychology. It is certain, however, that neither moral applause nor moral condemnation nor swift and easy universal prescriptions are of any value in deciding about sexual exclusivity.

People who are happily in love rarely pursue outside affairs actively. When they happen, they tend to happen as departures from the couple's intention. They can happen for any of the reasons we have discussed or for many others we have not.

We can wish that such problems did not arise in the course of our relationship. We can hope that they will not arise. And, indeed, they may not. If they do, wisdom asks that we do not allow this one upsetting event to cancel out all the values of our primary relationship; wisdom asks that we think before concluding that love is gone. There are too many uncertainties in life, too many unknowns, too many vicissitudes. Since we have no guarantee that there will never be storms, we need the wisdom to navigate through them.

Q. If my partner tells me that he (she) is sexually attracted to another person, how can I deal with this in a rational manner, without falling apart or behaving destructively?

A. While attacks, rebukes, vilifications, and other guilt-inducing strategies are to be avoided absolutely, we are not obliged to be a model of philosophical detachment and serenity either. We have a right to feel hurt, we have a right to feel agitated, we have a right to feel distress and to show it. And our partner needs to be mature enough to handle all that.

I love the answer Devers gave when someone at an Intensive asked what she would do if I ever told her I was strongly attracted to another woman. There was no implication that I was falling in love or wanted to leave Devers; the premise was that I couldn't get this woman off my mind.

Devers said, "First I'd want to know who the woman was, where he had met her, how long he had known her, information like that. Next and most important, I'd want to know whether or not he felt he was falling in love, because the possible loss of his love would be of far greater concern to me than any issue of sexual jealousy. Assuming he didn't feel he was falling in love, what would I do? Well, I'd probably feel shocked, upset, scared, perhaps, but then I think I would make this request of him. I would ask that before he initiated anything sexual with her, he would meet her for lunch or dinner two or three times—in other words, two or three meetings of a couple hours' duration to talk with her and get to know her. After the three meetings, I'd want to know what his feelings were. Many of us have slept with people we wouldn't have slept with if we had first had three conversations over lunch. We would have been disenchanted, or our curiosity would have been satisfied, and that would be that. So I would be hoping that after three meetings his interest would diminish. If it hadn't, if he still felt that he wanted to know her further, perhaps becoming sexually involved, I might go a little crazy.

"But I think I would have to find a way to accept it. I certainly would not deliver any ultimatums. It would not be in my self-interest to make him feel guilty, because that would only alienate us. And you can be sure I would not walk away and leave him to her. I would want him to talk about her, I would want to know what he found attractive, I would want to know what he felt she had to offer. I would want to know what might be lacking between us, if anything, and what I might be able to do about it. I would fight for our relationship, I would suffer a good deal, I'd probably throw a fit or two. But I would ask for that three-meeting agreement, and I would ask that he speak to me before he spoke to the other woman."

A woman indignant at Devers's answer spoke up: "You mean you'd sacrifice yourself for him? Just let him do whatever he likes?"

"It wouldn't be a sacrifice at all," Devers answered. "I want to save our relationship, but I don't own Nathaniel. He's not my slave; he's not my property. Becoming hysterical and uttering threats wouldn't help me save the relationship. Each of us must decide what we think will work for us and do it. The dynamics of each relationship are different, but I know one guideline that applies to all of them: honesty and straight talk between partners."

Then Devers added, "One other thing. I would be respectful of Nathaniel's feelings in such a situation, and I would certainly expect him to show respect and care for mine. I would expect him to take my feelings seriously, to have empathy and compassion. If he didn't, the whole situation would change, the problem would be far more difficult."

Someone else protested, "But what if he ends up falling in love with the other woman?"

"That's a risk that's always there," said Devers. "For me, and I suppose for most of us, that's scary. Still, I don't think threats are the answer. I'd have to let my partner know that I loved him, that I wanted to do whatever I could to save our relationship. I would put up with a lot of pain so long as I believed there was a chance of saving our relationship. I can't admire people who are so afraid of being hurt that they give up and walk away."

My own attitude, as you may have guessed, is precisely the same as Devers's in this matter. I might add that most of our students seem to approve and appreciate the sense of the three-lunch agreement. It's not an answer to everything, but it is a practical starting point.

Q. Wouldn't an outside sexual involvement be inevitably destructive to our relationship?

A. It would be naive to deny that affairs can threaten the best of primary relationships. We cannot know for certain what lies beyond the door until we open it and walk through. When we begin an affair, we cannot know in what ways our life may change. And we cannot afford to deceive ourselves about possible consequences.

We can think of cases (not very many, however) in which an affair has strengthened the primary relationship, leading the couple to a fresh appreciation of the bonds uniting them. We can also think of cases in which an outside affair destroyed the primary relationship. The hurt and pain were too much, or the person who had the affair fell in love with the new partner or decided, at any rate, that he or she wanted to be free.

Too much pain sometimes causes love to die. A couple having to cope with an outside affair do not have to separate. They may continue on different terms. The character of the relationship will have changed but may still include affection of some kind, even if the fire is gone.

There may be so much smoldering resentment on one or both sides that the couple's original happiness is lost irretrievably. And yet: "It took my wife's having an affair to make me realize how much I loved her," said a man at an Intensive, "and what a rotten husband I had been. She tried to reach me; I wouldn't listen. I didn't pay any attention to her needs. When a man came along who knew how to treat her, she was susceptible. I felt as if our house had fallen on my head when she told me, but looking back, I have to say it was worth it. It woke me up. It made me realize I was not about to lose this woman, no matter what I had to do."

"When my husband and I married," a woman said to us, "I had had considerably more sexual experience than he. When I found out about his affairs, the dishonesty enraged me most, the lies. We took a long time working that through. I have to admit, though, he got something from the other women, a confidence he didn't have before that I am benefiting from today."

Not all of the stories we hear end in reconciliation. "My affairs led me into a more and more private life," said a divorcee in one or our groups, "and left me more and more estranged from my husband. We just had less and less to say to each other. Something died. I can't explain, there are no words for it. It was as if I had injected poison into our marriage and couldn't get it out again. Maybe it was the affairs, maybe it was the lies, maybe it was both, but I felt guilty, defensive. We quarreled over trivial things. The distance between us grew until we could hardly recognize each other."

To say it once more: if our partner sleeps with someone else, we may legitimately feel hurt or angry, frightened or threatened, but whatever we may feel, we need to understand that attempting to hold and control our partner through guilt only drives our partner further away. The impulse to lash out feels very natural, but if we want to preserve the relationship, we need to recognize that lashing out is not healing. And neither is denying our pain or pretending indifference. What we need is understanding and an honest effort at communication.

Some couples, realizing that outside affairs can happen, agree in principle to accept them, providing there is full disclosure. Other couples prefer discretion and silence; they agree to accept such affairs in principle but ask not to be told about them. Both policies have their hazards.

We can think of many cases in which a policy of full disclosure worsened the estrangement and alienation, ultimately destroying the primary relationship. We can think of cases in which a policy of discretion and silence led to one or both partners living more outside the relationship than in it. Again, the estrangement and alienation reached a point where two people who had once adored each other found themselves to be more like old acquaintances than lovers.

The experiences we hear of convince us that it is extremely naive to deny that outside affairs pose a threat to romantic love. Any choice a couple makes will have consequences. Sometimes a couple will begin with one policy regarding sexual exclusivity, realize it does not work for them, and change to another. All we can say, both to those couples who are inclined to sexual exclusivity and to those who are not, is "Be as honest with each other as you can about your feelings, preferences, and actions. Don't lie to yourself. Don't lie to your partner. You'll discover what works for you and what doesn't."

We are convinced that deception poisons the best of relationships. Lies are unavoidably alienating because lies necessitate invisibility. They are the antithesis of mutual self-disclosure, which makes romantic love flourish.

Perhaps it is appropriate to mention, as an aside, an argument against outside relationships that we have seen demonstrated again and again: the trouble is that they sometimes make a bad relationship bearable. They keep a man and woman from confronting their frustration. Their affairs are not a solution but a painkiller, delaying the end of a primary relationship that should end if the individual man and woman are ever to be happy. For those who are tempted to outside affairs, it can be very important to ask: "How would I feel about this relationship if I were not to have outside affairs?"

To focus some of the points we have been making, the following excerpt from *The Psychology of Romantic Love* seems worth quoting:

> What seems to be changing today, and changing for the good, is an increasing unwillingness on the part of people to live with lies in this area—an increasing impatience with a life of deception, and a greater desire for the whole issue to be brought into the open.
>
> It seems clear that fewer and fewer couples today are willing or able to dedicate themselves to sexual exclusivity across a lifetime. Men and women will need the wisdom, early in their relationship, to face this issue squarely, to formulate a policy for dealing with it that each can live with. Ideally, they will formulate a policy *before* the issue arises. . . .
>
> It is easy enough to declare, dogmatically, that sexual exclusivity is the only workable lifestyle for everyone, or to declare, equally dogmatically, that

"open" sexual relationships are the only practical answer. Neither assertion shows adequate respect for the subtleties and complexities of relationships or the profound differences that exist among people.

Q. When contemplating the possibility of another sexual involvement, how should I deal with the pain I will be causing my primary partner?

A. Speak to your partner with empathy and compassion. One of the commonest errors men and women make in this situation is to allow their misgivings or feelings of guilt to turn into resentment. If we choose to become involved with someone else, the effect on our partner is part of the reality we must deal with. We do not think fear of our partner's pain should cause us to remain silent when we are contemplating an outside affair. If at all possible, we should talk with our partner before anything happens. The more honesty, dignity, and compassion we can bring to it, the better the chances that our primary relationship will survive.

Just the same considerations apply, of course, to how our partner handles the pain of his or her knowledge that we are considering such an involvement.

A woman we know loved her husband but was frustrated in her marriage. Her husband's failure to acknowledge this frustration precipitated her into an affair with another man who gave her what her husband would not. She did not wish to abandon her marriage, yet she needed the affair to make her life bearable. Her husband knew from the outset. He went through considerable anguish, before and during her affair, and she remained compassionate with him at all times. Within a few months, the affair ended. The compassion she maintained toward her husband, even while fighting for her right to her own needs, reached him as nothing else ever had, and he chose to come with her for marriage counseling.

She was guided by respect for his feelings and for her own from the very beginning: "Darling, I have something painful and frightening to tell you, painful and frightening for both of us. I have met a man I am strongly drawn to and want to have an affair with him. I know that this has got to be bad for you. It's what I feel I must do." During the affair, when she saw her husband behaving stoically, she would say, "How is it for you right now? Can we talk? Do you want to yell at me, strike out, or what?" Once, when her husband was weeping and confessing his fears of abandonment, she said, "Everything this man gives me I want from you. If I don't have some joy in my life, I'll die. So I need what I'm getting right now. I don't want to leave you. I don't want to make you suffer. I want to put my arms around you and tell you everything is all right. But I can't go back to what we had before, I just can't. Please help me to come back to you." This last sentence was decisive to his seeking marriage counseling.

Q. Should we always be honest with our partner about our sexual feelings and activities? That might destroy my marriage—or any marriage.

A. Being honest does not mean that we share with our partner every single sexual thought or fantasy that flickers through our mind. It does mean talking about matters that affect the relationship.

If I am walking down the street and I notice an attractive member of the opposite sex, I need hardly run home to report a momentary sexual response. If my mate were walking with me, I might comment, "That's a very attractive person." My mate would understand that such an observation might be accompanied by a moment of wondering what it would be like to experience that person sexually. I don't need to spell it out in detail. Indeed, unnecessary detail sometimes gives honesty a bad name.

One woman complained at an Intensive that her efforts at honesty with her husband only caused him to withdraw from her. Questioning them both further, Nathaniel learned that her idea of honesty was to point to some man and say to her husband, "God, that man is gorgeous. What a body. He really turns me on. I wonder what he's like in bed." She professed not to understand why this had an unpleasant effect on her husband.

We doubt that such over-explicitness is merely the result of ignorance; it is far more likely to be an expression of hurt or anger or both. We learned later that the woman was nonorgasmic and blamed her husband. Her remarks about other men were disguised reproaches. She was not practicing honesty, not even excessive honesty, since she was not communicating straightforwardly about what was really bothering her.

With regard to affairs, we have already expressed our conviction that lies as a way of life are poison to a relationship. Romantic love is sustained by intimacy and self-disclosure, and lies sabotage both. If our goal is to experience love, dishonesty is incompatible with that purpose.

Beyond that, we can only mention once again that different couples come to different understandings about the issue of sexual exclusivity. What matters most is to agree on a policy and adhere to it. An important part of honesty is not changing the agreement without the partner's knowledge and acceptance. If couples come to see that their agreement is not working for them, they are free to modify it.

We know a couple, very much in love, who married with very little prior sexual experience. One day the woman said to her husband, "I feel totally loved by you and you have made me feel very secure in our relationship. But whenever I try to tell myself that you will never have another woman in your whole life, it feels insane to me, almost against nature. I know that someday you are going to be tempted. That will be very painful for me. I want to spare you the burden of dishonesty. If a time comes when you feel that's what you need, you have my permission and acceptance. But I don't want to know about it."

The husband thought this over and said, "Okay. But then I want you to have the same freedom for yourself. I don't believe in a double standard."

"But I don't want that freedom."

"Well, this is for the future, just in case," he said. "I wouldn't feel right accepting this for myself if you didn't have the same rights."

The first affair did not occur until nearly three years after this conversation. Over several years each of them had a number of affairs, which they did not discuss with each other. Eventually the absence of any discussion of this aspect of their lives became alienating. They loved each other too much to allow the alienation to continue.

The husband chose to break their agreement and talk about his affairs, and his wife did the same. They both suffered considerably, but they regained the closeness that had originally made them so sure of each other. Both chose to return to a policy of sexual exclusivity.

Our chief objection to secret affairs when a couple has agreed on sexual exclusivity is that the person having the affair is unilaterally changing the contract with the partner. The partner is given no choice as to whether the new terms are acceptable. In business this would be fraud. Is it less objectionable in intimate relationships? We cannot escape the conviction that honesty, rationally understood, remains the best policy.

Q. I have lied to my partner about affairs in the past, but I want to correct the situation now and develop a good relationship again. How do I go about rebuilding trust?

A. To rebuild trust, you must first prepare yourself with patience and respect for your partner's process, all the natural stages your partner must go through, from hurt to anger to the desire to strike out at you. The first tentative opening up to you will almost certainly be followed by withdrawal, a new burst of suspiciousness and anger, which may yield to a longing to feel secure with you. There may be moments of passion, another withdrawal, and then another slow opening. In time your partner's trust will become stable.

Allow your partner this process. Do not demand an instant recovery. Do not let guilt lead you to new cruelties—insensitivity, lies, unwarranted accusations, coldness, remoteness.

Keep inviting your partner to talk about his or her feelings. Show that you understand. "I can see that you feel devastated and very angry at me. This must be so hard for you. I hope you'll talk to me about everything you're thinking and feeling. If there's anything I can do that will help right now, please tell me."

Understand that your partner is the one who must rebuild security and confidence. Your part is to provide an environment for this delicate work.

If you are going to be late arriving home, telephone your partner; don't wait for your partner to make this request of you, with the implication that he or she is checking up on you. Whenever possible, leave a phone number where you can be reached. Do everything possible, without being asked, to include your partner in your activities.

Above all, don't be evasive. Do nothing to create new reasons to doubt your honesty.

At times you too will feel hurt and angry; that is only natural. Communicate those feelings to your partner, without reproaches.

Ask periodically, "How are you feeling about us today?" Show your partner that you are concerned and that you care. Don't overdo it; don't make a big production out of being "a reformed sinner"; don't wear your partner out with your efforts to establish your virtue. Do try to see the problem in a realistic perspective.

A husband in therapy complained that patience was very difficult for him: "All my life I felt put down. Mother was always telling me I was wrong about something. So was my first wife. I know my present wife has a right to be hurt and angry with me, and yet . . . I'm tired of feeling guilty. I'm tired of apologizing."

"I wonder if you're able to separate your present wife from your former wife and from your mother," said Nathaniel.

"It's not easy," the man admitted.

"Without that separation, you can't live in the present. Not living in the present, you can't see your present wife. You can't see the present situation. You can't respond just in the here and now."

"Then what do I do?"

"Drop the idea of guilt. It's irrelevant here. Look at your wife's eyes, at her face. See that she is not your mother or any other person in your life. She is the woman you love. Look at her and breathe deeply. Come into the present. See that behind the anger on her face there is hurt, and behind the hurt there is love. Don't try to prove to her that you are not bad. That's not the issue. Think that you want to let her know it's safe for her to love you. That's what trust means here. She's so eager to belive it's safe. See that. And allow it to happen, that's all—just allow it."

Q. I was devastated to learn, after the fact, of my partner's affair with another person. How can I ever feel trust and confidence in him (her) again?

A. This, obviously, is the other side of the problem we have just been discussing—now considered from the perspective of the person who feels his or her trust has been betrayed.

We cannot rebuild trust alone, without help and cooperation from the other party involved. So we need to reapply everything we said about helping our partner trust us again. We are now looking at trust as a problem for the relationship rather than for either individual. It will help to say to our partner, "I want with all my heart to feel the trust and confidence I used to feel. Please help me."

Without attacking or vilifying, talk about your fear of trusting, your anxiety about the future, your concern about the depth of your partner's commitment to you. Let him or her in on your processes. Do not hide behind a wall of moral indignation or behind condescending psychology either. No matter how hurt you may be, you still need to remain open and vulnerable if the problem is to be solved.

If you do not deal directly with your anxiety over trusting, you will make your partner pay indirectly. You will hurt your partner, and you will hurt the relationship through disguised, unconsciously motivated revenge.

Do not torment your partner with intimate questions about the other person or the details of their sexual transactions. Such questions are either masochistic or sadistic. Neither is conducive to the rebirth of love.

Try to understand why the affair happened and why your partner waited so long to tell you. You don't need to know the size of the breasts (or the penis) of the other person. You need to know why your partner did not feel free to speak honestly with you from the start. Ask, "Is there anything I do that makes you afraid to be honest with me?"

Further, realize that you may have anxieties about trusting that began before your partner's affair and that his or her confession merely brought the problem to a crisis. So here honesty is needed from you.

Recently a woman came for counseling at the insistence

of a dictatorial husband. The woman had confessed to an affair some time earlier, and the husband had been lording it over her for months, insisting that he could trust her only after intensive psychotherapy (for her, of course). He would not accept her as his wife until she could provide him with a comprehensive account of the underlying motives for her act, "which you cannot hope to attain without the guidance of a psychologist." It was apparent to us that her affair was, at least in part, a rebellion against her domineering husband. His response is the most extreme example in our experience of how not to go about trusting our partner again. It's no good imposing demands that cast our partner in the role of a guilty sinner who must somehow crawl back to salvation.

The husband would have done far better to drop the mask of righteousness and face his wife as a friend and equal. But he was afraid to be vulnerable.

If this woman responds to therapy as we hope, she will break free of the role she has been cast in, and both she and her husband will approach the question of trust in an entirely new way.

How do we go about rebuilding trust in our partner when our partner has been dishonest with us? As we have already said, we cannot do it alone; we cannot do it by evoking shame or guilt; we cannot do it by demanding some humiliating atonement. We can do it only by continuing to share our feelings as honestly as possible, if our partner will allow it, and by letting our partner know how eager we are to trust again.

Q. When we first met and fell in love, my partner was married to someone else. Remembering this, I am sometimes fearful that the pattern will repeat itself. I am often jealous and suspicious. How can I deal with this?

A. We would want to know first whether your partner is doing anything in the present that makes you suspicious. If the answer is yes, you would have to deal with his or her behavior and with your response to it.

For example, if your partner has become irritable, or withdrawn, or uninterested in sex, obviously you will need to initiate a discussion of possible causes, preferably in a benevolent and non-accusing manner.

If the answer is no, if your partner's behavior has not changed, we would want to know whether you feel that your partner displayed a lack of integrity in the way he or she handled the transition from the marriage to the relationship with you. Was your partner's behavior comprehensible to you? Could you understand the reasons for the choices he or she made?

And are you comfortable with the way you behaved? It is possible that you are burdening your partner with some of the guilt you have never resolved in yourself. Perhaps you feel guilty for having taken your partner away from his or her former spouse. The only solution we can suggest is lots of conversation. Involve your partner in the search for a solution.

One woman in therapy said to us, "I don't blame my husband for the way he ended his earlier marriage, and I don't think I blame myself for their divorce. They were in trouble long before he and I met. And yet I keep saying to myself, 'If he left her for me, how can I know he won't leave me for someone else?' " Deeper questioning revealed that her fear of abandonment went back to childhood. The fact that her husband had left another woman merely brought the anxiety into focus. She resolved the problem by learning to talk about her fear of abandonment directly rather than demanding assurances from her husband that he could not possibly give. Her husband helped her with his patience and his willingness to listen without launching into self-justification, apology, or attack.

Q. Sometimes I feel a need to talk with my present partner about the pain or joy of a former relationship. Am I unreasonable to want to talk openly on such a subject?

A. The desire to share painful and happy experiences with someone we love is natural and can strengthen a relationship. Part of our motive may be to work through unfinished business, while another part almost certainly is to make ourselves more visible to our partner. Such sharing entails intimacy and trust, but we need the wisdom to know what to communicate and how to communicate it.

*   *   *

Our past is part of who we are today, and it is natural for our partner to have some curiosity about our past. We should never try to pretend that we were born on the day our current relationship began. The mistake some people make is in talking so much about the past that they create the impression that it has more emotional reality and importance for them than the present. Obviously this can hurt the present partner.

Making comparisons is another mistake: "George was so great in bed. He was the best lover I ever had. And you are almost as good."

Using the past to make a complaint about the present is a bad idea: "I used to love going skiing with Marilyn. She was a superb skier. And afterward, sitting by the fire, sipping a glass of wine, listening to music, it was heaven. God, I wish you were interested in skiing."

This issue is a bit difficult to discuss because the appropriateness of talking about past relationships depends to a great extent on sensitivity, good taste, and common sense. These are difficult to reduce to a set of rules or guidelines. It would probably be all right to say "I used to love skiing with Marilyn" and let it go at that. We don't want to re-create the setting in such intimate and immediate detail that our present partner feels like a third party, especially where sexual matters are concerned. Generally speaking (and of course there are exceptions), it is better not to regale our present partner with the sexual glories of the past. Most of us do not enjoy feeling we have become the third person in bed. When in doubt, ask: "Do you feel comfortable hearing me talk about this? May I tell you about this, or would you rather I didn't?"

We only need to be aware of how our remarks are likely to affect our listener. We might ask ourselves how we would feel listening to such revelations. And we might assess our partner's level of confidence—self-confidence and confidence in being loved by us. A moment's consideration will show us how to speak sensitively and appropriately.

When we raised this issue at an Intensive recently, a man said, "I feel complimented when my wife trusts me enough to talk about important incidents from the past. I feel I am being let in on her private world, and it makes me feel closer to her. I never feel she is comparing the past to the present. I just feel there are things she needs to talk about, and I am the person she chooses to talk to. I like that."

Q. A question frequently asked of Devers: Are you ever jealous of Nathaniel's love for his deceased wife Patrecia?

A. This question has been asked of me a remarkable number of times over the past several years, probably because of the depth of feeling with which Nathaniel wrote about Patrecia in *The Psychology of Romantic Love*. The matter is deeply personal for me. I hope my response will have value to those who are struggling with their version of this kind of issue.

When I moved into Nathaniel's home, a home he had shared with her for many years, there were pictures of Patrecia in many rooms of the house. Having lost a husband myself through accidental death many years ago, I felt I understood Nathaniel's motives: he was clinging to the memory of her in life in order to make the transition to accepting her death. I had done the same with my husband. So I could not resent a natural part of his healing. I knew that he would remove the pictures, as he did, when he felt ready.

There were many times when he felt the need to talk about Patrecia, but I never felt excluded. I always felt he was expanding the area of intimacy between us. He had an extraordinary ability, whether he was sharing happy memories or painful ones, to make me feel that he saw me, loved me, and had absolute confidence in our future. He told stories, created pictures before my eyes, took me more deeply into his life than he had ever taken anyone. He made me feel I had always been there. He remained aware of me, while taking me through all the years of his life that I had missed, introducing me to a woman who was not an enemy or a rival but a person I would like to have known.

Of course there were times it was painful, times I felt lonely, but such emotions were generally short-lived. If I was angry at Patrecia over anything, it wasn't because of Nathaniel's love or his memories but because of her death. I would like him to have come into my life under less tragic circumstances. I would like our relationship to have had a happier beginning. And sometimes when Nathaniel was gone from the house, I would look at Patrecia's picture and tell her so.

A love who has died can be more formidable than one who is still living. However, Nathaniel never drew inappropriate comparisons, nor did he say or do anything to make me compete with her. The message he conveyed was that Patrecia had been a unique human being, and so was I, and no rivalry between us was conceivable.

I was intensely interested to hear Nathaniel talk not only about Patrecia but about all of his life before we met. I knew that all of it would help me to understand the man I was in love with. If there were women who had been important to him, they were part of him, and I wanted to know him.

I would often encourage him to talk about Patrecia and about two earlier relationships that had been especially significant in his life: one with his first wife, Barbara, whom he married when he was twenty-two years old; the other with novelist-philosopher Ayn Rand, whom he personally admired and whose work he championed. During eighteen years this second relationship involved, at one time or another, virtually every emotion possible between a man and a woman. (They came to an explosive parting of the ways in 1968.) Together we went over letters, private diaries, memoirs extending back over thirty years, most of which no one had ever seen, with the partial exception of Patrecia.

On the occasion of his fiftieth birthday I presented him with a collage of over 150 photographs, mounted within a single large frame, that traced the course of his extraordinary life. It begins with the classic naked baby picture and ends with photographs taken at our wedding. There are pictures that trace his relationship with Patrecia. There are pictures of Nathaniel with Barbara. And there are pictures of Nathaniel and Ayn Rand. I hope that one day he will write about the stories behind these pictures, from the beginning to the present, because the stories are extraordinary in the way they are interwoven—like a well-constructed plot. It is Nathaniel's perspective on his own life, his sense that everything, joyful and painful, is important because it is part of his life—and his sensitivity, dignity, and candor in making me feel part of it all—that made creating the collage a rewarding experience for me selfishly.

I don't know how to explain more clearly than this why I am not jealous of memories.

Postscript. Since I wrote the preceding (in 1982), Nathaniel has begun working on a memoir (1986).

Nine
Balancing Work and Love

Of all human pursuits, work and love are the two sources of greatest happiness in our lives. Indeed, psychologists often measure emotional well-being by a person's ability to participate happily, energetically, and creatively in both work and love.

Through work I support my existence and personal autonomy. I give shape to my life, enrich my identity, and experience the pleasure and pride of using my distinctively human powers. Through romantic love I enjoy one of the highest emotional rewards of my efficacy and worth, not as a producer but as a person. Love is a celebration of what I am and what I have made of my resources and potentials.

These two values are so demanding and so important that men and women sometimes experience them as being in conflict. Many people feel that success in one comes only with sacrifice of the other.

In the past men spoke more about the problems of balancing the claims of work and love, but in today's world more and more women express the same concerns. Work can interfere with love, or love with work, in a hundred different ways: one partner is working while the other is not, or one partner is happy with his or her work while the other is not. Sometimes an individual feels more competent in work than in love or more competent in love than in work. Work can be a passion or just a means of earning a living.

Let us explore this territory.

Q. Doesn't the pursuit of a career always hurt love to some extent? Doesn't passionate involvement with another person always take something away from a career?

A. All significant values make significant demands on our time and attention, sometimes competing with each other. Having values thus compels us to make choices. We bear responsibility for finding the balance among these demands that will yield the most satisfying and fulfilling life.

To achieve an appropriate balance, we need to realize what our values are. We have to know whether we experience work and love as equally important or whether we experience one as more important than the other. One may seem more important during a particular period of our life. But if we know we want both and want to be happy in both, we must think very clearly about our priorities and monitor our commitments to work and to love on a fairly regular basis. We must take responsibility for watching over the health of both, making certain that neither suffers from neglect.

While both work and love require time, they do not literally require equal time. Love does not ordinarily require eight hours a day. It does require a very high place among our priorities, supported by the conviction that protecting and nourishing the relationship is of the first importance to us.

The head buyer for a large chain of department stores complained when she came for counseling that her work was endangering her relationship. She traveled a great deal and spent long hours on the job. She loved it. "Do I have to give up my career? Do I have to give up everything I enjoy and worked so hard for because my partner feels neglected?"

Nathaniel asked, "What are your options short of giving up your career?"

"I've tried to train several assistants."

Nathaniel saw an opening. "Many people feel responsible for every aspect of their work and like to oversee personally virtually all that goes on, far beyond the point of necessary supervision. Would you be willing to make a two-week log of everything you do and the time it takes, down to every detail? When you come back, let's look at it together."

When she came back, she knew the answer to her question. The log made her aware of how much time she was spending on matters it would be far more efficient to delegate. "I've started turning things over to my staff," she said, "and I keep seeing more things that I don't really have to do personally. I've been coming home earlier, leaving the office around five. My partner is pleased, and so am I. Some frantic rush inside me is beginning to subside. I can't believe it, but I'm beginning to enjoy leisure. I'm also beginning to see ways to cut down on the extent of my traveling. It's as if I've been trying to prove something all this time and it's beginning not to feel necessary any longer." She added, "I'm beginning to think more of vacations, going away with my partner for weekends, just having fun. I don't feel guilty either. Well, not very guilty."

At an Intensive a man remarked, "I let things slide in our marriage without noticing it for a long time. Part of the reason was that my wife and I were so comfortable together, no major conflicts to work through. I became more and more involved in the office, and we spent hardly any time alone together, the way we used to. Our conversations became shallow; sex kind of dropped off. I was pouring all my energies into some deals I was working on. Work is the main thing for men and marriage is very nice but secondary. I mean, if you work eighteen hours a day at the office and put together some fabulous deal, the world recognizes that as valuable—right? Suppose someone asks what you've been doing lately. 'Well, I've been spending a lot of time with my wife, playing, having a great time, making the two of us terrifically happy.' People would just look at you."

"So what's the end of the story?" someone asked. "What happened?"

"What happened," the man said, "is that my wife asked me would I be willing to have some sessions with Devers Branden before our marriage blew apart. I said sure, and we went to Devers. She took me through a kind of guided fantasy. The idea of the fantasy was that my work was a terrific success only my wife wasn't there anymore. I was all alone with my deals, and how did I feel? Miserable. Why should I give a good goddamn about anything if she isn't in the picture? So Devers said, 'Good. You've experienced the fantasy version. How would you feel about living it in real life?' I felt pretty stupid. I had to say, 'Nobody ever explained it to me like that before.' It all boiled down to making it real to myself how miserable I'd feel if my wife wasn't there. I can't forget that, not for a single day, no matter how exciting the deals get. If I had my wife but no work, I'd be miserable. If I had my work but no wife, I'd be miserable. You just learn to keep your mind on both.''

Even when we love our work, even when it is truly a passion, we often associate work fundamentally with survival. Having achieved a reasonable level of material comfort, men and women often continue to act as if life itself required their unbroken concentration on their job. They subordinate their interests and values, including love, to career. In many cases they absorbed this attitude from parents or grandparents, whose lives may have depended from day to day on work, but their more affluent children fail to notice that their own circumstances are entirely different. Material survival is usually not the issue.

We encountered a man in therapy who worked at his office twelve or thirteen hours every day and often on weekends. He enjoyed his work, but he also felt (rather than consciously believed) that survival for him and his family depended on long hours. His parents had known years of poverty as immigrants, and he had absorbed their attitudes uncritically, living as though everything he had achieved would disappear if he neglected his business for even one day. He loved his wife and children yet rarely spent time with them. He had no time. His wife threatened divorce unless he entered therapy with her.

Nathaniel told him to make a list of all his assets: "What would you have if you liquidated everything? Could you live comfortably for the rest of your life?"

"More than comfortably," he said, dazed.

"Then let's agree," said Nathaniel, "that the time you spend at work is a matter of choice, not of necessity. Agreed?"

"Agreed."

"You love your work, you love your wife and family,

and you say you want to keep both. Your wife says she has no reason to remain in the marriage if you continue to neglect her since she no longer feels married anyway. So what are your options?"

The man answered, "I have to cut down my time at the office and spend more time at home, and I'm willing to do that right now. But I'm realizing that I really don't know much about doing things just for fun. I was brought up to believe that life is work. Work is life."

"Me too."

"How did you ever break out of that?" the man asked.

"With a lot of help from my partner."

"Maybe I can get the same help from my wife." He was laughing now. He breathed a sigh.

Whether both partners work or only one, the principle of balancing our attention remains the same. We need to know each day what we value in our life and allocate our time accordingly.

Some jobs make it harder to reserve time for your partner than others, and both partners need to be aware of it. A woman who was planning to marry a physician wanted to have children, "but not if I'm married to you."

"Why?" he asked.

"Because I know what a doctor's life is like. There won't be much time when you're not working and I'm not working, and I want us to have it for ourselves alone." A painful decision. A choice. The answers are not always easy.

Musicians, actors and actresses, and people whose work requires long periods on the road face a nearly insoluble conflict between work and love if their partner cannot accompany them. We can't say that there is an ideal solution for every couple in every situation. We believe that for the majority there are solutions and that the element common to all solutions is the couple's determination to reconcile the demands of a career or two careers with the needs of romantic love.

The solution may entail the choice not to have children or the resolution to give our work so many hours a day and no more. It may man accepting limitations on how far we can go professionally. Sometimes the solution lies in giving so much care to the quality of the time spent with our partner that long periods of involvement with work become acceptable to both people. We cannot write out a simple formula. You have to decide with your partner.

Married women who do not work are the unhappiest group in our society (judged by the presence of emotional disorders and psychosomatic illness), while married women who work tend to experience more happiness in their lives. Studies, as well as our own observation, lead us to the conviction that the solution lies in finding the right balance, not in sacrificing one value to the other.

Q. My partner talks about the demands of his (her) work, but I suspect that he (she) is trying to cover up a fear of closeness with me. Can an excessive preoccupation with work be a smoke screen?

A. Indeed it can.
Many people deceive themselves with talk about the conflict of work and love, or intend to deceive others.

In *The Psychology of Romantic Love*, I discuss one aspect of self-deception, the fear of intimacy:

> Sometimes I have had a man or woman speak of love as a threat to their work. To surrender to love, they say, is to undermine their total commitment to their careers. As a man who has been achievement-oriented all his life and who knows rather a lot about what it means to love his work, I have never for a moment believed this argument. I am convinced it is a rationalization for fear of intimacy. Sometimes there is the additional fear that the lover will not respect their work needs [or] out of fear of displeasing the lover they will no longer give work its due. . . . [This] is a problem of inadequate self-assertion, inadequate autonomy. It is a problem of inadequate maturity. Of course, if a person has this problem and does not know how to resolve it, it is better that he or she face that fact consciously and not attempt intimate relationships. But this is rarely what such persons choose to do. They want love, they want relationships, they want marriage, but they do not want that which is logically entailed by a serious commitment: They do not want the obligation to

carry their own weight, they do not want to be
there, in the relationship, except at unpredictable moments, and they want their partner to accept that, to
absorb it uncomplainingly, and to support the pretense that they have a romance. What they want,
then, is a contradiction: to be in love and yet not to
be in love.

Earlier we mentioned the hazard of an extramarital affair that makes an unbearable marriage bearable. The person having the affair avoids confronting frustration in the
primary relationship through involvement with someone
else. Losing ourselves in our work, we can achieve the
same purpose. Long hours on the job won't make it possible to avoid the essential emptiness of the relationship or
to avoid painful conflicts with our partner. Work can be
employed as a defense against any repressed feeling. It is
always available as a means of distracting ourselves from
our inner life.

Q. My partner and I were both brought up on the
philosophy that work is the highest value, and
that's turning out to mean that as a person I am a lesser
value. It's making me angrier and angrier. Why should
love be second to anything?

A. We don't think it should be. It is not written that
love should or must be subordinate to work.

Right now we are writing this book under a deadline.
With the book, our work with therapy and marriage counseling, and our Intensives, there is not much leisure at
present. We would love to take off for a week or two, or
even a long weekend, just to be together and play. We
do spend time together in the evening, but we're often
tired.

But earlier this year, working under all the same pressures, I stopped. Devers had to have major surgery. I
chose to sleep most nights in her room at the hospital and
to spend most of my days there. Priorities.

I love my work passionately and cannot imagine life
without it. But I love Devers passionately and don't care
to imagine life without her. With values of the highest

importance, we do not think of one's being subordinate to the other. We look at the situation and choose.

I think I would not have understood this so clearly when I was younger. I might have wanted to take time off to be with Devers and drop all work on the book, but at the same time I might have felt uneasy, unsure whether this was the right thing to do. I might have thought it my duty to work regardless of adversity. Today I am certain that no value in my life is higher than love, and none is worth very much to me without love. Not everyone feels the same way. It is a good idea to know how you feel and how your partner feels about the priority of love before you commit yourself to another human being. If there are major differences, better to know before than after.

Let us assume that we are already in a relationship and we have come to feel that our partner values his or her work more than our relationship. It might mean that our partner does not feel *free* to value love as highly as work, as if love were some illicit pleasure of an inferior moral order. Men in particular often feel this way, secretly. The problem is not so much persuading them to value love as helping them to acknowledge that they already value love as much as work and that they are entitled to.

The sad thing is that some of us will not recognize how much love matters until it is too late, when our partner leaves us or dies. In a counseling session a man said to his lover, "I'm sorry. I've been happy with you, but I'm not certain we should stay together. Love seems to clutter up things; it gets me all tied up emotionally, gets in the way of work. I'm sitting in my office, looking at plans for a building, and thinking of you—I'm not sure I like that. It makes me feel strange. Do you think we could just be friends or something?"

She looked at him through a long, painful moment of silence. Then she stood up and said, "That's it. I'm finished. Goodbye." She walked out of the office.

The man looked as though he had been doused with ice water. He said, "Maybe it's for the best."

After he left, I said to Devers, "That man had better fall apart in the next twenty-four hours. It's his only hope."

He did. Next day, in a group session, he cried hysterically. "What have I done?" he shrieked. "What have I done?"

I shrugged and said, "No real man wants a woman hanging on his gun arm. Who needs her?"

"What are you talking about?" the man cried. "What's the sense of anything without her? Who gives a good goddamn about anything without her?"

"Oh, really?" I said "What are you going to do about it?"

"What can I do about it?" asked the man helplessly.

"I'm betting you'll think of something."

Next week both of them appeared in group, happy and smiling. He had thought of something.

Q. Your idea of balancing work and love seems to destroy spontaneity. Must everything be calculated and planned?

A. If handling your life and your relationship without planning works for you, there is no need to change your policy. Most people find that life does not spontaneously arrange itself the way they would like it to.

So we plan evenings to be together. We plan weekends and vacations. We plan for time uncommitted to anything but whatever we feel like doing when the moment comes.

No one wants to live by a plan all the time, and we don't recommend it. When we notice that we are spending enough time on work but neglecting our partner—spontaneously as it were—or spending enough time with our partner but putting off important moves in our career, then a little planning is in order.

We love spontaneity. We take the trouble to plan time in which we can be spontaneous.

Q. My partner seems always preoccupied with work, which annoys me. I want to help him achieve more control over his attention, but I don't know how to go about it. Do you have suggestions?

A. Most frequently wives ask this question about husbands, so our answer will assume a woman is asking about a man. Men do sometimes ask this question about their wives or lovers, and the principles behind our suggestions apply in those cases also.

*   *   *

The first step is to draw attention, without reproach, to the problem: "You seem very preoccupied. Something wrong at work? Tell me about it."

If he retreats from the offer to share his concerns with you, bear in mind that the popular notion of manhood encourages men to withdraw. You might say, "Do you feel I wouldn't be interested? I am interested. It feels lonely, sitting in the same room with you and knowing you're somewhere far away. I need to know what you're thinking." We need to apply everything from our chapter on communication about helping the partner to be more open.

Many different factors may be complicating what appears to be a simple refusal to talk.

"If I opened up to my wife and really talked, I'd have to face how bored and dissatisfied I am with my job. How could I stand it after that? Then how would I earn a living? So I just sit and stew and suffer and try not to feel anything."

Another man told us, "If I tried to talk, within two or three minutes she'd change the subject and we'd be talking about her. She only pretends to listen."

Another said, "It's so hard to admit you're scared—of the future, of the younger men rising in the company, of everything. I can't imagine my father admitting he was frightened about anything. I just keep my mouth shut and wonder what's going to happen."

Another said, "I'm never bored with my work, so it's hard to turn it off. And I'm scared of finding out I'm bored with my marriage."

Nothing good can happen until the man and woman find a way to restore direct communication.

After repeated efforts to get her husband to talk, a woman we know began making her own social plans for the evening. When her husband objected, she asked, "Why do you want me here? So you can ignore me? I'm willing to be home any time you're willing to be here with me." That was her way of forcing the door open and, at least in her case, the strategy succeeded.

Another woman finally said, "I don't want to take a lover, but I need someone to talk to. If not you, who will it be?" She succeeded in capturing her husband's attention.

Other strategies are less drastic and almost always useful: "I love you and I miss you. It's very hard for me when you're not here. It's worse when you're only physically present. You always seem preoccupied with work. What can I do that would make you want to spend real time with me?"

Or: "You feel the need to spend long hours in the evening and on weekends thinking about work. I am unhappy not really having a husband. What do you think we should do?"

Or. "Perhaps you'd rather live alone. Perhaps you don't really want to be married. I'm not being sarcastic, but often I feel as if I'm a burden and an inconvenience. Are you willing to talk about that?"

Or: "If you're having a hard time at the office, I will stand by you in every way I can. But I won't play the little woman who keeps herself busy in the kitchen with the children. That's not my idea of marriage. I know it's not yours either."

All of these approaches have proven themselves broadly effective. They indicate ways to begin talking. Where the discussion leads depends on the couple.

Q. Must I be interested in my partner's work?

A. There is no "must" about it, no question of duty. If we love someone, it seems natural to be interested in how he or she spends the major part of the day. We want to know something of the highs and lows, the struggles, difficulties, and joys of our partner's work because we are interested in our partner as a person. We assume here that the partner is interested in talking about his or her work.

This question is difficult for us because it is hard to imagine that two people can love each other and yet not be interested in each other's activities and concerns. Without such interest, how do they *sustain* a happy relationship?

In all likelihood, the lack of interest in our partner's work is a symptom of some other problem. If my partner talks only about his or her work and never about any other subject, after a while I become bored or resentful.

The real problem here is avoidance of contact by jamming personal and intimate communication with chatter. If my partner talks about his or her work while showing no interest in mine, again I feel bored or resentful after a while, but not because I have no interest in my partner's work. The issue is still two-way communication.

The way we talk about our work also makes a difference. One man we know talked about his work a good deal but always impersonally, abstractly, without ever indicating to his partner the personal meaning of his activities. In consequence, his discussions were colorless and remote. His partner said, "I guess I'm just not interested in insurance." She was one of those who asked us, "Must I be interested in my partner's work?" As it turned out, he learned to talk about what he enjoyed in his work. When he shared anecdotes that had personal meaning to him, allowing his own excitement to come through, he captured and held her full attention. She asked questions, because now it was not a discussion of his work but a discussion of his life.

Sometimes we are asked, "How can I get my partner interested in my work?" The preceding story anticipates our answer: make it personal. Your partner may not always follow the technical details of your profession, but he or she will understand the meaning of your work to you as a human being. That is the most important element to share. Talking about your partner's work and your work is simply another aspect of self-disclosure.

Q. My partner is reluctant to share his (her) thoughts and feelings about work. He (she) always says it's too involved to unravel for someone who wasn't there. How can I deal with this?

A. In light of what we have said throughout this book about communicating, we will limit ourselves here to the following story.

A while ago a friend of ours complained that her husband never shared his work with her. When she would ask, "How was your day?" he would reply, "Fine." If she would say, "Anything new or exciting?" he would reply, "You wouldn't understand the ramifications of all that goes on in a law office." She would ask him to tell her about some of the cases he was handling, and he would shrug her off.

Out of frustration, she went to the library, checked out a few books on law, and began studying some of the basics. She went to the Los Angeles courthouse to watch a number of different cases. She took notes.

After a few weeks she told him what she had been doing. She asked him some very specific questions about points she had not understood. As he answered her, he realized to his amazement that he could talk about his work; he was already talking about his work. On a day when he came home looking exhausted, she said, "What's the case that's giving you such a hard time?" He told her a little about it. Her responses were appropriate and incisive. So were her questions when she did not understand.

Naturally he was pleased that she had taken so much trouble to familiarize herself with this aspect of his life. More important, he recognized her effort as an act of love, which touched him deeply. It was as if she had given him a beautiful present.

Predictably, he was more in the mood to talk about his work on some days than others, but she no longer felt left out. He no longer felt alone in so important a part of his life.

All of us like to feel visible and appreciated. If our partner does not take the initiative in sharing his or her work, we might take the first step ourselves.

Q. **My husband does not regard maintaining a home and raising children as work. How can I achieve his respect for the work I do?**

A. Unfortunately there is a tendency in our culture to disregard work for which no payment is given. The person who cooks for wages works, whereas a woman who cooks for a family does not. Nurses, babysitters, chauffeurs, teachers, gardeners, dishwashers, decorators, caterers, janitors—they all work. But a woman who performs in all these capacities and more doesn't work; she *is* a housewife. (Calling her a "homemaker" doesn't change very much.)

*   *   *

Recently divorced men find out very quickly that you have to pay for all these services. Only then do they discover that a housewife does indeed work.

Short of divorce, how can you teach a husband that maintaining a home and raising children constitute work? Make a list of all your activities and invite your husband to find out what these skills command in the open market, or provide your husband with the figures (call the taxi company, call a housecleaning agency, call a decorator, etc.).

You might ask a husband to take over the household tasks for a few days; it is a sobering and educational experience, traumatic for some men.

One husband clarified the issue for himself by completing the stem "If I were to admit that what you do is work_____":

I might feel an obligation to help you sometimes.

I'd understand some of your resentment.

I'd thank and compliment you more.

I'd realize how much you protect me.

I'd wonder where you get the energy.

I wouldn't be such a prima donna.

We hope he has clarified the issue for some of our readers as well.

Q. My husband is all in favor of my working, so long as it doesn't interfere with all my duties at home. In effect, my emancipation consists of having two jobs. How do I get my husband to understand that I need help in running the house?

A. We once presented this problem at an Intensive to a group of men whose wives or girlfriends held jobs ranging from the secretarial to the executive. Most of them acknowledged feeling that regardless of any work a woman did outside, the home was her first responsibility.

We invited them to experiment with the sentence stem "If I were expected to be a homemaker in addition to

holding down a full time job_____." Amidst a good deal of
laughter and embarrassment, their endings included:

I'd say, "Are you kidding?"

I'd feel angry and exploited.

I'd feel overworked.

I'd probably be too tired for anything else.

*I'd wonder how come my partner only does one job while I
do two.*

I'd sure as hell understand the feminists better.

I'd start yelling for help.

I don't know what I'd do about it, but I'd be unhappy.

I'd wonder who made up the rules.

I'd say, "We've got to get a maid."

*I'd say, "My partner has to share some of the burdens at
home."*

I'd say, "What kind of racket is this?"

This sentence-completion exercise can be an interesting
place to begin for a husband who does not see that he
ought to help. If he comes to appreciate the inequity
involved, the next natural question is: "What do you
think we should do?"

Some working couples agree to share housework more
or less equally. Others budget money to hire someone to
take over some of the household chores. Some couples
acknowledge the inequity and choose to live with it. One
wife remarked, "I'm so much faster around the house
than my husband, I'm finishing while he's still getting
started. He helps with a few things, but the house remains basically my job. The truth is I don't especially
mind. In the future people will probably handle these
things differently. Right now, I can't get all that excited
about it, perhaps because our relationship is so good in
every other way."

Male/female relationships are changing as individual men
and women struggle to break free of sexually determined

roles, with varying degrees of success. Thus our answer to this question is unavoidably tentative and incomplete. It is impossible to review here all the strategies a couple may have to practice to erase or alter their programming, but Nathaniel will conclude with one cautionary observation for our male readers.

Gentlemen, we are going to have to bend, we are going to have to learn, because fewer and fewer women (in their right minds) are going to put up with our "helplessness." The best women, the most independent and the most admirable, won't be willing to live with the inequality we have always taken for granted. That game is just about over.

The attitudes we absorbed as children, while powerful, are not an excuse for doing nothing to change an unfair and undesirable status quo. "I know I should help you with the housework, but I never saw my father help my mother and it all seems too strange and unfamiliar to me." Simply not good enough, not anymore.

Q. My husband tells me he feels humiliated because I earn more money than he does. I appreciate his honesty, but I don't know what to do.

A. We have seen several cases like this. In one, the woman managed a dress shop; the man sold shoes. In another, the woman worked in advertising; the man repaired typewriters. In still another, the husband and wife were both psychologists, but the woman's therapy practice was considerably larger.

Even though women are generally underpaid in comparison to men, problems of this kind do arise, and it seems safe to predict that they will arise with more frequency in the future.

Many men identify money with manhood, and they may feel emasculated by a wife who enjoys superior earning power. This is a self-esteem problem, pure and simple. Without this diagnosis, it would be difficult for a wife to know how to respond effectively. While she can help her husband deal with his frustration, she cannot single-handedly change his perception of himself. Of course, if a woman shares her husband's view of money and competes with him, if she keeps calling attention to her success, then they both have a problem: measuring their self-worth on the wrong scale. Let us suppose for the purposes of this question that the problem is the man's and that the woman is not actively making it worse.

We hope you would encourage your husband to air his feelings honestly, to describe everything in as much detail as possible, without having to fear that you will ridicule or attack him. The idea is to transform an implicitly competitive relationship into one of benevolence and comradeship. When a person struggles with feelings he or she would like to be free of, the first step is to acknowledge them, experience them fully, not merely abstractly and cerebrally, express them so that, in effect, they have their day in court. (This process is liberating, as detailed in *The Disowned Self*.)

Show that you are not indifferent to your partner's pain. Communicating empathy and compassion contributes to his working toward a solution. Sacrificing your own career to appease your partner's insecurities does not contribute to the solution in any way beneficial to the relationship.

"I tried that for a while," said one wife at an Intensive. "I turned down promotions. I let other people take projects I really wanted. I even started to minimize the importance of my work in my husband's presence. I only grew to resent him. It was humiliating for both of us. I took a leave of absence for six months and then I began throwing up and getting headaches. So I went back to work at a lower-level job but that was no solution either. One day I decided: 'Enough. Whatever the consequences, I'm going to be who I am. If it's too much for my husband, so be it. It isn't love if I have to be somebody else—and somebody untalented at that.' "

A man in one of our groups said, "In a way I admire my partner for not giving in to my jealousy of her success, even though it hurts sometimes. I fell in love with her partly because she wasn't just a clinging vine. She sure isn't. Now I have to adjust. If I don't, I know I'm going to lose her, and that scares me more than anything. I'm just glad she's willing to come here with me and work on this."

This problem is not confined to couples who are mar-

ried. It arises with men and women who are going together or, in some cases, living together. Although this
chapter concerns itself chiefly with married couples, just
about every problem discussed applies to men and women
in any kind of serious relationship. And, of course, all the
principles of problem solving are the same.

Q. I usually do not enjoy socializing with my partner's professional friends. I appreciate that a lot
of this kind of socializing goes with the job, and I don't
want my lack of enthusiasm to hurt our relationship.
Should I ask to be left out of such gatherings, or should I
grin and bear it?

A. We have already established that every relationship occasionally requires compromise and accommodation, and they are vital here. In every relationship
there are times when we need to do things we don't enjoy
very much in order to assist or support our partner, whom
we do enjoy very much.

Privately, say to your partner that you do not find your
partner's associates particularly interesting or enjoyable,
but do not abuse or ridicule them. You achieve nothing by
putting your partner on the defensive about the people he
or she chooses to socialize with.

Many couples ameliorate the problem by inviting friends
of each partner to parties whenever possible. The mixture
of personalities makes it easier for the couple and, as an
added benefit, enriches the quality of the event.

Anyone who is serious about solving this problem will
take extra pains when visiting his or her friends to see
that his or her mate does not feel like an outsider. Do not
leave your partner with someone you regard as boring so
that you willl be free for the person you find really interesting. This is how the grievance often starts.

Some couples develop separate social lives, each person
going to certain kinds of events without the other. While
this policy can work as part of a solution, there is a risk in
too much of their leisure time being spent apart from each
other. They are sharing that much less of their lives.

There is no way to solve a problem of this kind without
good will, benevolence, and a genuine desire to find a

solution that will be as mutually satisfying as possible. A policy of demanding sacrifices, of demanding accommodations without being willing to make them, or of striving to see who will succeed in imposing whose will on whom can only mean harm to the relationship—no winners and two losers.

Good will and benevolence make it far easier to improvise solutions. We know an actor whose wife did not enjoy much of the socializing he felt compelled to do. He often arranged to bring along another couple, friends of his wife, when he wanted her to accompany him to some social event. In another case, a woman recognized that her partner did not enjoy a certain kind of socializing and promptly reduced it to the barest minimum. Her partner appreciated her consideration and attended that minimum cheerfully.

Some couples find it easier to reach a solution than others. Those who go out together alone on a regular basis, those who reserve leisure time by themselves, are far more successful in dealing with this problem. An unwillingness to accommodate our partner is often an expression of resentment of too little time allocated to the relationship itself. If you feel you're spending more time than you want to with your partner's friends, check on whether you're spending enough time with your partner.

Q. Nathaniel and Devers Branden, you are husband and wife, in addition to which you conduct workshops together, practice therapy together, and you're now writing a book together. How do you manage to survive so much togetherness? Won't too much of it eventually stifle love?

A. Devers said to me, "You answer this one, please." As a person who is used to working alone and who has never spent so much time in the presence of another person, I am amazed at how well this much togetherness works for us on all levels: intellectual, emotional, and sexual.

I am not prepared to say that it will always work for us; I know only that it does now. And I am certainly not prepared to recommend it as a general way of life for everyone. Some people seem to need far more time alone than either of us does right now, and each of us has certainly required more of it in the past.

We do know how to keep out of each other's way when one of us is preoccupied, as sometimes happens—especially with me.

On the other hand, sometimes Devers will bounce into my office, fling herself on the sofa, and say, "Ten minutes. Come here." I am generally fairly obedient in such situations. Sometimes I will bounce into her office, fling myself on the floor, and make the same request. She tends to be no less obedient.

I don't know that my answer is of any practical value to anyone, except perhaps to satisfy curiosity. We said earlier that solutions and lifestyles need to be custom tailored, not acquired off the rack. What we have works for us. Another couple, no less in love, may require more time apart to support a no-less-happy relationship.

Devers has come back for a final word, after all.

Nathaniel and I know couples who work together as we do but find that they spend leisure time discussing professional matters; they don't know when or how to turn work off. They end up being partners in the business sense but no longer in the romantic sense. As much as two people may love their work, there are still times when they need to protect their personal relationship against it.

Other couples we know have experimented with working together and have decided against it, not because of any frictions during the work day but because of the excitement of meeting in the evening. We recommend that amount of togetherness which makes a couple happiest.

Coming back to our own situation, we don't know if we will always work together in the future as much as we do now. We don't feel any need to know. Right now, working together is a thoroughly enjoyable way of life. It is fun, it is exciting, it is an adventure. If our needs and wants change in the future, then our attitude is: we will move on to a new adventure—a lifestyle that will better serve our relationship when and if our present way of life no longer proves satisfactory.

Ten
Stress, Conflict, Change

Even the best of relationships must weather stresses, conflicts, and changes from time to time. They challenge a couple's ability to adapt and thrive.

Differences of temperament that didn't seem to matter once matter now; familiar patterns of behavior no longer satisfy; one partner longs to move off in a direction the other experiences as foreign and frightening. Money, children, family—stress accompanies any significant change in our lives.

But change is inevitable. Our desires, needs, and interests shift as a normal part of life. Whether or not romantic love survives these challenges depends less on external circumstances than the responses we choose to make.

We may see change as a threat or as an opportunity for growth. We may see any setback as a calamity or as just a setback, to be overcome and transcended. We can be rigid, or we can be improvisational. Our manner of responding will have consequences for romantic love, as it will for ever aspect of our life.

Selecting our questions on the basis of which were asked more frequently and with the most intensity, we began with three relating to money.

Q. It's difficult to keep passion and excitement alive when we are continually worried about finances, yet some couples seem to manage it. How?

A. The money we have or do not have matters less than such factors as our self-esteem, our ability to find joy and satisfaction in our daily activities, and our general outlook on life.

Studies suggest that people who feel good self-esteem, fulfillment in their primary relationship, and optimism about the future worry far less about money than those afflicted with low self-esteem, discontent in their primary relationship, and a view of the future as a storehouse of potential catastrophes.

People with a strong disposition to worry rarely enjoy any aspect of their life. Their ability to enjoy their work, children, and recreation suffers along with their ability to love. Psychologists and students of human behavior generally agree that many arguments about money are in fact a smoke screen concealing hurt, resentment, anger, or conflict in other aspects of the relationship, such as sex. The classic example of this phenomenon is the woman who feels sexually neglected by her husband and outrages him by going on shopping sprees. Arguments about money can also represent conflicts of values or priorities, differences in how two individuals think money should be spent.

So there are two issues we need to address here: *anxieties* about money and *arguments* about money.

Let us first consider continual worrying about finances. If we wish to protect our romantic life against financial anxieties, we need to be aware of the danger of tying our sense of personal worth to our income. We need to keep our priorities clear so that we give time and attention to love—especially when other pressures threaten to distract us and fling us into anxiety or depression.

When I was twenty-two years old, I had two small children, and my husband (who was to die a year later) was working for a mining company. We had very little money at the time and anticipated a struggle for several years to come. Almost every morning we held each other, acknowledging our present difficulties but talking also of our goals and dreams for the future. We kept looking for ways to give ourselves and each other pleasures, big or small, that would help to keep alive our enthusiasm for life. Even for a dinner of hot dogs and beans, I would set the table with an attractive tablecloth, candles, and flowers, or whatever small items of delight I managed to find. For me, it was a way of preserving our sense of what *really* mattered, of what life is *really* about, even when we had no amenities. We believed in ourselves, we believed in each other, and we believed in life. That is how we were able to keep financial worries from swamping us.

As to the second category, arguments about how money is to be spent, it is one more area for compromise and accommodation. One person in a relationship should not make all the decisions; that much seems fairly obvious. Partners who want the relationship to work take the trouble to reach decisions that are mutually satisfying. For example, he wants a new stereo system; she wants a trip to Europe. They cannot have both in the same year. They can toss a coin, or they can explore the urgency of their feelings about these purchases, because one may turn out to be stronger than the other. They can negotiate other considerations, perhaps tipping the scale toward one decision or another. Without good will, the genuine desire to see each other happy and satisfied, mutually agreeable solutions do not come easily. An attitude shared by the couple is the important thing—not heroic unselfishness but rather a selfishness that includes the interests, satisfaction, and fulfillment of the other.

When a couple's arguments about money begin to look like a screen for problems in another area, we find sentence-completion exercises the fastest way to cut through it. "The good thing about spending money extravagantly is_____":

it drives you crazy.

it makes me feel loved.

I've got to have some pleasure in my life.

it's better than taking a lover.

it impresses Mother.

it makes our friends think we're really doing well financially.

it relieves the boredom of not doing anything all day.

"The good thing about overcontrolling how much money you can spend is_____":

it keeps you tied to me.

that's how my father always was.

it lets out my anger.

it makes up for a lot of things.

I'm the boss.

I want to have authority over something.

Conflicts whose roots go deep beneath the surface of awareness are obviously harder for couples to solve on their own. At the same time, couples who have learned sentence completion as a technique have achieved impressive results by adapting our exercises for their own use in solving problems at home. (We are planning a book to teach couples how to use sentence-completion exercises on their own to solve a variety of problems, such as fights over money.)*

Here are a few stems couples may wish to experiment with:

When I complain about your attitude toward money, what I'm really trying to say is_____

It might be easier for us to agree about money if only you would_____

If I were to respect your preferences about spending as much as my own_____

Maybe I would feel differently about money if only_____

Sometimes, when we fight about money, what I think we are really trying to tell each other is_____

Q. When we were struggling financially, we told ourselves that later we would be free to enjoy our relationship. Now we have made it, and our lives are overfilled with people, responsibilities, and commitments. When does the right time for love come, or does it?

If You Could Hear What I Cannot Say by Nathaniel Branden, Bantam Books trade paperback, 1983.

A. If a couple does not have a commitment to honor their love and to do whatever is required to protect the relationship, there will always be reasons for postponement and distraction of every kind: "We're struggling to earn a living. We have social obligations. Relatives are coming to visit. The children need us. We devote our spare time to charitable activities. Friends dropped by for a visit. Now that we're successful, the business is more demanding of our time than ever. Do you know how much work is involved in preparing a party for 300 people?"

A relationship can decay by such slow and subtle stages that resignation and despair may become a substantial part of it before either partner notices. By the time one cries out, "What is happening to us?" often the relationship has already undergone considerable degeneration. To make matters worse, there are always friends (and psychologists) to chime in, "Well, what did you expect? You don't really believe in romantic love, do you?"

We have already noted that for a man and woman to create happiness in their private life is generally not regarded as an achievement worthy of comment. And yet it is one of the rarest of all human attainments. Love is only for those who are aware of their priorities and are not afraid to place their relationship first among them. When does the right time for love come? Now. Today. Love is for those who understand that it is now or never.

In practical terms, honoring a commitment to love means setting aside certain evenings—say, every Monday—and perhaps every other weekend to be alone together. No social commitments of any kind: no friends, no visitors, no involvements with other people. If time alone together has already become a problem, the twelve-hour intimacy marathon may be in order. Now. Today. For any couple who feels they have lost their way or lost contact with each other, the twelve-hour intimacy marathon is probably the fastest way back.

Relationships are not like games with time in and time out. They go on every moment, getting better or getting worse. The time to experience the preciousness of love is while we still have it, not after we have lost it.

Perhaps we should mention one final point. When a

couple is starting out and struggling financially, that struggle can be a tactic to avoid pain and frustration in the relationship. Later, the social obligations and other commitments that come with success can accomplish the same purpose. As with extramarital affairs or excessive preoccupation with work, we can use just about any activity to divert ourselves from a recognition that our relationship may have no good reason to exist—or at least is in mortal danger.

"If I were to stop running to other women (men)/to the office/to parties/to charitable functions_____":

I would have to face how unhappy I am.

I would have to admit that our marriage gives me nothing.

I would feel the emptiness of my personal life.

I would have to look at how far apart we are now.

I would have to admit now how much you have hurt me.

I would have to face how many ways I have hurt you.

I would have to feel my rage and frustration.

I would have to decide how to connect with you again.

I would have to decide if that is still possible.

Q. My partner is extremely money-conscious and success-oriented, while I am not. Can love survive that conflict?

A. In our experience, the problem is not so much money and success but a corresponding imbalance in the importance each partner attaches to the relationship, as measured by the amount of time, energy, and care they are willing to give it. When there are differences of this kind, one partner usually wants more time devoted to the relationship than the other. The one preoccupied with money and success says, "Wait. Wait until I've made it. Later we'll have more time for our relationship." While we are waiting for the right time, the right time evaporates. Unresolved differences in this area can be very hazardous.

*   *   *

It is useful to know whether the questioner respects the other's attitude toward success and money. If not, good-bye love. If there is respect, and if both partners can agree to allot time for the relationship, then the difference in values need not be fatal.

Here is a further complication: a person whose self-esteem is tied to money and success often exists in a state of such tension that surrender to love (literally, relaxation) becomes extraordinarily difficult. Often he or she fears intimacy, fears anything that distracts from the pursuit of money and success. Romantic love requires our concentration as much as a successful career.

A couple would do well to resolve this kind of issue before getting married, even before living together.

A colleague of ours will ask a man and woman in premarital counseling to imagine what their relationship will be like five years in the future. This exercise in fantasy brings out undiscussed differences in values, lifestyles, and aspirations. Couples need to know whether they can live with each other's dreams and accommodate them in some mutually satisfying way. (Of course the issue extends to far more than money; add children, friends, careers, recreation, and so forth.)

A woman who values money and success more than her partner may end up belittling him for falling short of goals he never set for himself. A man who values money and success more than his partner may begin a self-escalating process of alienation by ignoring her efforts to draw his attention. The more he tries to concentrate on deals and accounts, the more her frustration increases.

We need to know today what our values are and where our relationship ranks among them. After that, survival of the relationship depends on the couple's flexibility and openness to change.

Q. I would like my partner to change in certain ways, and yet I do not want him (her) to feel that there is an obligation to live up to my expectations. How can I put this to my partner, or do I even have the right?

A. We appreciate the sensitivity and perceptiveness of this question. Many men and women manipulate their partner into change, never considering that their partner is entitled to make a choice.

Our partner does not owe it to us to be other than as he or she is. For that matter, no one is obliged to live up to our expectations, even if our expectations are reasonable, even if the other person would benefit and feel better. We stress this point at the outset.

Presumably we fell in love with our partner as he or she now is, not with a picture we drew of some future version.

Having made these observations, we acknowledge that as a relationship progresses, we may wish our partner were different in one respect or another. Perhaps we would like our partner to take more responsibility in our relationship, acquire a wider range of interests, become better educated, participate in new activities, or respond to needs in ourselves that we were not aware of in the past.

We can ask for what we want and ask how our partner thinks and feels about it. If appropriate, we can seek to engage our partner in new activities and hope that his or her own interests will catch fire independently.

Just as my partner is not obliged to change simply to please me, neither am I obliged to be happy for the rest of my life with the present state of affairs. I have a right to change, to grow, to acquire new preferences. If my partner has freedom, I also have freedom. If I am no longer able to enjoy my partner's habits or way of being, or if he or she develops in ways that are incompatible with my own standards and values, I need not condemn myself to a life of pretense and resignation.

We risk overemphasizing this point because so many men and women consistently fail to understand it, or act on it. My partner has the right to say yes or no; so do I. My partner has the right to say "This pleases me" or "This doesn't please me"; so do I. My partner has the right to say "I want to live this way" or "I don't want to live this way"; so do I. I will not force my values on my partner; I will not allow my partner to force his or hers on me.

When we see how free we are in this respect, we are in

a better position to evaluate whether differences are nego-
tiable, whether compromise and accommodation are
possible.

We need to realize also that not all changes are easy to
make, even if our partner is willing. Some require little
more than agreement; others reach far below the surface
of personality, so far that the individual may truly not
know how to generate the change. Can we command
ourselves to be interested in painting or baseball or poetry? Neither can we command our partner. All we can
reasonably do, if our partner is willing, is exercise our
ingenuity in finding ways to evoke and stimulate our
partner's interest.

As to the kind of changes that are appropriate to ask for
directly, changes that are within our partner's power to
provide, we offer the following story.

"Don't try to change me, I am who I am," said a
husband when his wife complained about the frequency
with which he brought home guests without informing
her in advance. Her repeated requests for a little more
consideration availed her nothing. One day, when her
husband arrived home with a half-dozen guests, the wife
greeted everyone pleasantly and then proceeded to walk
out. When she returned several hours later, the husband
asked, bewildered, "Where were you?"

"Went to the movies," she replied.

"The movies? I don't get it. How come?"

"Just felt like it."

"But we had guests!" her husband protested.

"Didn't feel like being with them," she responded.

He looked at her, thoroughly confused and frustrated.
"Well," he said, "that certainly wasn't very considerate of
you."

She answered, "Don't try to change me, I am who I
am."

"What do you mean?" he cried. "Aren't you part of a
relationship?"

"Aren't you?" she answered.

He became angry. She stood her ground.

"Well," he finally conceded, "I guess we really should
talk about these things, shouldn't we? Work out something we both can live with—right?"

She smiled pleasantly. "Right."

Not a model or confrontation suitable for everyone, true enough. But sometimes we need to take strong measures. No arguments, no attacks, no vilifications here—and the woman made her point.

Q. When we were first married, my partner and I seemed to want the same things out of life. Now we seem to be moving in different directions. We still feel love, but there is more strain and friction. Is there a limit to the differences we can accommodate and still be in love?

A. A woman in therapy said, "My husband and I no longer have anything in common. The kids are teenagers and go their own way. My husband and I have completely different interests. We seldom spend any meaningful time together, and except for mundane things we have nothing to talk about. He has his career and I do volunteer work, which I enjoy but he doesn't care about. He has his own friends, who are all unhappy in their own homes so they come to ours and he entertains them. We have been taking separate vacations for the past few years. I love getting away by myself or with friends of my own.

"Some years back, when we first sensed that we were growing apart, we tried doing things together—tennis, skiing, and so forth. And it was fun for a while, but in the end I just got tired of it, tired of it all. It felt like we were finding ways to keep busy rather than preserving anything important between us.

"There is the other side of it: we love and respect each other. We will never divorce. But there is no magic, not for either of us, no happy excitement of the kind you talk about and think is so important. He's frustrated and I'm frustrated, and there is nothing we can do. But we have too much between us to think of destroying the relationship. It may sound strange, but that's how I feel—too many years, lovely children, and all the kindness we have given each other and continue to give each other. We're good friends. It's not romantic love, not at all. But then I never grew up expecting romantic love anyway."

Has their relationship survived? Here it is a matter of definition. What does "survive" mean?

Millions of couples do not expect intensity of feeling in

their relationship and are perfectly willing to live without it. Others treat its absence or disappearance as cause for divorce. A couple's expectations may determine how much divergence their relationship can stand.

A man at an Intensive told us this story: "I don't think love is made up of shared interests. My wife and I started a business together when we were young, and for years we had lots to talk about and lots to share. When the business became successful, she got tired of it and wanted children instead. We hardly talked about the company after that. She acquired interests of her own, and yet we had great talks together, just strolling around the neighborhood, looking at trees, children, store windows. Everything would catch our attention, and we'd just have fun together.

"Do we share many interests? I don't know. An interest in each other, perhaps. Love is more than talking. It certainly goes deeper than hobbies, politics, careers, community work, and all the other stuff people talk about—even deeper than children, if you want to know the truth. When I wake up in the morning, I look at my wife and realize that I know her, even though she has changed. I know her as deeply as I know myself. We decided to celebrate our thirty-eighth wedding anniversary by coming to this Intensive. Do we have any interests in common? You folks tell me."

Sometimes people are bound by values so profound (even below consciousness) that no diversity of superficial interests can alienate them from one another. What they share is far more important to them, the sense of being joined at a deep level of being. In a sense, we have returned to expectations: couples who experience fundamental affinities simply do not care about divergence above this basic level.

One more story: "My husband and I met in graduate school and boom! we were madly in love. We were both getting our PhDs in psychology. We both wanted to teach, do research—the academic life in all its glory. We were lucky and got jobs at different universities in the same city. He loved it. I found what academia really meant: politics, vicious competition, publishing endless quantities of crap to stay in the game, being at the right conferences. I don't believe any other profession is more obsessed with status and prestige. I got sick of it and went into private practice. Of course, my husband looked down on that. Working with people isn't 'pure science.' When I tried to talk with him about my practice, he wasn't interested.

"We found ourselves reading different kinds of books, enjoying different kinds of people, going to different kinds of professional events, and the gulf between us kept widening. I'm not sure you'd even call it a divergence of interests; it was more of a discovery that we have very different values, which the divergence of interests gradually made apparent to us. One day I looked at him and realized we no longer had anything to talk about. I said I wanted a divorce. And that was that."

Let us conclude with this general observation: if there is no conflict of basic values, it is not necessary that a couple share all interests for a relationship to be happy. However, the fewer the interests they share, the higher the risk of alienation. Unresolved alienation does not necessarily entail the end of the marriage or the living arrangement, merely the end of romantic love.

Q. For a long time I have provided most of the emotional support in our relationship. Now I want to receive more emotional support, but I can see my partner is unprepared for such an adjustment. What can I do?

A. I would like to begin our answer by telling a story about Nathaniel and myself.

For the first couple of years of our relationship, Nathaniel was still in a fairly bad way emotionally over the loss of Patrecia. He needed far more emotional support than he was able to return. I was in a stronger emotional state than he most of the time. Generally, I had to take care of myself.

Then my daughter Vicki badly needed me because of a crisis of her own. Then other family problems arose. I felt enormous physical and emotional fatigue. Almost everyone I knew was drawing on my energy, and I was being stretched thinner and thinner.

I should have sat down to discuss the whole issue with Nathaniel openly and candidly. Instead I attempted, shyly,

awkwardly, and indirectly, to ask for emotional support.
If Nathaniel asked me how I was feeling, I would answer,
"Okay, but not great." And then I would pause expec-
tantly and finally say, "I need . . . Want to come over and
sit down beside me? How are *you* feeling?" When I didn't
immediately get the nurturing I wanted but had not asked
for clearly, I felt hurt and angry. Then I suddenly insisted
on my needs, not recognizing the abruptness of the change
in my behavior. I was hurting Nathaniel and getting no
comfort myself—all because I had not given enough thought
to establishing a transition to the changes I wanted in our
relationship.

The situation began to improve only after we partici-
pated in the twelve-hour intimacy marathon we so often
recommend to others. It gave us the opportunity to talk
about the rough time we had just come through, about
our relationship at present, and about our goals and needs
for the future.

Even so, the transition did not happen quickly. We
explored the problem with sentence-completion and role-
reversal exercises, in addition to holding each other, talking, and taking walks. Nathaniel became more and more
thoughtful and considerate, as his normal loving impulses
reawakened.

I noticed that the more straightforward and direct I was
about expressing my needs, the more spontaneous and
enthusiastic was the response elicited. But I had to be
willing to express what I wanted many times—many,
many times, in some cases—without bitterness or despair
when Nathaniel didn't heed my requests promptly. He
came around in the end because I projected the conviction
at all times that what I wanted was natural for him to
give. In other words, I made my belief in him and my
confidence in him clear; whatever was wrong was temporary. I was right about Nathaniel. Later he said. "Sorry to
have kept you waiting so long."

Summarizing what I learned from this experience, I
would offer this advice:

Acknowledge to your partner that you are asking for a
break in your former pattern; recognize the need for a
period of transition.

Anticipate and deal with any feelings of abandonment
your partner may experience.

Ask for what you want clearly, straightforwardly, and benevolently.

Communicate your conviction that of course your partner wishes to nurture you as you have nurtured your partner.

Communicate your confidence in your partner's ability to give what you ask for.

If your partner does not respond as you hope and you feel hurt or angry, allow yourself those feelings. Express them without attempting to evoke guilt in your partner.

Let your partner understand that you have feelings and your feelings are part of the reality with which he or she has to deal. Seek to communicate at all times your fundamental belief in the relationship, your conviction that *of course* you are going to give each other what you want and need—*that happiness and satisfaction with each other are inevitable*.

Be patient. Don't deny your hurt or anger, but just the same be patient.

Persevere; ask again and again. Don't surrender to passivity, cynicism, or despair. Have the determination to approach the problem again and again until your partner responds. The reward is worth it.

Q. I am in a relationship that feels totally wrong for me today, yet my partner insists it is right for him (her). That's hard for me to understand. Can a relationship be right for one person but wrong for the other?

A. We'll begin with a story.
A couple came for counseling. The husband was very much in love with his wife, and while she respected him and felt affection for him, she was no longer in love with him. He had come to us hoping that through therapy they could recapture the feeling they had once shared. He wanted to know what he could do to make her love him again.

As the wife spoke to us, her eyes filled with tears; she glanced at her husband, then down at the floor, and said, "Up until about eight or nine years ago, I suppose I would have said I felt very much in love with him. Gradually I realized that I wanted more out of life than being a wife and mother. I got a job. I began to feel a new sense of excitement and vitality each day. It was as if I had been asleep for years. I didn't even look forward to coming home anymore.

"I spent more and more time at work with my new friends and associates. Several times I invited him for lunch—." Her eyes met her husband's. "I felt he was invading my territory. He was an absolute doll, he did nothing wrong, and he's a wonderful husband and father. I ask myself all the time, 'What's wrong with me?' I love him in a way. He's my best friend, but I'm not in love with him. There's no passion or excitement, just . . . quiet affection, tired affection.

"He insisted that we come to therapy, but I really don't see that there's anything to work on. If I'm totally honest, I have to say I feel I've outgrown being a wife. If this doesn't sound too cruel, I should say I've outgrown being his wife. It's not him, it's me. My husband is a good man; he'd do anything I asked him to. I want to be just friends if that's possible. And God help me, I would even like him to keep the children and allow me to visit them. I'm so sorry. I wish I could feel differently, but it's all gone, and I just want to be free."

The man took his wife's hand and looked at us in bewilderment. "How could I love her so much and want us to stay together, knowing she wants out?"

Was the marriage wrong for the woman and right for the man?

After working with both of them, we had no doubt that the marriage was wrong for the woman. She needed to be free. The man said he would have been content to let things go on as they were for the rest of his life.

But on another level, can we say that a relationship is right for someone when the other party involved does not feel love, does not want to stay, does not want the relationship? We do not think so.

We do not think it is desirable to spend the balance of a lifetime with a person who does not love us and does not want to be with us. The fact that we may be desperately willing does not mean we are serving our best interests.

However, we have seen many situations of this kind where the person who wanted to continue the relationship later declared that the break was the best thing that ever happened to him or her. The partner who wanted to go first perceived the truth of the relationship first. We know a couple who had been married for twenty-one years when the husband, a physician, announced he wanted a divorce. The wife became hysterical, threatening suicide. Her whole sense of identity was tied up with being a doctor's wife. A year later, dressed in blue jeans, a sweater, and a new, very becoming hairdo, she appeared at one of our Intensives, flirting, laughing, enthusiastically describing the new career she was preparing for. She grinned at Nathaniel and said, "If you had dared to tell me then that I would be where I am today, feeling what I am feeling now, I think I'd have thrown you out the window."

As happens in most cases of this kind, a fear of change intensified her desire to remain in a relationship that her partner was ready to end. She was afraid she might not be able to evolve with changing circumstances; she was afraid she might turn out to be no one at all without her husband. Though the end of her marriage was a great loss, unquestionably she became a healthier and more admirable woman for having overcome her fears. Her case illustrates perfectly what we meant earlier about seeing change as a threat or as an opportunity for growth.

A word on behalf of the partner who feels that the relationship has become wrong for him or her: if my life and well-being require that I leave, I do not need to prove that the relationship is also wrong for you. If it is wrong for me, it is wrong. And facing it will require honesty, courage, and integrity from us both.

Q. My partner experiences my growth as a threat to our relationship and often appears to be sabotaging my efforts to evolve. What am I to do if I don't want to stop growing and I don't want to see my relationship destroyed?

A. The desire for permanence, especially when we are deeply happy, is thoroughly understandable, but we can't hold a moment forever. Love can be the most nearly permanent thing in our life; still, it is subject to change and motion like everything in the universe.

Sometimes a couple breaks up not because their growth and development require it, as they may tell themselves, but because one of them fought the process of the other's evolution. One of them tried to freeze a moment that had vanished, lacking the flexibility and inner security to allow the change to emerge. One resisted learning what new possibilities might open for them both.

To quote from *The Psychology of Romantic Love:*

> A man may have held the same job for fifteen years; suddenly or not so suddenly he is dissatisfied, he is bored, he feels unfulfilled—he wants a new challenge. His wife is bewildered and frightened. What will happen? Will they be as financially secure as they were in the past? Why is he losing interest in their friends? Why has he taken to reading so much? Is he going to become interested in other women next? She panics. When he tries to explain his feelings, she does not listen. She is terrified of losing what she has. And out of her terror she proceeds to lose it.
>
> A husband complains that his wife is scatterbrained, that she cannot even balance her checkbook. He loves her, he says, but how he wishes she were more mature! Something happens; through some mysterious process of growth he had not noticed, she becomes more responsible. She takes an interest in his business. She asks intelligent questions. She decides to start a business of her own. He is devastated; what has happend to the wonderful little girl he was so happy with? She looks into his eyes and sees an enemy, the enemy of her self-realization. She wants his love, she wants their marriage, but she wants to be a human being too. Shall she revert to being a little girl again—and hate her husband for the rest of her life? Shall she continue to fight for her own development—and drive her husband away? These are the kind of hard and painful choices that many a couple has to face.

We can help our partner understand our growth by doing everything in our power to share the process with him or her, talking about what it is like from the inside. We can seek to involve our partner in our adventure. If our partner is willing, we can welcome his or her participation as we expand our internal resources or cultivate new ones, test and challenge ourselves in new ways, explore unfamiliar aspects of life, discard habits, beliefs, and lifestyles that no longer seem appropriate—our growth will enrich our partner as well as ourselves.

We can invite our partner to talk about any of his or her fears relating to our new dreams and aspirations, and we can listen with empathy, compassion, and respect. Without apology or attack, we remain steadfast in our right to growth—and in our love for our partner. We allow our partner to see that the first does not undermine the second.

Every relationship is a system. And when one part in a system changes, the other parts must also change to maintain equilibrium. If I am growing and my partner is resisting growth, we have disequilibrium. Then there must follow a resolution or a divorce, or worse than a divorce: a long, slow disintegration.

If my partner tries to sabotage my growth, I have no choice but to point this out, calmly if possible, and refuse to cooperate.

When a woman we know went back to school to train for a career, her husband made jokes and belittling remarks: "How is the schoolgirl? What did you do during recess today? Did you play volleyball?" The wife chose not to respond but talked cheerfully about what she was learning. She sought unsuccessfully to convey to her husband some of her own excitement. Finally she said to him, "I'd like you to notice that you are making fun of my efforts to learn. That hurts. It's not going to stop me, but it hurts. Why do you do it?"

He got out from under her question for the moment. Later he began to ridicule her again. Again she drew his behavior to his attention. Eventually he confessed: "The truth is I'm scared. I'm very scared. Things were great the way they used to be. I don't want to lose you."

"Every time you make fun of me," she said to him, "you antagonize me. You don't draw me closer."

"I know," he sighed.

They came for marriage counseling, where he had the opportunity to explore his fears and insecurities. Today he boasts about his wife's accomplishments. If we have the self-confidence and the wisdom to be the friend of our partner's growth, then growth is no threat. If we set ourselves against it, we invite tragedy.

"From the day I began teaching at college," one woman told us, "my husband started chasing other women. I understood his motive. His ego was shattered and needed rebuilding, but nothing I could say helped. He wanted me to choose between him and teaching, and I lost respect for him. I thought there was more to him than that. When we divorced, I cried—not for the man I was leaving but for the man I thought I had married."

To quote once again from *The Psychology of Romantic Love*:

> Our greatest chance of permanence lies in our ability to handle change. Love has the greatest chance to endure when it does not fight the flow of life but learns to join with it.
>
> If my partner and I feel that we are truly the friends of each other's growth, then that is one more bond between us, one more force to support and strengthen our love. If my partner and I feel that, out of fear or bewilderment, we make ourselves the enemy of each other's growth, then that is but a short step from feeling that each is the enemy of the other's *self*.

The decision to share my life with another person is a decision to share a journey, to share an adventure, not to lock ourselves away in some false Eden.

In premarital counseling, we invite a couple to talk about their feelings toward change and growth in the future, stressing that such a change and growth are inevitable. Can this be frightening at times? Of course. But without them, where would be life's excitement? Where would be the stimulation that keeps love vital?

Eleven
Marriage, Children, Relatives

Although many of the questions and answers presented in this book contain references to marriage, our primary focus throughout has been on the romantic love relationship, not on marriage as such. We have tried to confine ourselves as much as possible to the essentials of a mutual commitment between man and woman, whether or not they are legally husband and wife.

Now it is time to address ourselves to a few questions that deal specifically with marriage, children, and the wider family setting in which man/woman relationships usually take place. Children and relatives could fill an entire book on the challenges of romantic love, though considerations of space confine us to only a few basics here.

Contrary to some reports, marriage is not going out of style. More people are marrying than at any other time in our history. Still, the question about marriage we hear most frequently, from men and women, is why marry?

Q. My partner and I are very much in love. We live together and feel totally committed to each other. We do not plan to have children. Why should we get married?

A. Marriage is not an obligation; it is a choice. As we see it, the essence of marriage is not legal but psychological. Through marriage, one of the most enduring of human institutions, we give external expression (social objectification) to the inner experience of commitment.

To quote from *The Psychology of Romantic Love:*

> When two people wish to commit themselves to each other, to share their joys and their struggles, and when they wish to make a statement to the world around them about the nature of their relationship, to give it social objectivity, they look to the form or structure of a marriage agreement as a means through which to express, solemnize, and objectify their choice. The institution of marriage, certainly as it exists today, is a response to our desire for and perhaps need of, structure. This does not mean that every couple who fall in love automatically think of marriage; many do not. More and more couples currently are choosing to live together without marriage in the legal sense. But if and when they do choose to marry, I think their motive is best understood in terms of a very human, very natural longing for structure.
>
> We can acknowledge the legal and financial considerations that often make marriage desirable, considerations having to do with the protection of children, questions of inheritance, and so forth. These practical considerations can obviously be important. But I do not believe they represent, for most people, the essence of marriage or the ultimate grounds for its existence. . . .

Though more and more men and women are choosing to live together without marriage, the fact remains that when the relationship reaches a certain level of commitment, the overwhelming majority choose to marry. Marriage seems to answer fairly basic human needs.

This observation by itelf should not persuade anyone to marry who doesn't wish to. Men and women who are sufficiently self-aware may recognize that they would not be comfortable with a long-term commitment and would be unlikely to sustain it. They wisely avoid marriage despite familial or social pressures. We need to know who we are before we fit ourselves into social roles. Marriage as social objectification involves making a statement to society, not giving in to society.

We know a man and woman who have been living together happily for seven years. Both have unhappy marriages behind them. We cannot imagine how they would act differently if they were legally married. But they choose not to be. They deflect any inquiries on the subject of marriage. Why should anyone insist that they change?

So much for our objective answer. We would now like to respond more personally.

Nathaniel: I love being married. I love the sense of structure and of sanctuary. The phrase "my wife," the most thrilling in the world to me, evokes my soulmate, my other self, my mirror, my spiritual partner.

When I knew how much I loved Devers, I knew I wanted us to be married, even though the pain of Patrecia's death was still with me. We were living together and could have gone on living together without marriage. But there was some powerful drive in me to make my feeling for Devers manifest: this is my woman; this is my choice; this is the human being who means more to me than anyone else in the world. I wanted my life to be organized in every possible way around my love for Devers. Once again I am back to the theme of structure and social objectification.

For some time, Devers was reluctant to marry, not because she doubted her feelings for me, but because she wondered whether I should have a period of testing and freedom before undertaking a new commitment. I knew what I wanted: a new beginning, a new commitment, a rebirth symbolized in marriage.

Devers: I had been single for fifteen years when I met Nathaniel and did not expect to marry again. My children were grown and neither Nathaniel nor I had any thought of starting a new family. When I decided to marry him, friends and family asked me why. I was financially self-sufficient and had been through most of my adult life. Being single had never troubled me. Living with Nathaniel, I was already happier than I had ever been. They wondered why we were not content to let things go on just as they were.

It wasn't easy to explain. Independence was my natural state. I had achieved a good deal of success and recognition in what people call "a man's world," and I knew something about how to create joy for myself. But I had never known the desire to say yes to a man from my deepest soul. I experienced the desire to surrender to my deepest emotions for the first time with Nathaniel. Marriage was the way to acknowledge and celebrate these feelings, and the day of our wedding, I made my statement to the whole world, to myself, and to Nathaniel.

This is what marriage means to me. If it means any less, I suspect we are ill-advised to marry.

It is not a good idea to marry because it would make Mother and Father happy.

It is not a good idea to marry because of pregnancy.

It is not a good idea to marry to prove that we are normal.

Then why marry? Marry because it is the best way to objectively enact your deepest feelings. Marry because it is the only sufficient expression of your commitment to another.

Q. Why would a person be afraid of marriage?

A. First of all, we refer you to Chapter 1, where we answered the question "Why do some people seem frightened of love?" Everything there applies there. As to fear of marriage in particular, the best way to respond is to list some of the sentence completions we hear for "The scary thing about marriage is_____":

every married couple I know is unhappy.

I won't be Daddy's little girl anymore.

the breakup of a marriage hurts worse than the breakup of an affair.

it would make Mother unhappy.

it's too hard, always having to think of the feelings of another person.

I like keeping my options open.

I won't belong to myself anymore.

*nobody could love me if they saw what I was like day by
day.*

I couldn't trust myself to be faithful.

I don't want to be responsible for a whole family.

I can't be sure my partner won't be unfaithful.

happiness doesn't last.

This list suggests that we need to penetrate to the roots
of our fear, to understand its cause. We may arrive at
some kind of resolution by exploring our feelings with our
lover or with a friend. Or we may need the assistance of a
psychotherapist.

By way of practical advice, we can only suggest a place
to begin. When the issue comes up in our premarital
counseling, we ask the couple to do a string of sentence
completions, beginning with the stem "The good thing
about getting married is_____" and following up with
"The bad thing about getting married is_____." We try to
elicit at least fifteen endings for each stem. Sometimes we
suggest that, instead of speaking aloud, they write out the
sentence completions in a notebook.

Readers who wish to experiment will find the exercise
clarifying; almost always it brings out major concerns that
linger beneath immediate consciousness. Sometimes awareness is enough to open the path toward resolution. A
woman found through sentence completion that she had
a great many things to say in favor of marrying her lover,
the strongest point against it being the possibility of hurting her mother (whose marriage was unhappy). Once she
understood what choice she was actually making, she
went ahead with the wedding. After four-and-a-half years
of marriage, she seems satisfied with her decision.

Q. I am in love and perfectly happy living with my
partner and I feel no interest in marriage. My
partner is eager to get married. Would I be wrong to
accommodate him (her)?

A. First we need to establish what marriage signifies
both to the partner who wishes to marry and to
the one who doesn't. To find out, there is no better

exercise than the sentence completions just mentioned, plus "Marriage, to me, means_____." Each partner works alone with a notebook, writing ten or fifteen endings for each stem and then comparing their responses. The comparison will form a basis for further exploration into their feelings and attitudes.

The person who wishes to get married may discover, for example, that the chief motive is to bind the partner to the relationship, the desire for marriage being a disguised fear of abandonment. He or she may then decide that doubt is not a valid reason for marriage.

The partner disinclined to marry may discover that marriage signifies social conformity or compliance with parental wishes. Having never considered marriage apart from the family and social pressures attached to it, this partner may then decide that there are good reasons to marry.

We are reluctant to recommend that anyone marry, no matter how much in love, when there is any resistance to marriage. If the marriage makes sense for a couple, it should not be that difficult to explore the ground of the resistance and to resolve it. To "accommodate" your partner without such exploration would probably be a mistake.

The following story illustrates why we should not brush aside or suppress a disinclination to marriage. After living together for five years, the man wanted to marry, the woman didn't. When asked to talk about her reasons, she said, "I love him with all my heart—that's not the problem. I just don't believe in marriage. Mom and Dad got divorced. Just about every couple I know seems to be getting divorced. There's something about marriage that doesn't work. I don't know why or what it is. Anyway, who needs it?"

Some time later, frictions that had been more or less dormant became quarrels over what they wanted out of life. Eventually they broke up. "I loved him, but I didn't always respect him. He was willing to float along, never really going anywhere. He treated me wonderfully. He was kind, thoughtful—an angel. One day that just wasn't enough. You want more.

"All my talk about marriage was just a way of avoiding what really bothered me. I'd like to get married one day, if I find the right man. Somewhere inside I always knew that the relationship with him, even though it went on for five years, was not meant to be forever. It was okay, because I cared for him more than anyone else I knew, but I didn't feel the kind of love you need for marriage. So I talked about not believing in marriage."

We suspect that this is a fairly common pattern.

A disinclination to marry may have any of several motives; whatever the motive, we need to examine it before we get to the altar.

Q. Will marriage change the quality of our relationship?

A. Sometimes hope accompanies this question, sometimes fear. People may marry in the belief that their problems will disappear after the wedding, or they may avoid marriage because they fear the wedding as an end of something precious in their relationship.

If a man and woman continually fight and frustrate each other while having an affair or living together, the odds are high that they will continue to fight and frustrate each other after the ceremony. Even worse, they may feel trapped.

If a man and woman have a strong and healthy relationship before marriage, then formalizing their commitment may lead them to a deeper and more satisfying experience of the relationship. It happened for us and for others we know. Saying "I do," with an awareness of everything it implies, may intensify love and devotion.

A friend said to us recently, "Because we had lived together for three years, neither my girlfriend nor I thought getting married would make any difference in how we felt. And for the first few months of marriage, I would have sworn it didn't. But, you know, something changes, something subtle that's hard to put into words. It's as if the relationship has grown deeper roots."

The fear that marriage may hurt a relationship often finds expression in one or more related apprehensions: that we may take each other for granted, that we will stay with each other out of duty, or that we have no choice but remaining in the relationship. If a man or a woman perceives marriage in this way, then of course the relationship may suffer. But the suffering is caused by the meaning of marriage for individuals; it is not intrinsic to marriage.

A couple who married after years of living together told us, "We took another vow, before the wedding. If we're not as happy married as we were before, we've sworn we'll get divorced and go back to living together again. We've had a great thing going, and we're not going to let anything wreck it, including marriage." We would guess that their attitude is itself protection against marriage wrecking their relationship.

All of us have heard stories of couples who got on marvelously for years, married and broke up with considerable disappointment and bitterness. Some people, perhaps, are unable or unwilling to make the adjustments and accommodations that marriage requires; they can love only while they feel single. But a man and a woman who have been together for some time may get married because they sense their relationship is in jeopardy. Marriage will save them somehow. When it doesn't, the marriage takes the blame.

Will marriage change the quality of a relationship? Everything affects the quality of the relationship. Change is inevitable. Marriage can provide a context for growth or for deterioration; it depends on the attitudes and behavior of the couple, not on the institution.

Q. My partner says our lives before marriage won't exist anymore after we are married. I am afraid I won't be able to talk about my experiences or bring my friends into my new life. Should I get married with this issue unresolved?

A. Emphatically, no.
If our partner tells us that everything that happened prior to our marriage "does not exist," he or she is asking us to disown our life—our memories, our friends, our struggles, our attainments, our values, everything that made us and makes us who we are. The issue is the same as in the last two questions of Chapter 5, which also have to do with our attitude toward our partner's past.

This particular case sounds to us like tyranny, which is incompatible with romantic love, and suggests a lack of self-esteem, in both the person who would make such a demand and in the person willing to accept it.

We know a young woman who thought her partner couldn't be serious, couldn't possibly mean it, and anyway she could straighten him out later. After they were married she was stunned to hear him tell one of her girlfriends, "I can't have you in our house. You're part of my wife's past." Eight months of marriage and two months of therapy later, the couple divorced. This is not an issue to debate after the wedding. It is an issue reasonable people need to resolve before they can even think of a wedding.

Q. What issues absolutely need to be settled before marriage?

A. We can't answer absolutely because the issue that is most important to one individual will be less important to another. We have different hierarchies of values. Let's approach this matter in a different way.

In considering marriage, ask yourself this question: if my partner were to remain essentially as he or she is now in attitude and behavior, can I see myself living happily? Or am I assuming that after the wedding he or she will change? While particular changes are always possible, they are by no means guaranteed. In contemplating marriage we need to be able to see ourselves happy with our partner *as he or she is*, not as he or she might be.

Marrying in haste, we lack the opportunity to learn the whole range of our partner's attitudes and to learn which are really important to our happiness—matters of personal character, implicit or explicit views of male/female relationships, attitudes toward intimacy, emotional communication, sex, money, recreation, friends, work and leisure, children, ways of expressing love and affection, ways of handling anger and other painful emotions, ways of responding to conflict, and so forth. All of these are matters we are wise to explore prior to marriage.

Given sufficient opportunity to talk and reflect, we may decide that we can live happily with certain traits, only to discover later that we can't. Or we may decide to accept certain of our partner's traits but overestimate our tolerance. We are none of us infallible. Being aware of such considerations, we at least give ourselves a better chance.

Q. I am very much in love with someone who says and shows he (she) is in love with me, too. He (she) is frightened of marriage, because of a painful marriage in the past. Is there any way to reach my partner on this issue?

A. A man and woman we know were very much in love. Having gone through an extremely painful marriage when he was young, the man swore he would never marry again. The woman loved him and wanted to be married but was willing to live with him on any terms he proposed, with or without marriage. Her simplicity and sincerity, her total commitment to him without the pressure to marry, so touched him that after a year of living together he insisted they marry.

Another man and woman we know found themselves in a similar predicament, except that it was the woman who opposed marriage. The man decided to give the relationship everything he could for a year, to be as kind, loving, and devoted as possible. If the woman was still against marriage after that year, he would end the relationship. She remained adamant and they parted. Seven months later she married another man.

When a person says, "I do not want to get married," he or she may not be aware—or may choose not to acknowledge—that it often means "I do not wish to be married to you."

Another man announced he would never marry because of the financial losses he had suffered through a previous marriage. His partner suggested a prenuptial agreement that would protect him against any such losses if their relationship failed. He promptly agreed. As of this writing, they have been married for three years.

Is your partner able to change his or her mind on the subject of marriage? That's worth finding out if you want to marry.

First, never quarrel with your partner's fears. Encourage your partner to express his or her feelings as openly and in as much detail as possible, perhaps using the sentence-completion exercises recommended earlier, and listen with attention and respect. Give your partner the opportunity to think the matter through on his or her own. Allow your partner to learn that he or she can trust you, is safe with you. Don't withdraw your love or coerce your partner into acting against his or her feelings.

If marriage is important to you, you may reach a point where the wisest thing to do is let go, accepting that marriage with this person is impossible, or at least impossible for you. This is the last decision we want to reach, and the hardest one. If you are in love and you are convinced your partner is in love with you, don't hasten to despair.

Q. I am forty-five years old and have never been married. I have never known intense love, much to my regret. Is it necessarily wrong to marry for companionship or even for financial security?

A. We think that it's wrong to deceive the person we marry, pretending a passion we do not feel. Where there is open recognition of the motives and considerations involved, only the man and woman can determine whether such a marriage is suitable for them.

We consider love the ideal basis for marriage, assuming psychological maturity. Given a choice between marrying for companionship and marrying for financial security, we think the former motive has a better chance of leading to some measure of happiness.

People who do not wish to take financial responsibility for their own existence generally lack self-reliance, and such people are usually not rewarding to deal with, let alone live with. A longing for companionship is more likely to yield a genuine exchange of affection, nurturing, kindness; it is far richer ground for discovering shared experiences that will be pleasurable.

Age makes a difference here. A twenty-year-old who spoke of marrying for companionship, in the absence of love, would raise many questions in our minds. A young person marrying for companionship or financial security must lack self-esteem so acutely that the relationship would have almost no chance.

As a charming example of the opposite tendency, we heard recently from a reader and admirer of Nathaniel's books, a gentleman of sixty-three. He arranged a long-distance telephone therapy appointment with Nathaniel to discuss the advisability of marrying for companionship. The woman was fifty-seven. They had been going together for three years.

"I am fond of her," the man said, "and she seems to like me quite a lot, and we get along just fine. I was madly in love once, when I was young. I know what that feels like, and this isn't it. I enjoy her company and I think it might be pleasant for us to live together."

"So why not just live together without marriage?" asked Nathaniel.

"Well," he said, "that would be fine with me and fine with her, but you see she's got children from a previous marriage and so have I, and I think that would embarrass them."

Sentence completion seemed appropriate at this point. Nathaniel gave him the stem "If I didn't have to think about our children's feelings_____."

His endings were rapid and consistent: "I'd have been living with her a year ago; we could just go our own merry way; we wouldn't be bothering about—." The man stopped abruptly. "Thank you very much, Dr. Branden. I don't think we'll be sending out wedding invitations."

Some people need only a little help in recognizing what they already know.

Q. **All my life I have heard that children are essential to the perfect fulfillment of romantic love. Do you agree?**

A. It is not hard to understand why two people who love each other would want to share the adventure of creating a new human life. But no, that experience is not essential to the fulfillment of romantic love.

There are men and women who will say their love reached a new level of fulfillment when they brought a child into the world. But there are other men and women, no less in love, who lead intensely fulfilled lives without children. When a couple thinks children are important to the relationship, children tend to be important; otherwise, not.

We should have children only for the right reasons: not out of a sense of duty, not to prove our femininity or masculinity, not to please our parents or friends, and not as insurance for our old age. If we are excited at the prospect of bringing new life into the world; inspired by the role of teaching; challenged by the responsibility of sustaining, guiding, and then releasing an independent human being; and if we truly know and feel that we have the time and love to spend on another life—then having and raising children can be a magnificently enriching experience.

In too many relationships, children obstruct rather than fulfill romantic love, and most couples find they must protect their love in some ways against the demands of raising children. Contrary to the popular myth, studies indicate that children do not help a marriage on the average but tend to make it harder for the marriage to proceed happily. Friction tends to increase with the birth of the first child and tends to decrease when the last child leaves home. Couples who plan to have children and preserve their romantic relationship should consider in advance exactly where the role of parent is going to conflict with the role of lover. If either partner has a serious doubt, the couple should probably not have children yet.

Couples in love who choose not to have children are often accused of selfishness, of wanting to live only for themselves. Papal condemnation of birth control, for instance, hangs on the charge of "selfishness." The implication is that our lives do belong not to us but to our families, to society, and to God. Our own happiness is not a proper moral purpose, so we have to justify our relationship (and our existence) by the production of offspring. We believe that a successful romantic relationship is its own justification. The idea that having children is a duty rather than a choice is fundamentally inconsistent with romantic love as we understand it.

A woman came to Devers for a consultation because she wondered if something was wrong with her and her husband. Through eleven years of marriage, neither had ever desired a family. She and her husband had always en-

joyed a satisfying relationship with a lifestyle that children
would have made difficult or impossible. Friends and
family kept asking when and if they planned to have
children; the woman's childbearing years were running
out. She and her husband both felt a mild guilt over their
lack of interest in children.

Devers asked, "Apart from whether it's right or wrong,
do you and your husband want to have children?"

"No," the woman replied firmly.

"Do you think it's right," Devers asked, "to bring children into the world when you don't want them?"

"Our lack of interest could mean something is wrong
with us," the woman said.

"Do you believe anything is wrong with either one of
you?"

"Our parents do."

"Do you?" Devers repeated.

"Do you?" the woman asked Devers.

"If you think this should be settled by vote, we'd better
call a few more people in here." The woman began to
laugh, so Devers pushed on. "If you like, I can telephone
my mother and a few of my aunts and uncles and ask
them all what they think."

Devers walked her over to the mirror and asked her to
play her mother giving a lecture on why she had no right
not to have children. The woman launched into: "Every
woman should have children. What's the matter with
you? Who do you think you are, being so selfish? Don't
think it was always fun for your father and me. There
were a lot of things we couldn't do because we were
taking care of you and your brothers. Why should you . . ."

"Go on," said Devers.

Her voice went low with fury. *"Why should you get off
easier than I did?"*

The woman turned to Devers in astonishment. "Wow!"

"Wow," said Devers.

Q. I want to have children and my future spouse
doesn't. Is it safe for us to marry with this question unresolved?

A. No. This issue is important to both of you. Do not
assume that it will all sort itself out later. People

change their minds. Men and women marry deciding they want to have children and decide later they don't want them. They also marry with no intention of having children, deciding later they want children after all. But don't count on it. And don't wait until after marriage to discuss a difference that will affect the rest of your lives, directly or indirectly, in just about every possible aspect.

Suppose you can't reach a resolution and marriage is your first priority. The person who wants to have children should be willing to forgo that desire if he or she cannot persuade the partner, now or later, because it is wrong to bring a child into the world unwanted.

Even with an agreement about children prior to marriage, one or the other partners may change his or her mind. Just as it is inadvisable to marry unless both parties are enthusiastic, we think it is inadvisable to have children without enthusiasm. Agreeing to have a child to accommodate our partner is an act of cruelty, crippling the child and eventually the relationship itself.

In spite of our best efforts, the question may raise itself in all sorts of unforeseen ways, putting the relationship in jeopardy. What if a couple discovers that they can't have children and only one partner favors adoption? What if the man is sterile and the woman wants to bear a child, but the man feels uncomfortable about artificial insemination?

It isn't possible to resolve all such matters prior to the wedding. We are back to negotiation, as we always are sooner or later, because conflict is woven into the very fabric of our existence. We need to struggle for answers in such a way as to protect romantic love and at the same time respect our other values and needs. We have to struggle as best we can.

Q. How can I involve my husband more actively in caring for and raising our children?

A. The time to ask this question is when a couple first considers having children. They need to discuss how they see their respective roles and how much each is prepared to contribute. Unfortunately, few couples do so, and by the time this question is asked, the father is already out of the picture as far as raising the children is concerned.

The first step toward a solution is communicating that there is a problem.

"I would love to have more participation from you in bringing up our children. They love you and they need you. I want them to have a male influence. You have something to give them I cannot give them. I need help. I feel abandoned at times when I don't get it."

Some fathers become more responsive when they see they are *needed*, as a father as well as a relief man.

If his resistance continues, we might say, "I feel incapable of raising the children competently alone. What do you think we should do? Are there any circumstances or conditions under which you would be willing to participate more in raising our children?"

Now we are moving into an area where the principles of effective communication set forth earlier in the book apply fully.

One ingenious mother instituted an after-dinner event she called Family Roundtable Discussion Time. Before anyone rose from the table, she encouraged the children to talk about their day, ask questions of Mother or Father, discuss any problems, communicate gripes, air differences with siblings, talk about anything, ask about anything. The general rule was "There are no forbidden thoughts and no forbidden feelings." Later, each child chose a parent to put him or her to bed on that particular night. The procedure made it impossible for Father not to participate.

When we told this story at an Intensive two years ago, another woman added an interesting idea for reorienting a somewhat reluctant father. She taught her family sentence-completion exercises. At the dinner table, Father heard sentence completions beginning with such stems as "One of the things I want from you, Daddy, and don't know how to ask for is_____"; he surrendered willingly to his children's love and need for him. (While this woman's success is intriguing, we must warn against the danger of involving the children inappropriately. Sentence completion is a tool of communication, not coercion.)

Fathers are generally more willing to participate in the fun of raising children than in the mundane and messy aspects. This selective participation is easy to resent, but it can provide a basis from which to expand the father's role. While cuddling the baby, for example, he may be open to the idea of changing the baby, if the suggestion is made without resentment.

However, cultural tradition and upbringing play a powerful part in determining how a man perceives his role as a father. Attitudes change slowly. We suspect that each succeeding generation of fathers will find it a bit more comfortable to help with the children than the preceding generation.

"Do you feel it was ordained by nature that changing diapers should be woman's work?" one wife asked her husband.

"No," he replied.

"Then would you be willing to help me sometimes?"

He gulped, "Sure."

She laughed, telling us about it. "I took one look at his face, at the pained expression he was trying so hard to conceal, and I decided it just wasn't worth it. Oh well."

Q. My husband feels jealous of the time I spend with our children. How can I deal with this?

A. As always, we begin by inviting our partner to air his or her feelings, without arguing, counterattacking, or becoming defensive.

It may be well to remember how Jane solved that problem in the old Tarzan movie where they "find" a son, Boy. At first Tarzan is a little put out by Jane's involvement with the child. Sensing this, Jane almost immediately engages Tarzan in caring for the child. She leaves them alone together, so that Boy becomes their son and not merely hers.

When a wife is feeling a little frustrated with her husband, she turns naturally enough to the new baby for comfort, and the husband senses the raising of some mysterious barrier. One husband complained to us, "I felt as if I wasn't needed anymore, as if I had served my purpose. From the moment she became pregnant, my wife became preoccupied with her own body. With all the attention she was getting, I felt it wasn't our baby, it was her baby."

If her husband shows signs of jealousy, the woman should ask herself if she is doing anything to provoke jealousy. Let her also ask her husband, "Am I doing anything that makes you feel excluded? Do you feel that I love and care about you less than I used to?"

Once again, we stress the importance of engaging our partner in the search for a solution. "It's a fact that the baby needs time and attention. We also need time and attention for ourselves. What would you like to have us do?"

When I was pregnant with my younger daughter Lori and taking care of my daughter Vicki, I noticed one day that my husband was acting almost like a child, following me around, almost hanging on my apron strings. When I asked him what he was feeling, he replied, "Left out."

That was all it took. I spoke of my love for him more often. I became more attentive, more aware of his adjustment to the arrival of the second child. I created time when he and I could be alone together. After Lori was born, I would say, "I had fun today, swimming and playing with the kids, but I was wishing you were there. I missed you." I kept our communications centered around him and me as much as possible. I was always a wife first, a mother second.

I did not allow the children to exhaust me so much that I had no time or energy to be his lover and companion. That had to be paramount, not only for his sake but for mine.

No matter how much we love our children, every parent has to recognize that children can endanger the romance in a marriage. When a mother begins thinking of herself as a mother first, the marriage is in trouble—at least, the kind of marriage we would admire.

At a recent Intensive, a young woman offered an interesting perspective on this subject. She said, "I learned a lot about how to be a woman from my mother. I love the fact that she loved my father as much as she did, that she was physically affectionate, even. . . . How shall I express this? Cheerfully sexual, if you know what I mean. I didn't feel neglected, but I did feel that Dad was the supreme thing in her life. Seeing her happiness was an inspiration for me."

Q. **How can we respond to our child's jealousy when my partner and I express affection for each other?**

A. A child who reacts with jealousy at the sight of Mother and Father kissing, hugging, or holding hands is almost certainly a child who is feeling left out and insecure. The first step, then, is to give the child the experience of being fully loved and treasured. We create that experience by creating time focused solely on the child's interests and needs.

How parents react to jealousy has a great deal to do with whether it disappears or escalates. We have the power to diminish jealousy, and we have the power to reinforce it. We need to be aware of which we are doing. By way of illustration, we offer the following two stories.

A couple and their two children visited us for the weekend at our home in Lake Arrowhead. There were plenty of activities to keep the children cheerfully occupied, but the older child, a girl of nine, somehow knew whenever Mother and Father had their arms around each other. She would rush into the room to interrupt, infallibly. In a voice of thinly disguised irritation, one of her parents would say, "Honey,"—a sigh of exhaustion—"can't you . . ."—a sigh of exasperation—"can't you find something to do? Go down and watch television, or do something with your books . . . or something." And the daughter would reply by whining. "No, it's boring. Everything here is boring. I want you to come and play with me."

After several variations on this theme, Nathaniel cut in gently. "Sweetheart, your parents have come up here to spend time with us. We need to be by ourselves for a while. I think you can find a way to keep yourself entertained." She paused to see if her parents would say anything. She made a clown's face and said, "Oh, well," and walked away. A few minutes later we heard her playing downstairs.

On another occasion a couple brought their eight-year-old son on a visit. We four were playing music and dancing in the living room. The boy kept jumping between his parents, interrupting and demanding attention. The father laughed and pulled the boy in to include him in the dancing. When the music stopped, his mother smiled down on him and said, "Now scram. Right now this room is for grownups. You brought twelve million things with you to do up here. Go do one of them."

"But Mom."

His mother bent down to press her nose against his. "Listen. Mom and Dad love each other. Got that?"

"Yeah."

"And this is our time. Got that?"

"Yeah."

"See you later," said his father. And the boy withdrew to the lower level of the house. No arguments, no reproaches, no yielding to the child's manipulations: love, respect, and firmness were enough to handle the situation. Later, we all had dinner together, and the boy was laughing with no trace of resentment or jealousy in his manner.

The first couple reinforced their child's jealousy and her misbehavior. The second couple dealt with the jealousy and the misbehavior in turn, with much better results. The second couple didn't end the problem forever, but they demonstrated a pattern of response that will, in time, dissolve a child's jealousy.

Q. Sometimes I'm a little bit jealous of my husband's relationship with our daughter, just as he is a little jealous of my relationship with our son. We wonder about the meaning of this and how we might best deal with it.

A. To begin with, we are most likely to be jealous of our partner's relationship to a child when we feel that our child is receiving some form of care, attention, or nurturing we are not. This comes out very clearly in therapy when we hear a husband say, "She has more energy and enthusiasm for our son than she has for me," or when we hear a mother say, "He is more responsive to our daughter than to me."

If our partner is jealous, the difficulty probably lies not in the relationship to the child but in the relationship between husband and wife. Sentence-completion exercises may help bring the issue into the open: "One of the things I want from you and don't know how to get is_____" or "One of the things you give our daughter (son) I wish you would give me is_____."

When a husband and wife have been hurting each other for a long time, they may direct their unmet needs, unconsciously or consciously, at one of their children, often a child of the opposite sex. We see the problem of the so-called Oedipus complex originating far more often with the parent than with the child. A frustrated wife says to her son, "You're Mommy's little man." A frustrated husband says to his daughter, "You're Daddy's number one girl."

The children are generally quite unprepared to cope with emotional needs in their parents. Feeling that Mommy or Daddy wants something they are powerless to provide can produce helplessness or inadequacy in dealings with the opposite sex as these children grow older.

This problem exists in its most acute form when a parent, sexually frustrated or insecure, behaves seductively toward a child, evoking sexual feelings in the child which distort his or her development. If the child becomes "hooked," participating unconsciously in a "romance" with the parent of the opposite sex, it is no wonder the other parent feels distress, even if he or she does not fully understand what is happening.

The point is that we cannot afford to ignore jealousy when its causes and consequences are so serious for parents and child alike. The possibility for a solution lies entirely in the willingness of the adults to confront their frustration and examine its effects on their relationship to their children.

Counseling a couple who were caught in this problem, we gave the mother the sentence stem "One of the things I get from our son that I don't get from you is_____." Her endings included:

he adores me.

he enjoys being held.

we play together.

I can let out my affection with him.

he enjoys my attention.

I feel someone loves me all the way.

These endings were sufficient to make her husband aware that they were sitting on a powder keg. Further therapy was indicated.

There is one other aspect of jealousy we want to comment on: children can provoke jealousy in their parents. A little girl can feel very flattered, and very powerful, at the thought that she gives Daddy something Mommy does not; a little boy can find it intoxicating, if somewhat frightening, that Mommy sometimes turns to him in preference to Daddy. Having once noticed their power, some children play one parent against the other, igniting jealousy and effectively controlling life in the home. It is a thoroughly understandable survival strategy, given a child's view of the world, but it is not a strategy to cooperate with.

Avoid any temptation to make a child an ally in conflicts with your partner. Don't make your child the confidant to your conjugal unhappiness. Understand and respect a child's needs for *parents*, not symbolic lovers.

Q. My wife consults her parents on everything we do. If we quarrel, she discusses it with them. I don't know how to deal with their continual presence in our marriage.

A. This problem almost certainly reflects a lack of maturity in the person still attached to his or her parents; in more technical terms, it reveals a lack of adequate separation and individuation.

Deal with the situation by communicating your unhappiness and frustration. Tell your partner that you feel uncomfortable when she shares with her parents what you regard as the intimate, private business of your marriage. Invite her to do some sentence completions: "The good thing about telling Mother and Father everything is_____." Chances are her answers will speak for themselves and will perhaps shock her a little:

it keeps me their little girl.

I can feel young.

I have a place to go.

I get back at you.

I feel I have two homes.

they like to feel needed.

I'm the center of everyone's attention.

I get you angry.

I don't have to make my own decisions.

Follow up with "If I didn't keep running to my parents_____":

they might feel I wasn't their daughter anymore.

I'd have to be a woman.

I'd be on my own.

I'd lose Mother.

I'd lose Father.

we might be happier.

I'd feel free.

we would have more fun.

we'd quarrel less.

we'd really be married.

We can't lay out all the steps that might be necessary to correct the problem, but we know that men and women who have learned the basics of the sentence-completion method have solved such problems on their own.

Not long ago a husband guided his wife through some sentence completions, and she came up with just the kind of endings we listed above. She realized that she liked the idea of remaining Father's little girl. She agreed not to seek advice from her parents or discuss marital quarrels with them for one month, just to see how it felt. She anticipated anxiety but was surprised to feel relief and a new freedom. Her husband was happy to be trusted as he had never felt trusted before.

Q. My husband and I love our parents and each other's parents, but we don't want them meddling in
our lives. Is there a loving way to tell parents not to
interfere?

A. Let's begin with a simple story that involves a
one-on-one encounter between a married son and
his mother.

I (Nathaniel) remember an incident that occurred some
years ago, when I was forty, and my mother was still
living. The day before I was due to fly from Los Angeles
to New York City she telephoned me to let me know that
it was snowing in New York and I should be sure and
take galoshes. (Everyone in Beverly Hills owns a pair of
galoshes, of course.) I did not lecture my mother, I did
not protest, I did not ask why she was still treating me as
a child. "You know, Mother, I'm probably the luckiest
man on the West Coast."

"Why?" she asked.

"There must be a thousand forty-year-old men preparing to fly to New York right now, and I'll bet their moth-
ers are not phoning them from three thousand miles away
to remind them to take galoshes. I am really well looked after."

My mother laughed, something she rarely did, and
then she sighed. "I guess you know how to take care of
yourself."

Humor proved to be the best method of communication
in this case, rejecting my mother's premise without possibility of debate, and without hurting her.

One of the most common errors made by not-quite-
grownups is to announce, "I am now an adult. Please
stop treating me as if I were five years old." No full adult
ever announces that he or she is an adult. Taking it for
granted that they are grown up, they do not regard the
matter as open to debate or discussion. They are confident
enough to be relaxed and good-natured about it, if and
when their parents occasionally slip.

A number of couples have asked about parents who slip
more than occasionally, and though solutions have to be
tailored to individuals, the experience of one couple we
know should prove broadly illuminating.

After some coaching from us, they arranged a family

dinner, husband, wife, and both set of parents. As everyone sat around the table drinking coffee or tea, the son smiled benevolently at his parents and in-laws and said, "You know, it's really wonderful to have had parents who not only brought us into the world but prepared us so well for functioning as adults."

"Not everyone has the advantages we've had," the daughter added cheerfully.

"And I am absolutely convinced," the son went on, "that when loving parents give advice to their grown up children, it's always well intended, even when unnecessary."

"And I am absolutely convinced," the daughter smiled, "that you would agree that you've done a terrific job in raising us."

Both sets of parents listened with a growing sense of bewilderment.

"I can't imagine," the son said, "that loving parents would knowingly and deliberately cause their children pain, humiliation, anguish, or upset in their marriage."

"And I can't imagine," the daughter said warmly, "that parents would want their children to feel inadequate."

"If things began going wrong in a marriage," the son asked, "what parent would want to feel that he or she was partially responsible?"

"It's good to know," said the daughter, "that if we came to you for advice, you would do your best. And we would be very grateful if, in the future, you would wait for us to ask."

"I want to compliment all of you," said the son, "on having done such a fine job that now we don't need to rely so often on your counsel. I mean, some people never grow up, never learn to make decisions on their own. That must be a serious disappointment to parents who care for their children deeply."

"Anyway," the daughter concluded, "we both feel very confident that you understand and agree with what we're saying, and it's nice to feel that."

They spoke in a consistently warm, affectionate, and benevolent manner. As the couple later described the scene to us, both sets of parents went from disorientation to relaxation to pleasure. At the end they were nodding and beaming. Any future intrusion, after that evening's conversation, would become equivalent to acknowledging that they had not done a good job as parents, an admission few parents are eager to make.

Of course such dialogue sounds strange to our ears; it is not the way people ordinarily speak. Devers and I thoroughly enjoyed rehearsing them. For this family, it was the right approach; it succeeded.

With another couple we worked differently. Their parents, it seemed, would ask how things were, sifting the answer from any opportunity to give advice. They were so persistent, ignoring all requests to abstain from unsolicited advice, that we had to recommend a kind of retraining.

The moment a parent gave unsolicited advice, the son or daughter would say, "Well, I've got to go now. Talk to you again." The idea was to link the start of advice giving with the end of the conversation. Soon the parents noticed that if they wished to continue a conversation with their children, they had to abstain from giving advice.

As in the two preceding stories, the humor in the couple's strategy did not escape the parents, but it was too good natured to take offense at. We are partial to humor and benevolent noncooperation when it comes to dealing with parental interference.

Parents sometimes hang onto their children too long, not out of any ill intent but out of a desire to feel they are still connected with their children. The better we understand this longing, the less defensive and angry we feel. If we are secure in the knowledge that we are indeed grownup, we don't need to fight our parents for our independence. We can allow them a place in our existence without feeling threatened.

While loving our parents, we need to become adults in our own right; we need to say goodbye to them before we can greet the person we will fall in love with. To say goodbye in the sense we mean does not imply indifference or rejection. We merely say goodbye to the child/parent relationship as it existed when we were truly dependent on our parents for survival and well-being. Until that dependence ends, we are not ready for romantic love.

Q. I am about to get married, but my parents don't approve of my choice and are making my life miserable. Can they ruin my relationship if I marry against their wishes?

A. This depends entirely on the psychology of the individual. The more mature he or she is, the less likely it is that parental disapproval will taint the marriage.

A thirty-year-old man we know went through several bad months because his parents disapproved of the woman he had chosen to marry. The young man avoided quarrels but made his position clear one day to his father: "Look Dad, I understand that the girl I have chosen isn't one you would have chosen for yourself. She's not at all like Mom. She has different values. You're contented with the way Mom is. I wouldn't be. To be happy, I need to marry a different kind of person. The question is should I marry the woman I can be happy with or the woman you could be happy with?" His father accepted the young man's right to choose, and his mother followed shortly thereafter.

A dependent man or woman may marry against parental wishes and then subconsciously sabotage the relationship to prove the parents right, thus remaining a good boy or good girl. Again we turn to the issue of separation and individuation, essential for happiness and for success in romantic love.

We greatly admire a young woman who married a songwriter; her parents looked down on songwriters for some reason. When her father made a sarcastic crack right after the wedding, his daughter said to him, "No one is allowed to speak with disrespect about my husband in my presence. What you think is your business. But what you say about my husband in my presence is mine. Never again, Dad, or it's the end between us."

In romantic love, and certainly in marriage, my primary allegiance belongs to my partner. No other relationship ranks higher in my scale of values. I may feel hurt and disappointed if my parents cannot accept my partner, but I have already accepted my partner fully. If my parents can make me doubt, I am not ready for marriage. This is the principle of saying goodbye to my past to say hello to my present and future.

Q. My spouse spends an incredible amount of time giving help and advice to our relatives. He (she) has very little time for us. What's going on here?

A. A man who avoids his wife is very probably avoiding intimacy with his wife. The same is likely to be true when a woman avoids her husband. Sentence completion in these cases yields the same pattern of endings with remarkable consistency. "The good thing about spending so much time with relatives is_____":

I don't have to face frustrations at home.

I don't have to deal with my partner's loneliness.

I keep myself from being too vulnerable.

I don't have to look at what's wrong in our marriage.

I keep everyone at a distance.

I feel important.

I feel safe.

I work off my anger at my wife (husband).

I am in control.

I'm like a character in a story my wife (husband) can love from a distance.

After a couple has identified the problem, it is common for the person to agree that his or her behavior is wrong—and then go on doing it.

In therapy we seat the couple facing each other, and the partner who has admitted to avoiding his or her mate answers one question, "What are you willing to do to correct the situation?" After the response, the question comes back again: "And what else are you willing to do to correct the situation?" Repetition of the question provides a structure, or boundary, that prevents the couple from wandering to some other issue, and it compels the answering partner to become more and more specific about the commitment to change. We have them ask and answer the question ten, fifteen, twenty times, each time adding new details until they have enough to implement a satisfactory resolution. Since all our clients tape-record their sessions, they can review their agreement as many times as is necessary to solve the problem.

Q. Our relatives have a habit of dropping in uninvited, even after we have asked them to telephone in advance. What else can we do?

A. One couple solves this problem with admirable simplicity. They painted an elegant sign for their front door: "We do not appreciate unexpected visitors. If you have not telephoned in advance, please do not ring the doorbell."

From a strategically placed window they saw one of the relatives read the sign and ring the bell. The couple did not answer. One by one their relatives learned that the new policy was in earnest. The unexpected calls stopped.

A response of this kind requires a good deal of self-assertiveness, but then so does almost everything we have been advocating in this book.

Self-assertiveness need not be hostile; it can be cheerful and, as we have seen, even humorous. It must be firm. We must be willing to take a position and stick with it, if we respect our right to happiness.

Twelve
Letting Go

We have already noted that change and growth are inevitable in life and in love. One of the painful realities of romantic love is the possibility of having to say goodbye, because the relationship no longer works for one or both partners or because one of them has died. No discussion of romantic love is complete that does not address itself to the breakup of relationships, to the process of endings. We have to know how to let go so that we can open ourselves once more to love.

If we recognize that change and growth are the very essence of life, then we understand that two human beings pursuing separate paths of development may encounter each other at a time when their desires and needs coincide. They may share their journey over a period of years. When their paths diverge, when urgent needs and values impel them in different directions, they must part. Leaving is painful, undeniably. We want to cling, we want to hang on. We sometimes passionately resist the forces within ourselves that urge us into our future, because it is unfamiliar.

The Psychology of Romantic Love mentions an illustrative case:

> I am thinking of a romance I witnessed between a twenty-two-year-old woman and a forty-one-year-old man. He had recently come out of an unhappy marriage, she out of a highly frustrating relationship

258

with a very immature youth. Looking at the older
man, she saw a maturity she had never experienced
in a man, combined with an excitement for life that
seemed to match her own; looking at her, he saw in
her eyes an appreciation of his excitement and a
radiant excitement of her own that he had not experienced with his wife. They fell in love. For a while
they were ecstatically happy together. Time passed
and frictions slowly and subtly developed between
them. She wanted to be free, to play, to experiment—
in a word, to be young; he wanted the stability of a
firm commitment. Gradually they saw how different
were their respective stages of development and,
consequently, many of their wants and needs. They
felt compelled to say goodbye. But was their relationship a failure? I do not think they would say so.
Each one of them gave the other something beautiful, something nourishing and memorable.

It is an error to assume that a relationship is invalidated
if it does not last forever. The value of a relationship lies
in the joy it affords, not in its longevity. (There is nothing
admirable about two people remaining together, thoroughly
frustrated and miserable, for fifty years.) The ending of a
relationship does not mean that someone has failed. It
means only that someone has changed, perhaps for the
better.

As we shall see, letting go is an essential part of life in
many senses. Let us consider some of the problems it
poses.

Q. I understand that in every relationship people
have to compromise, but I want to know if there
are values that should not be compromised, not even to
save a relationship.

A. There had better be.
"I have no values I won't sacrifice to keep my
partner with me, neither my integrity nor my self-esteem
nor my mental or physical health": there is no way in the
world to reconcile such a statement with a happy love life.
A person taking this position would have to be so deficient in any sense of personal identity, so lacking in any

genuine experience of self, that we would have to wonder who was there to love or be loved.

Since the question is abstract, let us say as a matter of principle: yes, there are values we must not relinquish, not even to save a relationship.

Now we can proceed more specifically, pointing out that different people draw the line at different places, depending on their hierarchy of values. One woman told us she had tolerated her husband's drinking and verbal abuse for many years for the sake of the qualities he possessed when he was sober. When she discovered he was hitting their children, she left him, taking the children with her. A man spoke of forgiving his wife her many infidelities, but he couldn't accept her chronic lying. Another woman could put up with her husband's dishonesties in business but not with his sexual rejection of her. And so on.

We would divide personal values in two categories, optional and nonoptional. Differences in optional values are matters of preference and choice: I don't like it, but I can live with it. Differences in nonoptional values go deeper than preference and offer no real choice: accommodation entails self-destruction. Surrendering to physical abuse is the most available example of a violation of nonoptional values.

Suppose my partner lies to me about how he or she earns a living, giving absurd explanations for abrupt absences lasting days or weeks. In order to preserve the relationship, I struggle to make myself believe everything. I doubt my own awareness, I contradict my reason; in effect, I make myself crazy to keep the relationship going. Of course, it won't keep going, no matter how hard I try to cancel part of my humanity.

No relationshp is worth the sacrifice of our self-esteem. A challenge to our integrity may come in the form of a philosophical, religious, or political code, physical violence, excessive drinking, gambling, sexual humiliation. We can recognize it by the feeling of contempt it inspires in us. If our partner imposes fundamentally offensive values on us, we must challenge him or her, insist on immediate change—or else leave.

One might imagine that differences of this kind would

emerge and resolve themselves long before marriage; not so. The fear of confrontation and the hope that somehow things will work out keep too many men and women silent in situations which call for strong, unequivocal words.

For twenty-three years a woman remained with a man whom she knew it was a mistake to marry only a week after the wedding. He was an indifferent husband, a philanderer, an inveterate gambler; his sole asset appeared to be a kind of manly charm. As a girl she had been trained to be "feminine," passive, accommodating. For twenty-three years she lived in anguish, frustration, emotional impoverishment, and continual humiliation. Her self-respect receded almost to the vanishing point. In the twenty-third year of her marriage, when their son was an adult, she suffered a heart attack. Only then did she ask for a divorce. Her family was appalled and tried to change her mind.

"Every marriage has its rough spots."

"Who's that happy, anyway?"

"Marriage isn't a bowl of cherries."

She said to them, "If I don't get away from this man, I'm going to die." She got her divorce.

A man remained married for eleven years to a woman who continually rejected him sexually. She said she loved him but did not find him exciting "on a physical level." She created a beautiful home for him, she was highly regarded as a hostess, she was the picture of "a good wife"; he was quietly miserable. Infidelity did not enter his mind. He wanted her. He kept telling himself that somehow, someday, things would change.

He decided to enter therapy for personal growth. He begged his wife to join him, but she refused. In therapy the anger he felt against his wife exploded. He began to recognize the strain and rage to which he had acclimated himself. He made one last attempt to persuade his wife to join him in therapy. She refused, saying, "I don't believe in it. It's for weak people." She became hysterical when he told her he wanted a divorce. "What will I tell my friends?" He moved out of the house the next day.

There are differences we cannot live with. When a man and woman find themselves in a conflict that they can neither resolve nor endure, then it is time to say goodbye.

Q. I feel that the love between me and my partner has died or is near death. Is it possible to rekindle love?

A. There are people who, on the basis of their own experience, would say no—or yes. Many people try and fail; some people, feeling their love has died or nearly died, come through it to feel passion enter their lives once more.

This general observation is not very helpful, because when they ask this question people want to know whether there is a specific procedure by which they might reasonably hope to rekindle their love. And when the question is put that way, we have to answer in the negative.

We have already spoken about why love dies—because of hurt, frustration, and anger left too long unresolved; because of vanished respect for our partner; or because of new or subtly changed needs that carry us in different directions.

There is a pattern common to every case we know of where love was all but dead and then reborn: at some level the couple said goodbye, whether or not they physically separated, passing through a period during which they no longer thought of themselves as a couple. Some time later, they experienced themselves and each other as significantly different than they had once been.

In other words, we have never seen the passage from death to rebirth without some radical psychological break: separation, divorce, affairs, or separate lives under one roof. They experience the rekindling of love as a new relationship rather than a continuation of an old one.

We have the impression that some relationships perish because the lovers are afraid to let go, thus closing themselves off from the possibility of meeting on new ground. Our fear of saying goodbye can hasten the demise of a relationship if our fear leads us to ignore, deny, repress, disown experiences that are important to our well-being. We end up in a state of numbness from which there is no recovery, at least not with that partner.

We counseled a couple who had separated after twenty years of marriage and were contemplating divorce. During this period they dated other people. After several

months of estrangement, the husband telephoned his wife
to ask for a date. When they met, she was beautifully
dressed, had a new hairdo, and was ten pounds lighter
than when he had last seen her. She thought he looked
"gorgeous." They laughed a bit nervously and both said,
"You never looked this good when we were together."
They were shy, like teenagers.

They dated for several months. He sent her flowers,
cards. They had better sex than they ever had in the past.
They looked forward to their meetings with more and
more eagerness—until they raised the question of living
together as man and wife. Then everything exploded. All
the old angers reawakened. All the problems in communication reappeared.

They decided to seek marriage counseling. We can say
that their love has definitely revived. We cannot say
whether they will ever live happily together. Too much
still remains unresolved between them. We are absolutely
convinced that without their separation they would never
have reached even the hope for a future together.

"Letting go" sounds like such a tragic phrase. Letting
go of a relationship. Letting go of a dream. Letting go of
home. Letting go of a station in life. Letting go of a stage
of development. Letting go of a long-held viewpoint that now
seems invalid. Letting go of the longing for a time that
can never come again. And yet, letting go need not be tragic
at all. Somewhere in those words we may hear the promise
of adventure ahead, the promise of a new beginning.

Q. I have been trying without very much success to
make my relationship work. How do I know when
it's time to stop trying?

A. Before delivering an address to a men's organiza-
tion, I took a walk with the gentleman who had
invited me to speak, and he struck up a conversation
about marriage and divorce. "I am in a marvelous marriage now, but my first was a disaster. I stayed in it much
too long, trying to work things out."

"You know," I said, "I've heard that statement so many
times, yet the thought just now strikes me: has anyone
ever felt he or she left a marriage at just the right time?

Most of us hang on too long, just to be sure it's really hopeless. In retrospect, after we knew it was hopeless, it's natural to say we stayed too long.''

There seem to be two errors people commonly make when their relationship is not working. One is to hang on too long. The other is to give up too soon. Under what circumstances do we stop trying?

We stop trying when we feel we have no more energy to give a relationship, when we feel the love we had with our partner is irretrievably lost, when we experience the present as unbearable. We stop trying when we have lost so much regard and respect for our partner that we don't know anymore why the relationship was worth fighting for. And, very often, we stop trying because we have met someone else with whom we see a better chance for happiness.

In struggling with the question of when to stop trying, we should ask ourselves, "What are the reasons for continuing to try?" If I am miserable, if my partner shows no interest in changing, if I feel the relationship is destroying me, then "I love him (her)" doesn't seem like a satisfactory answer. It's perfectly reasonable to feel that we don't want to walk away until we've tried everything, but what are we doing when we hang on without really knowing what else to try?

For years a wife complained that her husband neglected her and the children in favor of his work and business associates. When she tried to discuss the matter, he would listen silently but rarely responded. If she persisted, he would answer, "This is the kind of person I am." When she asked him what they should do, he said, "Whatever you think best." He said he didn't have time to join her in seeing a marriage counselor. She told him they were heading for divorce. He said, "Oh, I hope not."

One day she screamed at him, "I think you're trying to make me the one who asks for a divorce."

"Oh, I wouldn't say that. But psychology's not my field. Can't we just go on without all this fighting?"

"I give up." She was now willing to be the one to ask for a divorce. She would let him win the game. If he wasn't playing a game, he was hopeless.

As he saw her packing, he said, "I hope you're not

really going." He had no suggestions to offer, no solutions, no promises even to make an effort.

So long as we love our partner, so long as we see any evidence of change or any reasonable hope for change, so long as the joy in the relationship outweighs the pain, it is wrong to walk away. The time to stop trying is when suffering has driven out the joy. That is safe enough as a general formula; the problem lies in applying it, in being able to recognize when you've reached the moment.

Our reluctance to recognize that moment may spring from our fears: fear of failing, fear of being alone, fear that living outside the relationship will be even more painful.

I very much admire Devers's maternal grandmother who, after forty-six years of marriage, separated from her husband because "he's too domineering and controlling and doesn't care about my needs. He doesn't treat me right, and I'm not happy with him." Her children were scandalized, but she insisted she would live on her own. She seemed much happier.

Devers: I think of my grandmother when women clients who really need to get out of their marriages, women in their twenties or thirties, talk to me about their fear of being alone.

We wish there were simple rules to prescribe. The truth is that knowing when to cut your losses is always a matter of personal responsibility and courage.

Q. My partner and I both recognize that our relationship has ended, yet saying goodbye is extremely painful for us both. Since we both accept its necessity, I don't understand why it should be so difficult.

A. The breakup of any relationship that began with love and deep commitment entails some sense of loss. There is always the thought, and the feeling that goes with it, "This is not how I thought our story would end." Even when we recognize that separation or divorce is a necessity, we are letting go of a vision of what our life was to be.

The problem may be compounded by a sense of failure. If we had only had the wisdom to act differently, the relationship would have survived. Sometimes our self-esteem is hurt, if only temporarily.

Our relationship may have become part of our sense of personal identity. Separation or divorce means that we are losing a part of ourselves. We feel diminished.

Then there is the fear of being alone, of facing the world without the support of the relationship, however flawed. For some of us the prospect is devastating.

Even under these "best of possible circumstances," where both partners are reconciled to the necessity of going their separate ways, there is pain.

Q. Is it more difficult for married people to let go? I'm not married and I can't imagine anyone feeling more anguish than I do at the prospect of separating from my partner.

A. When we think of the breakup of marriage, we tend to think of a relationship of longer standing and deeper commitment, and we may add the complications associated with children. We are inclined to say broadly that letting go is harder for married people than for single. Is this always the case? Not necessarily.

A couple had been lovers for seven years. When he met and fell in love with someone else, the woman who had been his constant companion went through just about every kind of anguish that is part of letting go. She felt their relationship was for life. She had to go through precisely the same kind of mourning as any divorcee.

And, like many divorcees, she recovered, and she fell in love again.

Q. Is it realistic for me to hope to be friends with my former partner?

A. That depends on the quality of the relationship you had while you were together and on the reason for your break.

If your relationship was solidly grounded in the first place, not principally based on fantasy, the day may come in the future when you can be friends again. If the relationship was never based on any real perception and appreciation of who the other was, if neither of you ever experienced much visibility with the other, then the likelihood of your ever becoming friends is slight.

If you leave the relationship still respecting each other, still admiring each other, again there is some possibility for friendship. Otherwise, there is not.

If you leave the relationship with one or both of you feeling enormously hurt by the other, with none of the hurt resolved, there isn't much chance for friendship. If the pain has been satisfactorily dealt with, so that you can take your leave of each other in peace, tranquility, and dignity, friendship may be possible.

If one of you is still deeply in love with the other, while the other is no longer in love at all, friendship is probably not feasible. If neither of you is in love any longer, but you continue to feel affection, friendship may be possible.

Partners who have both made new lives for themselves and are happy have the best chance to become friends later.

Most people do not find it easy to demote a relationship, to live comfortably on a lower level of feeling after they have known the higher. Even under the best of circumstances, former lovers or spouses rarely maintain friendships with each other.

If I take full responsibility for having chosen my partner in the first place, I am less susceptible to blaming him or her for the breakup. I do not see myself as a victim. If I keep myself aware that I had choices and that I am responsible for the choices I made, then I do not see my former partner as a persecutor or exploiter. Then I may be able to accept my former spouse or lover as a friend. Too often people indulge themselves in blaming the former partner, taking little responsibility for their own role in the unraveling. They protect themselves by putting as much psychological distance between them and their former partner as possible, which means forgetting or denying the values that initially brought them together and disowning the love they once felt. Aside from putting friendship out of the question, this defensiveness bodes ill for any future relationship.

Q. How do I recover from the breakup of a relationship when I am still in love with my former partner?

A. Whenever there is loss, there is a psychological need for mourning, a period during which we allow ourselves to experience the pain fully, reflecting on what is gone from our life and how we are affected by the absence. This is not self-pity but an essential step in the healing process.

In *The Psychology of Romantic Love* I wrote about my own mourning for the death of Patrecia. That discussion will supplement what we say here.

It sounds strange, but most people do not know how to mourn. They resist, struggle, lecture themselves, trying to cheer up while they go on suffering. We need time to feel our loss. We need to experience just how deeply we wish things were different before we can recover. We cannot be free of a pain we have never allowed ourselves to feel fully. We cannot leave a place until we have been there.

A paradox: if you want to conquer a pain, surrender to it. To surrender does not mean letting the pain rule and control your life. It means owning and experiencing the pain as a precondition of getting rid of it.

At an Intensive, a woman asked Nathanial about getting over the breakup of a relationship. He asked her, "What have you done to recover so far?"

She looked puzzled. "I don't know. Nothing, I suppose."

"Have you wept?"

"No."

"I suggest," said Nathaniel, "that you begin there."

The woman looked surprised and relieved, as if she had been given unexpected permission. Her smile said that she understood. "I've been trying to be strong," she said.

"I don't know who was the first person who said this," Nathaniel answered, "but the way out is through."

The way out is through: that is how we deal successfully with the pain of a breakup—or any pain.

Allow a period to meditate on the relationship, to remember the happy times as well as the unhappy, the joy as well as the hurt. Allow yourself to feel gratitude for an experience that contributed to your sense of being alive. Ask yourself: would you rather that you had never known this person at all? Your answer to that question will be worth thinking about.

Sometimes, of course, we *want* to suffer. Suffering over a past breakup can keep us far too busy for the challenge of a new relationship. I can wrap my pain around me and hide from the world for a very long time if I want to.

If our self-concept contains the vision of ourselves as a tragic figure, we may use our suffering to manipulate our friends. We owe it to ourselves and to our friends to keep a careful scrutiny in this respect, honoring real pain but never using the display of pain to stimulate martyrdom.

We may unconsciously imagine that if we suffer enough our partner's heart will melt. This kind of childish fantasy can only prolong suffering. If by some chance he or she does come back, it will be for the wrong reasons and not for long.

We have seen in our therapy groups that people who use pain manipulatively almost never enter their pain completely, almost always play on the edges of it. A few tears here, a few tears there; they avoid the cleansing, liberating power of total surrender.

Even if I am not still in love with my former partner, I may still need some period of mourning. While conducting a therapy group not long ago we were a little astonished when a man, who had two weeks earlier broken off with his girlfriend of five years, said, "I don't know what's wrong with me. It bothers me to think of her sleeping with other men. I was the one who ended our relationship." We were astonished by the assumption that he didn't need time to let go emotionally after five years of being committed emotionally. There was no awareness of, let alone respect for, the processes by which we assimilate change and internally reorganize, recharge, and rejuvenate.

We are not machines. Our emotions aren't wired to on/off switches. We are feeling organisms. We need time to adjust, to change, and when the change is painful, we need time to mourn.

Q. **If the person I love leaves me for someone else, how can I protect my ego from being damaged?**

A. In such a situation, it is normal to suffer a sense of loss. But it is a disastrous error to tie our self-esteem to another person's love for us. One of the essential characteristics of maturity and autonomy is that self-approval is generated internally, so that my sense of worth depends on my judgment and my actions, not someone else's.

We best protect our self-esteem by not internalizing rejection as part of our self-concept. Avoiding both self-blame and blame of our partner—realizing that we cannot demand love as an act of self-sacrifice—we seek to understand *why* the breakup occurred. If we feel part of the responsibility was ours, we think about how we might behave differently in a future relationship.

Convert the situation into a learning and growth experience. The first step in self-healing is emotional honesty: allow yourself to experience your pain fully—don't pretend that you don't care or are "above" such reactions—but do not allow it to shut you off emotionally. Remain open; remain vulnerable. We protect our egos by staying responsive to life, not by escaping into numbness, bitterness, and despair.

Q. I feel my ability to love died when my partner died. How do I awaken that part of myself?

A. Once again: the way out is through. If I try to bear the pain of my loss by tightening against it rather than relaxing into it, by repressing it rather than surrendering to it, I keep it prisoner forever.

There is a life force within that will bring us back, if we keep out of the way, if we let the process of recovery happen. And the way to allow the process to happen, as we keep stressing, is never to fight our feelings, and never to act on them blindly. Acknowledge them.

Often what we call "feeling dead emotionally" is better described as "being afraid to feel." We shut down so as not to feel pain. At the same time we cut off the possibility of future joy.

We dread exposing ourselves ever again to the trauma we experienced at our first loss and so numb ourselves, saying it is because we cannot let go of the great love behind us.

A woman told us she had adored her husband so much that any future love was inconceivable. She wanted to talk about what a fine man he was but not about what the loss meant to her personally.

We placed her in front of an empty chair and asked her to imagine that her husband was sitting there. We asked her to talk to him. At first, she resisted. Slowly, with much encouragement, she spoke of how much she had loved him, then of how much she missed him, then of how angry she was at him for abandoning her. She spoke again of how much she loved and needed him, weeping deeply. "This pain is too much for me to bear."

She came back. We took her through many similar exercises. We taught her to do them on her own at home. We taught her not to fear pain but to taste it, touch, embrace it until it had no power to paralyze her. We saw her face become softer, more alive. One day she said, "I'm going on my first vacation alone. It's scary. Anyway, I'm ready. Who knows what's ahead?" Who indeed.

Nathaniel: A person once told me something that shocked me, hurt me, bewildered me, something that I have never been able to forget. "When a person we love dies, it is a tragedy, but it is also a gift, a gift that is very hard for us to recognize and accept. Suddenly new doors open, new possibilities emerge, and we are flung forward along a path we might never have found." It was not easy for me to hear this, a year after Patrecia's death.

Today, I know it is true.

Thirteen
Romantic Love in Later Years

At a lecture Nathaniel was delivering on man/woman relationships, a gentleman stood up and said, "I'm seventy-five years old, widowed, and I love to go on trips. I enjoy sexual adventure, and I'm looking to fall in love again. My children and grandchildren think I'm nuts. What do you think?" Nathaniel raised his water glass in a toast, took a long drink, and said, "That's what I think." The audience, which contained a good many people middle-aged and older, burst into applause.

"One of the few times I particularly appreciate having grey hair," said Nathaniel, "is when I'm lecturing on love. I'm not the person you should tell that romantic love is just for the young. Compared to you, sir, I am pretty young, a mere lad of fifty-one. I salute you." Once again the auditorium exploded with laughter and applause.

The director of the lecture series was surprised that this talk on romantic love had attracted middle-aged people in larger numbers than any other talk in the history of the program. We were not surprised. We know—as many others have known even longer—that love is not just for the young.

The questions in this chapter are distinctive in that they mostly come from men and women in their sixties and seventies who are actively interested in issues and questions pertaining to romantic relationships. Story-book notions of romantic love may not include such people, yet romantic love sets no age limits.

Q. I never experienced passionate love when I was young. Am I being realistic to yearn for it now in middle age?

A. When we mentioned this question to a psychologist of our acquaintance, she commented, "I had the most exciting, intensive love affair of my life when I was fifty-eight years old."

Taking another perspective on the question, we might consider why a person never experienced passionate love when younger. The most common reasons are fear of vulnerability, fear of losing control, fear of intimacy, perhaps compounded by emotional repression, sexual anxiety, poor self-esteem, or even an excessively conventional outlook on life.

As we grow older, we become more able to let go of many of these inhibiting attitudes, and we learn to worry less about what others might think. We are less afraid of being hurt, and we may thus learn to open ourselves to love. If we have expanded our self-assurance and our freedom, middle age can be the most exciting time of our life.

"I was married at fifteen and widowed at fifty-two," a woman said to us. "All my life I was encouraged to think of myself as belonging to someone else—to my parents, my husband, my children. My husband's death brought on a terrible period of crisis for me. Who was I? I didn't know anymore. I met a man. Can you imagine having your first affair at fifty-six? It didn't last, but I thought, 'My God, I'm a woman.' What a time to discover it! So many things that had mattered for so many years—what my family thought, how I might appear to others—faded into insignificance. I felt frightened, and free. I had several more relationships; they were intoxicating. I had just turned sixty-three when I took your Intensive, *Self-Esteem and the Art of Being.* You know who I met there. We're mad about each other. Maybe we'll get married, maybe we'll just go on living together. That doesn't seem very important right now. Do you ever have the feeling that the young don't know how to appreciate love?"

Fears that blocked us from passionate love may, on the other hand, become more entrenched through the years, and then love becomes harder and harder to find. Moreover, the capacity for experiencing passion is clearly more developed in some people than in others, no matter what their age. The issue is not age but inner development. To experience passionate love, we must first be willing and able to experience passion.

"I'm forty-seven years old," a lawyer said to us at an Intensive. "By nine o'clock in the evening, I like to be asleep. Sex hasn't interested me since I was forty. As far as I'm concerned, it's for kids. When I listen to you—I say this with all the respect and good will in the world—I honestly don't know what you're talking about. I can't relate any of it to my own experience."

Late in life the availability of an appropriate person often makes the difference for romantic love, but we have to be ready to recognize that appropriate person whether we are seventy or twenty. Attitude is decisive. Unfortunately, our culture encourages inhumane attitudes about the elderly.

"I am so goddamn mad," said a businessman of seventy-four, "at the way films and books portray elderly people. Either we're adorable, cutesy criminals or else helpless dreamers longing for days long gone by. Or else we're mean, ornery, and frightening, dead to all ordinary human feeling. How I'd like to see a serious love story about people in their sixties or seventies." When the participants at the Intensive began to applaud, he put up his hand to hush them. "You know why I really appreciate love at my age? Because in the background I always hear the clock ticking. Each moment of joy is precious."

Q. I am having an affair with someone a little more than half my age. Is this normal?

A. Both men and women ask this question of us (in case people think only males ask such questions). The fact is that many men and women in middle age become aware of a desire for a younger lover, and there is nothing unnatural about it.

We cannot see anything intrinsically objectionable in relationships between older men and younger women or older women and younger men; they have worthwhile things to give each other. It is hardly an argument to say that the relationship may not be "forever," since fewer and fewer relationships between contemporaries are "forever."

It is easy enough to understand the attraction of age to youth, since we tend to associate youth not only with beauty but also with health, vitality, energy, enthusiasm, excitement: why wouldn't we find such traits appealing and, under some circumstances, sexually stimulating? And why wouldn't youth, under some circumstances, be attracted to the maturity, knowledge, and stability associated with age?

Of course, there are many reasons why we may be drawn sexually to someone a good deal younger than ourselves. Sometimes, we may be attracted by the enthusiasm of youth, the energy, the excitement for life, and the lack of cynicism. Sometimes, because youth is not yet mired down in so many of the problems associated with age. Sometimes, we are charmed by the role of teacher, the chance to share what we know, and what we have lived, with someone eager and interested. Sometimes, it is a means of denying our own age, of reassuring ourselves that we are still young. Sometimes, we desire the gratification of knowing that even if we are no longer young ourselves we still have appeal for those who are. Sexual involvement with a younger person may give us an opportunity to recapture the excitement of our youth. When we have seen a number of our contemporaries die, it can be a desperate (if unconscious) strategy to deny not our age but our mortality.

All of these motives are human, some are foolish; none of them is abnormal.

One of our clients lost her father when she was very young. In her twenties, she carried on an affair of some years with a man in his fifties. He was kind, nurturing, protective—part lover, part father figure. The relationship had to end, and they both knew it, but when she announced her decision he was devastated. A year after it was over he said to us, "Sure, I knew I was kidding myself a little. I knew it wouldn't go on forever, but I kept thinking, 'Give me one more year. Just one more year.' Now we're friends again, just friends, and I'm learning to accept that. It was beautiful and it didn't last forever. I sure as hell wouldn't have been happier if I'd never met her. I always thought she was a fantastic human being, and I still think so. And I know I gave her something very special. And I got something very special back. Look, I'm telling you about it right now and I'm smiling, so it can't be such a tragedy, can it?''

We may be especially vulnerable to youth if we perceive our partner as aging more rapidly than ourselves. A younger person may have the energy to keep up with us, whereas our partner no longer seems able to. Yet it is easy to deceive ourselves, especially in the frantic struggle to keep up with the younger person who attracted us with his or her energy.

Having spoken already about the pros and cons of extramarital affairs, we can point out briefly that we are not obligated to act on our every sexual impulse. The experience of sexual attraction to a younger person does not mean that I must go to bed with him or her. Looking at the consequences such an affair may have on the rest of my life, I may well decide it's not worth it. Life consists of choices.

We stress this point because today many believe they are committing some sort of inexcusable crime against the self if they do not experience every possibility that life offers them. In fact, such a notion of self-fulfillment is inherently contradictory: As soon as I exercise an option, I necessarily exclude other options, other experiences. If I choose, for example, to experience every sexually attractive person I meet, I automatically forgo the possibility of experiencing sexual exclusivity. There is no way to have it all.

We do not mean to deny that different solutions are appropriate for different individuals and couples; we are acutely aware of the danger of writing universal prescriptions. But personal growth always entails the responsibility of choice.

We asked one of the most happily married women we know—she is in her late forties—how she would react if her husband were to find himself sexually attracted to a younger woman. She said, "I don't know for certain, but here's how I feel right now. If he felt he really needed that experience, sleeping with a younger woman, I think our accumulated years of happiness together would hold the balance for me against a sexual adventure of that kind. I think I could accept it. I love him.

"Now if he left me for a younger woman, what would I do? After going out of my mind for a while, well, I'd probably go out and get a face lift, go on a shopping spree, cry my eyes out, try to date him or be friends somehow. So long as I'm alive, I plan on being alive. After all the hurt and anger was over, though it probably never would be, and after I'd waited as long as I could for him to come back, I'd probably go out and try somebody young for myself!"

"And how would you react?" we asked her husband.

He smiled. "Probably the same way."

Q. My partner and I feel less interest in sex. Does this mean a diminished capacity for romantic love?

A. If a man and woman know how to cherish and comfort one another, and if there is a good foundation of respect and appreciation between them, the diminishing frequency of sexual intercourse need not undermine romantic love at all.

This is especially true when the couple has enjoyed a good sexual relationship in the past. Partners who once made love several times a week may now make love only once in two or three weeks, and yet their love for each other is no less deep and the relationship no less beautiful.

It is a fallacy, at any age, to assume that more is better. A couple can make love every day and do so perfunctorily. Another couple can make love much less frequently but make each encounter an exquisite experience.

In later years, when the capacity for intercourse may (although not necessarily) diminish, the capacity for touching, caressing, holding, fondling remains unabated so that sensual and affectionate expressions of love are always possible. Often older people expand their range of sexual expression to include many activities not directly related to intercourse: other forms of body contact as well as simple awareness and eye contact.

We do not want to make too much of the issue of

diminished sexual capacity because it is an area surrounded by misconceptions. A healthy couple is capable of enjoying sex well into old age. Indeed, some homes for the elderly have great difficulty in the practical management of strong sexual feelings that erupt between men and women in their seventies and eighties. (Try telling the staff in such homes that passion is only for the young.)

Aside from health, two factors seem particularly relevant to our capacity for sex as we grow older: our history and our attitude. If we have been sexually active throughout our life, we tend to remain sexually active into old age; otherwise, not. And if we think of ourselves as sexual beings, we tend to be sexual beings, regardless of age. If we believe that we are finished sexually at fifty or sixty or seventy, then our expectations can readily turn into realities.

If sexual problems do occur for one or both partners, we can help by continuing to see the other as sexual and as sexually desirable, projecting the conviction that sex remains an active element in our experience of the relationship.

"Obviously we don't make love the way we did when we were younger," said a man in his eighties, "but we're not indifferent either. Sex still matters. And sex includes more now. Just touching is sex. Just looking. It's all in the mind. When I'm ready to die, I expect to be able to look at my wife and know I'm looking at a woman."

We think that may be the ultimate triumph of our sexuality: to be able to retain that experience of our partner when the physical is no longer available to us. That may also be the triumph of love.

Q. I'm in my sixties, my lover is in her late fifties, and we're thinking of living together and perhaps marrying. Isn't it more difficult for people of our age to make the adjustments necessary for living under the same roof?

A. It can hardly be denied that we tend to become more set in our ways as we grow older, less flexible about new ways and styles of living. But we think it's an error to make too much of this. The question as stated doesn't mention emotional needs, which the relationship might satisfy and which might outweigh matters of taste and custom.

* * *

A man we know had been widowed for a long time. He lived his own life, did things his own way, and he was lonely. At the age of sixty-eight he fell in love with a woman he wanted to marry. She perceived him as set in his ways, and many of his ways were not hers. He adored her so much that he began doing things he had never done before—taking walks along the beach, seeing plays, going away for weekend vacations—all because he was determined to marry this woman and determined that she would be happy with him. After the marriage, he did not fall back into old habits. He had learned from his courtship that this new wife could introduce him to experiences he had never known, and to his surprise he enjoyed them, not only for her but with her. He learned it was more fun being pliant than brittle.

On the other hand, we know a woman with grown children who discovered, some time after her husband died, that she liked the freedom of coming and going as she pleased. She launched into a more active social life than she had had when she was younger and met a man she might have fallen in love with. Taking a closer look at his lifestyle—he was a bookkeeper and a bit of a workaholic—she decided that while she enjoyed having an affair with him, she did not want to live with him or marry him. Anything more than an affair would ruin their relationship. In an affair, she could see him when he was emotionally able and willing to see her; living with him, she would be forever waiting for those brief moments when he could take his mind away from his desk. Both in their fifties, they seem to be conducting a very enjoyable romance combining the advantages of maturity and the "irresponsibility" of teenagers. We suspect this woman has made the right choice, at least for her.

When we come together with another person in later life, we don't expect that our partner will make as many adjustments and accommodations as we might hope for in our twenties. With experience we tend to be more tolerant of differences in personality. And if we find someone we can truly love and admire, we are wise to appreciate what we have without crying for something else.

A woman of sixty-three living with a man of seventy

said to us, "What the heck, you can't have everything. But between everything and nothing there's an awful lot of space to negotiate."

Q. As a couple now in our sixties, we are especially interested in how romantic love most often goes wrong among people in our age group. We want to keep the fires burning.

A. The most common errors people make as they grow older seem to involve forgetting the importance of expressing appreciation, admiration, and love.

Being complimented on our appearance is very enjoyable in our thirties. Being told we are a source of delight is still a pleasure in our sixties, though with a fuller meaning. Our bodies are no longer what they once were, and we may be too willing to disown our need to feel desirable, especially if we are neglected. Being appreciated physically renews us.

The same principle applies to expressions of delight in lovemaking: if we feel taken for granted sexually, we may lose interest in sex. And then we have lost one aspect of intimacy, which is at the heart of romantic love. We need to see sensual and amorous response in our partner.

We hasten to add that expressions of appreciation concerning our intelligence, achievements, kindness, humor, and thoughtfulness *all* contribute to the vitality of romantic love.

The key concepts are awareness, appreciation, and communication: they fuel romantic love at any age.

Good questions to ask ourselves. What am I doing (*not* what have I done in the past) to make my partner feel loved, appreciated, visible? And: What am I sharing of myself, what am I inviting my partner to share?

Most people, when they fall in love and marry, imagine living out their lives together. We think this is a beautiful dream and one to be treasured. We greatly admire the people who have learned to embrace the last years of the life cycle, as rewarding in their own way as the earlier years. We think this perspective is one of the characteristics of men and women who truly love life in all its phases— not just its youthful phases—and whose minds and feelings are in harmony with the natural order of things.

To say "I love you" at the age of twenty may not be unusual. To say it at eighty-five, and to feel it, is to have mastered something essential about the meaning of life.

Q. Are there any final reflections you can offer for lovers of all ages?

A. This question was a final request from our editor Janice Gallagher (at J. P. Tarcher, Inc., publisher of the hardcover first edition of this work), whose original suggestions and counsel contributed so much.

First she asked us to conclude the book with a question on how Devers and I felt about ending our days together.

I protested, "I'm fifty-one and Devers is forty-seven. Don't you think that question's a bit premature?"

"You've told us a little about yourselves throughout the book. Why not say something about how you see the future?"

"I can't see why that would be of interest to anyone."

Janice said, "Well, what I would like is one final piece of wisdom."

"Thank you," I replied.

I called Devers into my office and invited her reaction. "Do you see us together twenty or thirty years from now?"

"I hope we'll be together forever."

"I do, too."

"But that isn't what matters," said Devers. "All we can know about, all we can have, is now. That's what we have to be responsible for."

I hope we'll have a chance to grow old together, I thought silently. I want that more than anything else in the world. I remembered the man who spoke about hearing the clock ticking. It's ticking for all of us. The realization did not feel tragic, but it did feel solemn.

"I feel grateful to life," said Devers, "for every day we have. I do my best to take care of it. Each day. Each moment. That's all I know how to do. That's all I can tell anyone."

Let that statement be our final reflection.

Appendix

Recommendations for Further Study

The purpose of this book has been to illuminate the meaning of romantic love and to deal with the most burning issues and questions in the lives of men and women struggling to make love work.

The underlying premise of this discussion is the supreme importance of high self-esteem to human well-being. I hope you will choose to pursue this subject further.

My most comprehensive discussion of self-esteem is *Honoring the Self*. This book sums up my nearly three decades of work in the field.

For an examination of my theoretical starting point, with particular emphasis on philosophical foundations, I refer you to my earlier book, *The Psychology of Self-Esteem*.

For an exploration of the childhood origins of negative self-concepts, illustrated by many cases taken from my clinical practice, see *Breaking Free*.

For the problem of self-alienation, and a discussion of the relation between reason and emotion, see *The Disowned Self*.

For the most comprehensive discussion of the nature and meaning of romantic love, see *The Psychology of Romantic Love*. This is the logical book to read after (or before) the present volume.

If You Could Hear What I Cannot Say is a workbook which teaches the reader how to use my sentence-completion technique to resolve problems in the area of intimate relationships. *To See What I See and Know What I Know* is a workbook which teaches the uses of sentence completion of self-understanding, self-discovery, and self-healing.

How to Raise Your Self-Esteem teaches specific exercises and behaviors that raise self-confidence and self-respect. It is the translation of my theory of self-esteem into practical action.

All these works are published by Bantam Books.

In addition, I have been developing a series of self-actualization audiocassettes, aimed specifically at carrying forward in new ways the material presented in all the above writings. You may obtain information about these cassettes, as well as other related matters—lectures, seminars, workshops, and the like—by writing to: The Biocentric Institute, P.O. Box 2609, Beverly Hills, California 90213.

Selected Bibliography

By Nathaniel Branden

Hardcover

A Nathaniel Branden Anthology. (Contains *The Psychology of Self-Esteem; Breaking Free; The Disowned Self*) Los Angeles: J. P. Tarcher, 1980.

The Psychology of Romantic Love. Los Angeles: J. P. Tarcher, 1980.

Paperback

Breaking Free. New York: Bantam Books, 1972.

The Disowned Self. New York: Bantam Books, 1973.

The Psychology of Romantic Love. New York: Bantam Books, 1981.

The Psychology of Self-Esteem. New York: Bantam Books, 1971.

On Communication

Bandler, Richard; Grinder, John; and Satir, Virginia. *Changing with Families.* Palo Alto, Calif.: Science and Behavior Books, 1976.

Becvar, Raphael, J. *Skills for Effective Communication.* New York: John Wiley and Sons, 1974.

Cameron-Bandler, Leslie. *They Lived Happily Ever After.* Cupertino, Calif.: Meta Publications, 1978.

Faber, Adele, and Mazelish, Elaine. *Liberated Parents, Liberated Children.* New York: Grosset and Dunlap, 1974.

_____. *How to Talk So Kids Will Listen & Listen So Kids Will Talk.* New York: Rawson, Wade Publishers, 1980.

Ginott, H. *Between Parent and Child*. New York: Macmillan, 1965.

———. *Between Parent and Teenager*. New York: Macmillan, 1969.

———. *Teacher and Child*. New York: Macmillan, 1972.

Johnson, David W. *Reaching Out*. 2d ed. Englewood Cliffs. N.J.: Prentice-Hall, 1981.

Miller, S.; Nunnally, E. W.; and Wackman, D. B. *Alive and Aware: How to Improve Your Relationships Through Better Communication*. Minneapolis: Interpersonal Communication Program, 1975.

Sex, Love, Marriage

Barbach, Lonnie Garfield. *For Yourself: The Fulfillment of Female Sexuality*. New York: Signet, 1975.

Brecher, Ruth, and Brecher, Edward. *An Analysis of Human Sexual Response*. New York: Signet, 1966.

Carrera, Michael. *Sex: The Facts, the Acts, and Your Feelings*. New York: Crown Publishers, 1981.

Castleman, Michael. *Sexual Solutions*. New York: Simon & Schuster, 1980.

Comfort, Alex. *The Joy of Sex*. New York: Simon & Schuster, 1972.

Freedman, Jonathan. *Happy People: What Happiness Is, Who Has It, and Why*. New York: Harcourt Brace Jovanovich, 1978.

Hunt, Morton. *Sexual Behavior in the 1970s*. New York: Dell, 1974.

Kaplan, Helen Singer. *Disorders of Sexual Desire*. New York: Simon & Schuster, 1979.

———. *The Illustrated Manual of Sex Therapy*. New York: Quadrangle/New York Times Book Company, 1975.

———. *The New Sex Therapy*. New York: Brunner/Mazel, 1974.

Lehrman, Nate. *Masters and Johnson Explained*. Chicago: Playboy Press, 1976.

LoPiccolo, Joseph, and LoPiccolo, Leslie. *Handbook of Sex Therapy*. New York: Plenum Press, 1978.

Masters, W., and Johnson, V. *Human Sexual Inadequacy*. Boston: Little, Brown, 1970.

———. With Robert J. Levin. *The Pleasure Bond*. New York: Bantam Books, 1976.

Murstein, Bernard I. *Love, Sex and Marriage Through the Ages*. New York: Springer Publishing, 1974.

O'Neill, Nena. *The Marriage Premise*. Philadelphia: M. Evans and Co., 1977.

Otto, Herbert A. Editor. *Love Today*. New York: Association Press, 1972.

Rosenberg, Jack L. *Total Orgasm*. New York: Random House/Bookworks, 1973.

Schneider, I. *The World of Love*, 2 Vols. New York: George Braziller, 1964.

Taylor, G. Rattray. *Sex in History*. New York: Harper Torchbooks, 1973.

Zilbengeld, Bernie. *Male Sexuality*. Boston: Little, Brown, 1978.

Index

*A*uthor of *The Psychology of Self-Esteem, Breaking Free, The Disowned Self, The Psychology of Romantic Love, What Love Asks of Us* (with E. Devers Branden), *If You Could Hear What I Cannot Say, Honoring the Self, To See What I See and Know What I Know,* and *How to Raise Your Self-Esteem,* Nathaniel Branden is a pioneer in his studies of self-esteem, personal transformation, and man/woman relationships. His works have been published in French, German, Portuguese, Dutch, Hebrew, Greek, Japanese, Swedish, and Italian. Dr. Branden is in private practice in Los Angeles and lives in Lake Arrowhead, California.

As director of the Biocentric Institute in Los Angeles, he offers Intensive Workshops throughout the United States in self-esteem and man/woman relationships. He also conducts professional training workshops for mental health professionals in his approach to personal growth and development.

Communications to Dr. Branden or requests for information about his various lectures, seminars, and Intensive Workshops should be addressed to The Biocentric Institute, P.O. Box 2609, Beverly Hills, CA. 90213–2609.

*D*EVERS BRANDEN is a psychotherapist in private practice at the Biocentric Institute in Los Angeles. Devers Branden also co-leads many seminars and workshops with Dr. Branden, as well as his training programs for mental health professionals. She is the innovator of many therapeutic techniques in "the Biocentric Approach."

"Who am I?" remains the ultimate question we are continually challenged to answer as we go on evolving. Now, Dr. Nathaniel Branden offers his guide to self-discovery:

TO SEE WHAT I SEE AND KNOW WHAT I KNOW
☐ (34235-5 • $8.95)
A Trade Paperback

In this book, Dr. Branden guides the reader through a series of sentence completion exercises of which the goal is to provide a path to the personal exploration of thoughts, emotions, behavior, and—ultimately—to generate change where change is desired.

And Bantam has these other fine titles by Dr. Branden to offer:

Bantam

On Psychology

☐ 26507	**MEN WHO HATE WOMEN & THE WOMEN WHO LOVE THEM** Dr. Susan Forward	$4.50
☐ 34366	**SIGNALS** Allen Pease (A Large Format Book)	$7.95
☐ 25119	**HONORING THE SELF** Nathaniel Branden	$3.95
☐ 26401	**MORE HOPE AND HELP FOR YOUR NERVES** Claire Weekes	$3.95
☐ 23767	**HOPE AND HELP FOR YOUR NERVES** Claire Weekes	$3.95
☐ 26754	**PEACE FROM NERVOUS SUFFERING** Claire Weekes	$4.50
☐ 26005	**HOW TO BREAK YOUR ADDICTION TO A PERSON** Howard M. Halpern, Ph.D.	$4.50
☐ 27084	**PATHFINDERS** Gail Sheehy	$5.50
☐ 24754	**PASSAGES: PREDICTABLE CRISES OF ADULT LIFE** Gail Sheehy	$4.95
☐ 27043	**THE POWER OF YOUR SUBCONSCIOUS MIND** Dr. J. Murphy	$4.50
☐ 34574	**GOODBYE TO GUILT** Gerald Jampolsky, M.D. (A Large Format Book)	$9.95
☐ 34367	**TEACH ONLY LOVE** Gerald Jampolsky, M.D. (A Large Format Book)	$7.95
☐ 27333	**LOVE IS LETTING GO OF FEAR** Gerald Jampolsky, M.D.	$3.95
☐ 25822	**WHAT DO YOU SAY AFTER YOU SAY HELLO?** Eric Berne, M.D.	$4.95
☐ 27158	**PSYCHO-CYBERNETICS AND SELF-FULFILLMENT** Maxwell Maltz, M.D.	$4.95
☐ 27087	**CUTTING LOOSE: An Adult Guide for Coming to Terms With Your Parents** Howard Halpern	$4.50
☐ 26390	**WHEN I SAY NO, I FEEL GUILTY** Manuel Smith	$4.95

Prices and availability subject to change without notice.

Buy them at your local bookstore or use this convenient coupon for ordering:

- -

Bantam Books, Dept. ME, 414 East Golf Road, Des Plaines, IL 60016

Please send me the books I have checked above. I am enclosing $_____
(please add $2.00 to cover postage and handling). Send check or money order
—no cash or C.O.D.s please.

Mr/Ms _____

Address_____

City/State _____ Zip _____
Please allow four to six weeks for delivery. This offer expires 11/88.